SPIRITUALITY OF
THE THIRD WORLD

SPIRITUALITY OF THE THIRD WORLD

A CRY FOR LIFE

Papers and Reflections from the Third General Assembly
of the Ecumenical Association of Third World Theologians
January, 1992, Nairobi, Kenya

Edited by
K. C. Abraham
and
Bernadette Mbuy-Beya

BIP–95

ORBIS BOOKS

Maryknoll, New York 10545

The Catholic Foreign Mission Society of America (Maryknoll) recruits and trains people for overseas missionary service. Through Orbis Books, Maryknoll aims to foster the international dialogue that is essential to mission. The books published, however, reflect the opinions of their authors and are not meant to represent the official position of the society.

ORBIS/ISBN 0-88344-977-3

Contents

SPIRITUALITY OF
THE THIRD WORLD

Introduction

K. C. ABRAHAM

The Third General Assembly of the Ecumenical Association of Third World Theologians (EATWOT) met in Nairobi, Kenya, January 6-13, 1992. The Nairobi Conference firmly declared that Third World theology should be decisively shaped by the spirituality of the marginalized—women, indigenous people, Minjung and Dalits. *Spirituality of the Third World* articulates this creative and life-affirming spirituality that is at the very center of the life and struggles of the poor.

I begin by presenting an analysis of the situation of the Third World today. Although the first two essays (Part I: The Changing Context of the Third World) were not presented at the conference, they describe and capture the mood of our new context. The collapse of socialism and the dominance of a market economy have emerged as new realities in the Third World. Although state monopolies in our countries have often been unproductive, it seems to us totally false to believe that a market economy will solve all of our economic problems. The poor in our countries demand that we ask: Who controls the market? Who dictates the terms of development? Whose interests are served by the new economic policies?

In the past, the countries of the Third World could perceive the socialist model as a viable option, even though they knew full well that the existing patterns of socialism were far from perfect. Today, however, any talk of socialist alternatives is problematic. Is a market economy the *only* alternative left? Yet the crisis of socialism has weakened the Third World and at the same time it has weakened the possibilities of survival for our people.

This emerging new context and the sense of helplessness of the poor in our Third World countries have led us theologians to search more intensely for alternatives. It is our conviction that a new paradigm for just development must emerge from the experiences of the poor and the marginalized. In preparing for the Nairobi Conference, we worked to identify different expressions of the spiritualities of people of the Third World—those spiritual resources that sustain people who struggle for meaningful life against great odds. Part II of this book, The Search for Spirituality, includes a selection of these background materials. They are voices that represent

1

vastly different experiences, but voices that speak of the vision and vitality of the life of the poor. Can these voices be the basis for a new society? Can they form the basis of a new paradigm of hope? How do we respond to the challenges and questions they bring to the task of theologizing?

Part III, The Theological Response, includes papers and discussion from the conference itself. Presentations on the spirituality of Native Americans and of feminists, most particularly, called us to task. Use of symbol, ritual, and dance project both a vision and a value system oriented to the recovery of wholeness in the human experience, a celebration of the gift of life, the sacredness of body and bodily functions, and a renewed emphasis on our dependence on the earth, the delicate partner of us human beings.

Other papers attempt to clarify the links between theology and spirituality by exploring biblical perspectives on spirituality and the spirituality of Jesus and the early church, and by relating them to the spiritualities of other faiths. Another major paper reflects on the nature and direction of our commitment to the poor. The concluding "Statement of the Assembly" brings together the concerns expressed at the Nairobi Conference. This will provide, we hope, the beginning of a new stage in EATWOT's search for a theology for our time.

Preparation for the Nairobi Conference was entrusted to EATWOT's Theological Commission. We are including the commission's introductory statement in its entirety (below) because it identifies many of the crucial questions and concerns we need to face.

THE CRY OF THE THIRD WORLD

The cry of the Third World is a cry for life. It is a cry for freedom and dignity that constitute life as human. It is a cry for the rice and bread that sustain life, as well as for the community that symbolizes and grows from rice and bread eaten in company.

A Cry Uttered from the Midst of Misery

The cry is uttered from the midst of misery, from situations in which the forces of death are rampant and in which children die by the thousands from diseases related to malnutrition; yet elsewhere, food is wasted, milk and grain are destroyed, and resources are hijacked to provide luxuries and to produce weapons of annihilation.

We cry from the midst of the politics of the powerful who rule by torture, assassination, and by contriving the disappearance of women and men, and who commit aggression through proxy wars. Our cry rises from the midst of structures designed for our subjugation, marginalization, and extinction, through distorted priorities, skewed agricultural policies, unjust trade arrangements, and inhuman economic manipulations and pressure tactics—all practiced and imposed in brutal and subtle ways by neo-colonialism and the international imperialism of money built up through the atrocities, cruelties and robberies of the era of military colonialism. We cry from places where people are killed every day for holding that the poor have a right to live and for believing that children must be given food and justice must be practiced. We cry from within situations in which domination is transnational with allies within our midst.

From within such situations we cry for life and rice and bread. Rice and bread for one person alone may not be spiritual because it may be selfish. As ancient Indian scriptures say, "The person who cooks for him or herself alone eats sin." Or as Korean poet Kim Chi Ha has written,

> Food is heaven
> As we eat
> God enters us
> Food is heaven
>
> Oh, food
> Should be shared and eaten by all.

Or, in the words of Nicholas Berdyev, rice for myself alone may be unspiritual, but rice for my hungry sister and brother is spiritual. Thus, our cry for life is a cry for the bread and rice of life and for the spirituality of all the activities, processes, and relationships bound up with producing and sharing rice and bread. Ours is a cry for a spirituality of and for life.

Long ago in Egypt Pharaoh's empire condemned its Third World people to slavery and forced labor and their babies to death. The oppressed people cried out for life and withstood death. In the process they discovered in their midst a presence urging and energizing them to resist and dissent, and calling on them to revolt and walk out into freedom and to life in dignity. They found this presence open to their cry, moved by their suffering, and eager to identify with them. This encounter imparted to the oppressed people a fresh life-impulse; it gave them a new sense of everyday realities as having unsuspected depth; it provided their history with a new horizon of meaning.

So the people not only cried, but revolted and set the empire aside. The women hid the babies and refused to kill them. Women and men organized for combat. It is thus that within the encounter with the presence and the working out of the project of liberation a spirituality took shape: an openness and responsibility to the demands and possibilities of life in a community of freedom and dignity.

Further reflection deepened this spirituality and nurtured it to flower and fruit. Part of this fruit is a new religion that expresses itself in the belief that no power in heaven or on earth is to be honored or saluted except the one that liberates and honors human beings and gives them life. This spirituality and religion, betrayed and distorted in many ways in the course of time, have nonetheless preserved the direction and purity of its main current—namely, the commitment to life in freedom, justice, and dignity in community.

Jesus stood solidly within this tradition. Jesus declared in deed and word that the purpose of his coming was to give life in abundance and fullness to everyone. He came to look at the flowers and the birds, and to learn from them how the Father cares for the world. Jesus came to make the lame walk and the blind see, and to bring honor to the outcast and rebuild the pride of the humiliated. He came to throw prisons open and to let captives go, to smash chains and to set free the downtrodden. Then Jesus would lead them to rich pastures and tables laid with rich bread and rice. He loved life, and he loved the earth and he placed the earth at the heart of his prayer, with the yearning that to this earth and on this earth divine realities like the kingdom of God should happen, and that everybody of this earth should have rice and bread every day, and a share in the resources of the earth required to make life meaningful and creative. Therefore, he said, love one another and break bread with one another and share rice and give to each other freedom and life. Jesus thus presents and represents a spirituality of and for life. It is for this we cry when we cry, "Abba, Father, who are in heaven. . ."

Discovery and Appropriation

Is not such a spirituality present in a latent form in the prayer of the poor for life and bread? In their struggles for freedom and dignity? In their struggles for their children's lives, in their refusal to give up and surrender? In the courage with which they endure and give life a chance? In their hope that some day they will overcome the powers of death and domination and will change the world and give shape to a new age? Our cry, then, for a spirituality for life is not primarily for something yet to be created out of nothing. Our cry is rather for the discovery, and a deeper awareness and fuller appropriation of the spirituality already present, at least in solution and hidden ways and latent forms, in the life, the love, the caring, the struggle, the joy, the endurance, and the hope of the oppressed and suffering people. A discovery and appropriation which could then enhance their struggle and their hope, and strengthen their arms for continued combat till the day dawns and the shadows pass.

The cry is also to discover and take conscious possession of the relation which struggle for freedom and justice has to the presence that enjoins liberation, to the ultimate horizon meaning and ground of existence, to the Absolute Justice whose demand for interpersonal justice on our earth cannot be fought nor silenced. That means, the cry is for the discovery and conscious appropriation of the religious faith latent in all sides with life and justice and shared freedom, and in all struggles for life's liberation and creative growth.

Meaning and Types

We wish to explore the spirituality or spiritualities that are operative in the Third World and which animate, inspire, sustain, strengthen, enthuse, or domesticate and tranquilize people. What is it that controls people's consciousness? By what spiritualities do Third World people live? This project poses some preliminary theoretical questions.

How is spirituality to be understood? How is its specificity to be described? What are its parameters and components? Is being spiritual the same as being human? And what does "being human" mean? Is spirituality a matter of the quality of life, personal as well as social? How does it relate to modern values such as democracy, socialism, or other egalitarian ideas of social existence? Can it be identified with values such as justice, compassion, and commitment in community? Do we have models of spirituality in our Third World history? Could these be models at all in a world of diverse cultures and in a history in process? What would be some of the more telling paradigms of spirituality in the Bible? There is in the Bible mystery, prophecy and institution (of king, priest, temple). Do these represent distinct spiritualities?

There is the spirituality of indigenous peoples, of tribal and aboriginal groups, of Dalits, of women, of the poor. Do these differ among themselves, and from the spirituality of the rich, of men (males), of the urban elite? One speaks of a spirituality of and for protest, resistance, combat, revolution. One hears of a different spirituality or a non-spirituality of imperialist programs of world domination, or worship of profit or of a market economy, or of commodity fetishism and consumerism. How are these evaluated?

Is there a spirituality of ecology, a creation spirituality lived in the Third World, but betrayed by world domination, and needing exploration and redemption?

How is spirituality related to religion and mysticism? And to ethical practice?

Is the word "spirituality" itself usable today after it has gathered around it, down through the centuries, connotations of withdrawal to interiority, of flight from the world, of contempt of matter and history, and of an abstract other-worldliness? What better term could be suggested? Or is the word to be redeemed? Is it true that the church (and analogically the many religions) has today left behind its traditions of being Christendom (with coercive power and wealth and pomp), also its tradition of being Christianity (with concentration in doctrine, discipline and ritual) and is in the process of becoming Christianness—a movement, an energy, a lifestyle, a leaven, a spirituality, a fragrance?

We want to thank all our contributors. Many of our members were involved in the preparation of the conference. The Theological Commission provided the basic framework and the introductory statement. We receive with gratitude their contributions.

Orbis Books has agreed to publish the materials. Our special thanks are due to Robert Gormley, Robert Ellsberg, and Susan Perry without whose help and encouragement we would not have been able to publish it.

Part I

The Changing Context of the Third World

1

Changes in the Relationships Between Third World Countries and First World Countries

FRANZ J. HINKELAMMERT

I wish to develop some theses on the changes in the relationship between Third World countries and First World countries, which have been strongly affected by the crisis of socialism in the Soviet Union and in the Eastern European countries. It is a profound change, which came about in the '80s but which had already been developing in the decades prior to that.

First Thesis

I believe, and this will be my first thesis, that in recent years there has been a transformation in world capitalism, which came to light at the most dramatic moment of the crisis of socialism, that is to say, with the fall of the Berlin wall in November 1989. I was at that moment in the Federal Republic of Germany and I could see a strong symbolic connection between the fall of the wall and the massacre of the Jesuit community in San Salvador, which took place only a week later. What specially struck me was that the European media concentrated almost exclusively on the fall of the wall, while the other event, which showed so clearly what the Third World had become, was reduced to some marginal news items on the radio and in a few newspapers. What had happened in San Salvador was an "extermination" in the classic style of totalitarianism of the '30s, when one of the

This paper was published originally in the journal *Pasos*, July–August 1990. Reproduced here by courtesy of the publishers.

liberation theology centres of the western world was "eliminated." The western media reacted as the media of the totalitarianisms of the '30s had reacted. The government of the USA, through the FBI, kidnapped the most important witness and obliged her, through threats, to change her testimony. Consequently the other western government also collaborated to cover up this fact.[1] One month later the military invasion of Panama took place, with the approval of all western societies. There was also little or no news about this event.

The control of the media was once more brought about by the classic methods of the totalitarianism of the '30s. On the afternoon of the first day of the invasion a Spanish reporter from Spain's newspaper *El Pais* was killed, which was a sufficient warning to all the members of the media who were there at the time.

There isn't necessarily a connection between the two events—the fall of the Berlin wall and the Jesuits' massacre in San Salvador—though one cannot help wondering at the timing. Few historical moments in recent years have been as propitious for the massacre which took place in San Salvador as this one was. But even if there is no connection, there is no doubt that an undeniably symbolic relationship exists between the two. This proves to us that a capitalism which tried to appear, between the '50s and the '70s as a capitalism with a human face, needs no longer try to do so. It can now once again appear as a capitalism without a human face.

Capitalism today feels it can say "We have won." A philosophy of the State Department of the US government emerges, which talks of the end of history (and, relating it to Hegel, of the reality of the absolute idea) and which promises a future in which there is no longer any history or essential conflict, and in which the First World has found its peace and the Third World is no longer relevant.[2]

The world which now appears and announces itself is a world where there is only "one lord" and "master," and where there is only one system. We have a world with only one empire which extends everywhere; this empire covers and includes the whole world. It suddenly becomes clear that there is no place of asylum. With only one empire there cannot be any refuge. The empire is everywhere. It has total power and it knows it. Everywhere the empire announces that it has all the power. The self-proclaimed "open society" constituted the first closed society, from which there is no escape to the outside.

This means that for the first time the Third World finds itself completely alone. In its conflict with the First World of central capitalistic countries, it can count on the support of no other country. It can no longer resort to any Second World which in some way could be in solidarity with it. To the degree in which the Second World of the socialist countries continues to exist, it no longer offers any solidarity to the Third World, and has become part of the North confronting the South. It has been said in many parts of Latin America that the Second World cannot prosper if it is not admitted by the First World to that banquet where the Third World is devoured.

Together with all this there is a deeper conviction whose importance is undeniable and that is that the consciousness of an alternative is lost. It seems there are no longer any alternatives, and the "Totality" which is how the First World proclaims itself, is the expression of this state of consciousness. We are a world which is the Absolute Idea! When Kolakowski confronted Stalinism in the '50s he criticised it for being a blackmail with only one alternative"(!)[3]

However, he couldn't imagine what happens when this blackmail with only one alternative is put into effect and executed by a world system which has absolute worldwide power. Actually, we have arrived at a situation in which blackmail with only one alternative can be brought about without restrictions. Today this blackmail has been imposed on the whole world.

The crisis of socialism did not only take away from the Third World the possibility to seek solidarity in its conflict with the First World. It now can no longer resort to socialism as it seeks alternatives. It can now no longer use socialism to demonstrate that there really is an alternative however imperfect it may be. It can now no longer say that there is an alternative which can be improved and has a future; it can no longer say that it is possible to have another future, to have in the future something that is different from the present.

Capitalism in the '50s and '60s was a capitalism of social and economic reforms which also was concerned with the development of Third World countries so as not to allow alternative movements to flourish. But this capitalism believes that today there is no alternative, whatever it does. Therefore it again becomes wild capitalism—capitalism without a human face.

Most of us know that we are on a roller-coaster heading for the abyss. However, capitalism does not even try to put the brakes on. It says to us: "Do you have an alternative?" At the same time it continues to do all it can to prevent an alternative to this death trap from being found.

This is our first thesis: the crisis of socialism has extremely weakened the Third World but at the same time has weakened the possibilities of survival for humanity itself.

Second Thesis

This phenomenon of the weakening of the Third World is complemented by another which we could discuss starting with the following question: Does the First World still need the Third World?

We know that the production structures of the Third World have developed on the basis of its labour force, used in the production and exportation of its raw materials. The importance of the Third World has consisted in the development of its raw materials produced by the existing labour force. Where there wasn't enough labour force, the First World obtained it through forced slave labour. These raw materials were the basis of the development of today's developed countries.

Without a doubt, today we experience certain trends towards the loss of importance of the production of raw materials of the Third World. Many "natural" raw materials are substituted by "synthetic" raw materials, which also makes the labour force which produced them redundant. Many raw materials are still produced in the Third World but it becomes more and more difficult to use all the available labour force in their production.

This results in a restructuring of the Third World. From a world in which raw materials were exploited by exploiting the existing labour force, it has become a world where the population itself has been made redundant. Differently to what happened up to 100 years ago, the most important aspect in relation to the population of the Third World today is that it is a redundant population from the point of view of the First World and its economic needs. The Third World is still needed—its seas, its air, its nature, even if only as a garbage dump for the First World's poisonous garbage. Its raw materials are still needed as well. In spite of some raw materials losing their importance, the Third World continues to be of vital importance for the development of the First World. What is no longer needed is the greater part of the population of the Third World.

This is the reason why the First World does not withdraw from the Third World but now develops an image of it as a world where there is an excess of population. This redundant population, which is referred to in terms of population explosion, is seen as dangerous and no longer as something to be exploited. Actually technical development today is such that it cannot exploit this population. The structure of capitalism is such that it can no longer exploit the world's population. However, it considers population which it can no longer exploit as redundant. It is a population which is seen as overpopulation and which should not even exist but it is nevertheless there. This capitalism has nothing to do with the fate of that population.

The concept of exploitation now changes. As we know, the classic concept of exploitation refers to an available labour force which is effectively used in production and from which is taken the product it makes. We are referring to the concept of surplus exploitation as it was developed in the Marxist tradition. However, there now arises a situation in which a population no longer can be used for capitalistic production and where there is no intention of using it, or any possibility of doing so in the future. A world emerges where to be exploited becomes a privilege.

To be precise, this concept of exploitation appeared at the beginning of the 19th century in Europe. That was a world in which, during periods of great economic activity, there was full employment for the labour force and therefore when activity slowed down the workers alternated between employment and unemployment. But, in present day capitalism, this situation has changed. There is a situation where growing segments of the population of the Third World are no longer "exploited" in this sense. The more the population appears to be redundant, the less this concept of exploitation exists. This is why it has become less important. This is also observed in the conscience of the worker himself. He feels less and less that he is exploited when he realises that he is privileged compared to all those who are redundant. The whole relationship with exploitation then changes. This happens just as much in the industrialised world, although it is much more extreme in the Third World.

This also means that the redundant population of the Third World has no power at all. Those who are redundant cannot go on strike, they have no bargaining power, cannot threaten. The proud saying of the 19th century worker: "All wheels stop if your strong hand desires it" can no longer be spoken by the population of the Third World, even though it did seem possible during times of crisis. However it happened in a few specific countries and in exceptional conditions, at an also exceptional moment. The same can be said of the slogan "Proletariat of the world, unite." This was the cry of groups who felt they had the bargaining power which arose out of unity. Today this theme also is in a state of collapse. The peoples of the Third World have such a minimum bargaining power that they cannot demand their participation. The situation of the redundant population has become a situation in which their very existence is threatened.

This is the second thesis: the rich First World countries continue to need the Third World countries, but no longer need this population.

Third Thesis

In this situation the Third World countries lose the capacity to carry out any development policy.

In the present situation, the only possibility of development of Third World countries is in the development related to the world market which really means related to the market of the industrialised countries. This relationship is restricted to the production of raw materials. Although these become less important, there is nevertheless an ever growing competition among the Third World countries for these limited markets. The result is a drop in prices. With exports being greater in quantity, the availability of foreign currency becomes blocked or diminishes. Therefore, based on this traditional structure of production, development of Latin American and other Third World countries in general daily becomes less possible. For development, which would include the existing population, to be possible it would have to be based on the rapid growth of industrial production which would be integrated in the world division of labour.

There is clear evidence that the rich countries do not accept this type of development. We can see the systematic destruction of all the steps that lead to it. In spite of a few small countries managing to escape this fate imposed by the rich countries, the evident tendency of the Third World is towards destruction or slowdown of the industries which appeared be-

tween the '50s and '70s. The rich countries do not expect any advantages
to come out of the development of the Third World, only disadvantages.

The more environmental issues enter these considerations, the worse
the situation becomes. It is known that sensible development of the Third
World can no longer be a replica of the development of the presently
developed countries. The environment would not be able to stand it. It is
also known that a sustainable development would oblige the First World
to change all its production structures and its technical decisions in order
to make it adequate to the conditions for survival of the whole of humanity
within the framework of nature as it exists today. Since there is no will to
do this, the First World prepares itself to use the destruction of the Third
World environment for its own gain in order to guarantee its own survival
for as long as possible. We are faced with a "heroism" of collective suicide.

Here lies the importance of the Third World's foreign debt, which allows
the First World countries to control the development possibilities of the
Third World countries with a view to obstructing their success. This debt
has become the decisive tool with which to dictate economic and development policy to the countries which are in debt. If we were to observe the
trends of the imposed "structural adjustments" we would see that, obviously, the central conditioning consists in obstructing the energy, through
industrial products, of the underdeveloped countries into the world division of labour.

The Third World's foreign debt is an ideal tool with which to attain this
objective. The development of the Third World is suppressed in the name
of goals which, directly and apparently, have nothing to do with it. The
objective becomes invisible. What is visible is the debt these countries have,
and their obligation to pay it. However, the result is that the Third World
countries are reduced to a desperate production of raw materials which
suppresses its potential for industrial development.

If one wants to explain this policy in a few words which would express
what today dominates the First World like a phobia, one could say: Japan
never again! Japan happened once, but will never again happen! Or do we
seriously believe that we are prepared to accept a Japan as large as Brazil
or India?

This is our third thesis: the rich capitalistic countries have lost interest
in a development policy for the Third World and have opted to block it as
much as they can.

Consequently, we have three theses:

1) Capitalism once again becomes wild capitalism; it no longer fears
that alternatives are possible and therefore does not want to compromise.

2) The Third World is economically necessary for the rich countries
but its population is not needed.

3) The rich countries consider development based on industrial

integration in the world market as a threat; the foreign debt of the Third World works as an instrument to regulate control and eventually block this type of development.

The Search for Alternatives

As we view the situation described in the above three theses, and which has no apparent solution, it is necessary to reflect on the possible alternatives. It must be frankly admitted that we still have no thought-out alternative. But this should not be an obstacle to start in our own way. It is necessary to start gathering the rough materials now. I want to propose an important element in this process of building a new alternative. It is the need to create ties between the poor and the excluded themselves, to strengthen the unity between groups and institutions in the First World and the Third World, and to think of a new model of development. The soul of this model of a new alternative should be solidarity, understood in a different way than it was experienced in the past.

At present there is a type of solidarity emerging which is different from the workers' solidarity in the 19th century. Workers' solidarity was the foundation of the power of the workers themselves, which was the result of their unity. That is why it was able to be essentially solid, so as to confront capital, which was a destructive force. The solidarity of a population reduced to a redundant population cannot now have this characteristic. It does not constitute bargaining power. However it is, like workers' solidarity also was, a solidarity of mutual help. Nevertheless, for the last decade or two it does not constitute power anymore. It is the solidarity of the poor, not of the proletariat.

It can constitute power only to the degree in which there is the solidarity of groups which are integrated in the society with those who are excluded. It cannot limit itself to being the solidarity of a group that struggles, but it must be a human solidarity beyond any group, which includes the excluded as a basic condition. We are talking of the solidarity of the preferential option for the poor.

The trends of present-day capitalism, as we have seen, do not only develop the denial of solidarity, but the denial of the very possibility of solidarity as well. Solidarity today presupposes confronting this capitalism with the need for a just society which is participative and ecologically sustainable. Solidarity today will simply be a dream if it does not put into action this alternative to present-day capitalism and its destructive tendencies. However capitalism denies it, as it also denies the possibility of this alternative, the very possibility of human solidarity. As it struggles to the death against all possible alternatives, it struggles to the death against the possibility of solidarity itself. It declares it to be an illusion, a bad habit, because if all alternatives are illusory, then solidarity is as well. It then persecutes the very intention of being in solidarity as something that is either ignorant or criminal. Solidarity is persecuted as a destructive "utopia."

Present-day bourgeois thinking transforms solidarity into something diabolical. To the degree in which their solidarity expresses what in Christian tradition is love of neighbour, it now considers that very preaching of love as diabolical preaching, a demonic temptation.[4]

This carries with it the extreme denial of any human dignity. Since solidarity and the love of neighbour are proclaimed as diabolical, the recovery of human dignity is diabolical as well. For bourgeois society, even Jesus himself is now transformed into the devil, which needs to be fought.

Human dignity is denied when solidarity is denied. This is not a simple declaration of abstract principles, but a very real matter. Human dignity is based on the possibility of living with dignity. The acknowledgement of this is necessarily the acknowledgement of the right to live with dignity. This means to eat, to have a home, education, health, and so on. If there is no acknowledgement of this as a human right, there is no possible acknowledgement of human dignity.

However, the aim to live with dignity is a possible alternative only if an alternative exists. If I deny the possibility of any alternative, I deny the person the possibility of being able to live with dignity. Thus I deny the person his or her dignity in every concrete way—and I transform human dignity into an abstract principle, with no content. It is clear that human beings who have been made redundant and who consequently consider themselves redundant no longer have human dignity; thousands of declarations will not alter this fact. The exploited are violated in their human dignity, but the redundant are not even given a dignity that can be violated. And here it is clear why the remarkable name "cancer" is used to describe all liberation movements in the western world. I cannot recall one single liberation movement which was not called a cancer in Washington or in Europe. A cancer which must be cut out. This is the way the bourgeois world relates to liberation movements. The last time a cancer was mentioned in Latin America was in reference to Nicaragua and the Frente Sandinista. But it was also used in the case of Libya and Chile, and before that, I believe it was used for the first time in Indonesia in 1965. The word cancer replaced a word that was key to the Nazis: "parasites." This word was in reference to the same phenomenon. Substituted by the word cancer, it is today ever-present in the repression of the liberation movements in the Third World and, beyond those, in the repression of any form of dissidence.

If one were to take seriously this relationship between the existence of alternatives and human dignity, one would also see that the struggle of the bourgeoisie against any alternative, in order to destroy it, is also a struggle for the destruction of human dignity itself. People are not given the right to live with dignity. They can live, and live well, if they are able to find the space in the market to do so. If they do not achieve it, the market proves that they also don't have human dignity nor the right to claim it. Therefore in the process of the destruction of alternatives, and in the production of redundant people, attempts are made to destroy the very human meaning of human dignity to such a degree that these human beings who are made redundant see themselves as redundant. I believe that the whole ideological struggle today revolves around this. This is the content of psychological war. I also believe that the crisis of socialism has made it possible to really achieve this denial of human dignity.

This is not true exclusively in the "production of redundant people" in the Third World. A similar process is occurring in the First World, although at a lower level. Deep down, the psychological war, which at least in the Third World is widespread, tries to convince people who are made redundant that they indeed are redundant and consequently they destroy each other instead of being in solidarity among themselves. I think the first author to really understand this process and describe it was Nietzche. It is surprising to what degree he understood that people who are made redundant have to see themselves as such in order to destroy their very own selves and one another.[5]

Situations such as these are found today in many societies in Latin America: in the Dominican Republic, Honduras, Colombia, Peru, Argentina and others.

These processes show that to be in solidarity today is different from what it was in previous times, and there is no doubt that it has become once again of great importance. It is not simply a question of a call to unite and help. It requires the total restoration of human dignity which has been denied at its very roots. It must be made clear that the denial of alternatives is the denial of human dignity, and we insist on that dignity.

It does not mean we have the alternatives already worked out and up our sleeves. Is the genocide in the Third World legitimate if the victim population does not dispose of the means to develop an alternative for the Third World and First World countries? If at present we do not have a developed alternative to the destruction of the Amazon or the Himalayas, is this destruction legitimate? We know that this destruction of humanity and of nature must end, and everyone has a duty to find alternatives. Capitalism is embarking on the collective suicide of the whole of humankind. Can it be that it is legitimate only because nobody has found an alternative? An alternative needs to be developed.

Many proposals for alternatives have been broken. However, I can see no reason for the victory which the bourgeoisie celebrates today. Every broken alternative is a loss of hope in being able to escape from the collective suicide which the bourgeois society is planning. Alternatives are not developed quickly in a congress or in a secluded office. It will become ever more difficult to develop alternatives because any alternative must include technical considerations which cannot be developed superficially. However, the bourgeoisie has monopolised the very technical capacity required to develop them.

What we must prove is that there will be no human survival if all alternatives to the system which so obstreperously seems to be triumphing are not found. The alternatives cannot emerge unless the whole world's population demands them, because they know that they need them. Alternatives are not produced like sausages, to be offered later. There has to be an awareness that without them we are lost. Only thus will they be found. We will never have an alternative in recipe form because the alternative can only emerge when humanity realises that it needs it.

In spite of this the basic elements for this alternative are known. We are talking of a new economic and financial world order, an order for the marketing of raw materials. We are also talking of the re-establishment of an economic policy in relation to labour and the distribution of income; a universal policy of education and health and the establishment of an ecological order which would channel markets so that economic growth would respect nature's reproduction. However, an alternative can only come from this if it is effectively embraced by the whole of society in order to put it into practice in its daily exercise of power.

At the moment it cannot be an alternative for one class only. We are talking of an alternative for all humanity. But the search for it, and the insistence on it, continue to be a class problem. This is a class struggle above which hangs the denial of an alternative. The bourgeoisie no longer has an adversary grouped into a class. Nevertheless, it continues to be the dominant class which acts as in a class struggle, in spite of this coming only from above. This position of the bourgeoisie needs to be destroyed in order to be able to discuss and act clearly. If the bourgeoisie does not give in in this class struggle, there will be no alternative. It has the power to destroy anybody and today there is no way to defeat it by means of a response on the level of this very same class struggle. If it does not give in, we will go to the abyss.

There only remains the resistance to lead our society to a re-structuring of itself. I would like to end with a few words spoken by Mark Edelman, one of the leaders of the Warsaw Uprising in 1944: "It is better to do something than to do nothing." This something is what we must do.

Notes

1. The media in western democracies actually spoke more of the writer Rushdie. He had been threatened with death in Teheran. Living in London, he received Mrs. Thatcher's protection and he survived. At the same time, that is to say during several months in 1989, there was a press campaign in El Salvador which threatened the life of the Jesuits. They however continued in El Salvador under much heavier threats. The news agencies of the western democracies are as well represented in San Salvador as in Teheran. But they hardly spoke up. They did not do it after the massacre either, and yet they continued to speak of Rushdie who was already quite safe. Margaret Thatcher also showed practically no interest in the Jesuits. In Latin America there are many Rushdies; but they never have any protection. They are

killed, and no western democracy bothers. The well-known French philosopher Glucksmann, who was awarded the peace prize by German booksellers, in his "laudatio" for Havel, spoke of *three* heroes in the struggle against totalitarianism in 1989: Solzhenitzyn, Rushdie and Havel (See *Friedenspreis des Deutschen Buchhandels 1989*, Vaclav Havel, *Ansprachen aus Anlass der Verleihung* (Addresses on the Occasion of the Investiture), Frankfurt a.M. 1989, pp. 35-36).

However, these "heroes" whom I respect, are all alive today. Those who struggled for freedom in Latin America and the Third World however, are murdered. They were killed by the western democracies in El Salvador, Brazil, Colombia, Venezuela, and Honduras, which can count on the indiscriminate support of the western democracies of Europe and the United States. The massacre of the Jesuits is only one of the many cases. Are they not the real heroes of the struggle against totalitarianism in 1989? Western democracies proclaim and at the same time celebrate their peace prizes, without even mentioning the war that they themselves are bringing about.

Glucksmann said: "Take a good look: in the year 1989 the end of this century is being announced" (p. 36). Is it not the massacre in San Salvador that warns us of things to come?

2. See: Fukuyama, Francis, "The End of History?" *The National Interest*, Summer, October 1989. See: Gallardo, Helio, *Francis Fukuyama y el triunfo del capitalismo burgues. El final de la historia o el deseo de finalizar el ser humano?* in *Pasos*, DEI, San Jose, 1990, No. 27. Also: Gallardo, Helio, *Francis Fukuyama: el final de la historia y el Tercer Mundo, Pasos*, 1990, No. 28.

3. Kolakowski, *El hombre sin alternativa*, 1956. Unfortunately, he did not speak of the problem again after he moved to England. He no longer says that he again lives in a society without an alternative.

4. Popper puts it like this: We are all quite sure that nobody will be miserable in the beautiful and perfect community of our dreams, and there is also no doubt that it would not be difficult to bring heaven down on earth if we loved one another. But. . . the attempt to bring heaven on earth invariably produces hell as a result. It causes intolerance, religious wars and the saving of souls by means of the Inquisition (Popper, Karl: *La sociedad abierta y sus enemigos*, Paidos Studio, Buenos Aires, 1981, Tomo II, capitulo XIV, p. 403).

5. Nietzsche, Friedrich, *La voluntad de poderio*, EDAF, Madrid, 1981, No. 55, p. 60.

2

Global Solidarity for the Future: Where Do We Go from Here in South-North Relations?

LAWRENCE SURENDRA

State of South-North Relations

As this century with its blood-stained record draws to a close, the nineteenth century dream of one world has re-emerged, this time as a nightmare. It haunts us with the prospect of a fully homogenized, technologically controlled, absolutely hierarchized world, defined by polarities like the modern and the primitive, the secular and the non-secular, the scientific and the unscientific, the expert and the layman, the normal and the abnormal, the developed and the unde-veloped, the vanguard and the led, the liberated and the savable.

> Ashish Nandy
> in The Intimate Enemy—Loss and
> Recovery of Self Under Colonialism

Introduction

The disappearance of the Second World (the Socialist Bloc) has in effect meant also the disappearance of the Third World. The disappearance of the two worlds, has not led to the creation of a new One World—but only to a world in which the First World now totally and completely dominates the rest of the world. It is also a world in which, given the manner in which Eastern Europe and the Soviet Union have crumbled, the West dominates. This domination has so far meant more of gloating by the West about its superiority than seeking seriously, ways to bring western institutions and values in the construction of a more pluralist, just and peaceful world order.

The world today, looked at from the vantage point of the South, is a world in which the gap between "rich" and "poor" countries has become greater; this gap is no longer a relatively surmountable gap, but absolute in terms of access to key factors of production such as capital (including technology). Gloom, despair and despondency stalk many parts of the South. The famine, poverty and destitution in countries such as Ethiopia, Somalia, regions such as sub-Saharan Africa, present a grim picture of the future. In other parts, including parts of Asia, deepening poverty is leading to endemic violence and terrorism of both the non-state and state variety. Almost the whole of the South is moving into situations where health standards and environmental conditions are rapidly deteriorating.

At one level, among the poor and marginalized, there is a growing sense of hopelessness and powerlessness. At another level, fortunately one must say, there is still hope. Countless individuals and organizations are struggling against contemporary debilitating international and national processes. They are joining hands with people in their struggle for empowerment, hope and a better future—the struggle for a New One World of all peoples; a world of justice, peace and equality for all peoples. To be part of this struggle calls for serious analysis and understanding of the state of the world, particularly the nature of South-North relations. Emotional, knee-jerk or pietistic charity type responses are not only insufficient, they mock the millions who are kept for no choice of their own in an inhuman state. There is no greater challenge, for people on the globe today, than that of changing the South-North relations; a challenge to global humanity nearing the end of the 20th century that raises the fundamental question, "does humanity lie at the heart of human action?" It is in such a perspective that we propose to look at the future of global solidarity and where we go from here in South-North relations.

The Economy

The state of economic relations, the sucking out of the wealth, of capital—human and economic—is perhaps a good starting point for looking at the South-North relations. For the poorest of the world's nations, those of sub-Saharan Africa, the terms of trade for the period 1980-1987 deteriorated by fourteen percent. In 1987, this fourteen percent represented a loss of purchasing power amounting to US$ 3.5 billion compared with 1980, most of which benefited OECD countries. "Foreign debt rose from $6 billion in 1970 to $134 billion in 1980. Although this is only a tenth of the total debt of all developing countries, it represents three to four times the value of total exports from sub-Saharan Africa and is almost equal to the total Gross Domestic Product (GDP), which in itself is comparable to that of a country like Belgium. Annual debt service now amounts to $18 billion. Roughly $9 billion of this is actually paid and this represents the greater part of the total exports of goods and services."[1]

With the fall in most commodity prices by 20 percent and more, countries of the South had to engage in a severe cut-throat competition among themselves, leading to further disastrous consequences to the poorest. The General Agreement on Trade and Tariff (GATT) expects the volume of world trade to rise by between 5 and 6 percent in 1990. This is not different from the average growth in the 1970s and actually slightly lower than the average in the 1980s. The current deficit in 1990 of all developing countries was $16.3 billion, more than double the 1989 figure. Inequality of income distribution among countries has also increased since 1960. In 1990, the GDP averaged $12,490 in developed market economies while it was $980 in developing countries (using 1980 dollar values for both developed and developing countries). Thus, compared to an average rich country per capita income in an average developing country was only 7.8 percent in 1990 whereas in 1960 it was 10.1 percent.[2]

It is important to bear in mind that even these average developing country incomes are distorted by the inclusion of a large number of oil exporters. If we were to take countries that depend on the export of other raw materials, and take especially the 42 least developed countries' (LDCs) per capita income of $241 per annum, then these incomes are actually one-fiftieth of the income of the industrial world. A further point that needs to be kept in mind is that when one talks of "average income" it equally hides the position of the poorest groups, whose incomes are way below the average income.

What we have here touched upon is only the tip of the iceberg of issues of trade, economy and income distribution globally and vis-à-vis developing and developed countries. In referring to countries of the South and North, we cannot avoid mention of the transnational corporations (TNCs). This despite the magic performed by Maurice Strong, the Canadian billionaire, and UNCED, where in the 1000-page Agenda 21 at the Rio Summit, all mention of TNCs was taken out. TNCs control 70 percent of world trade, 80 percent of foreign investment and 30 per cent of global GDP. It is in such a context of the first world stranglehold, that developing countries get IMF-World Bank advice to "develop." To "develop" of course you need capital, but if developing countries were to borrow, it would cost them 71 percent in real terms, whereas it would be only 4 percent in a developed country. Need anything more be said about the One World we humans inhabit, and how the First World, to maintain its domination, uses every unfair means at its disposal?

Debt and Reverse Capital Flows

Central to the kind of unjust and perverse economic relations that the North maintains over the South is the debt situation of developing countries. Third World debt is now around $1.3 trillion, which accounts for 44 percent of its GNP. The net flow annually from developing countries to developed countries, from South to North, is $50 billion. The money lent by the World Bank in 1989 as concessional aid was only $28 billion. In effect, the South has been subsidizing the high consumption growth of the North, as a result of the debt crises of the South. According to Susan George, "OECD figures show that the debtors are reimbursing their loans at the rate of over $3 billion a week. Even more astonishing, they have sustained this rate of repayment over a decade."[3]

Since the debt crisis erupted in 1982, Latin America has sent northwards an average of $4 billion every month in the past nine years. Even the poorest region of the world, namely sub-Saharan Africa, has been contributing $10 billion annually by way of reverse transfer of capital to the North, with its Debt/GDP ratio at 106.1 percent! Debt has not only been used as the most ruthless technique of sucking away of the capital endowments and resources of developing countries, it has also been used as the "crowbar" (a la Carla Hills, the US Secretary of Trade) by the North to wrench open the economies of the South for further exploitation and impoverishment by the economic forces of the North such as the TNCs.

Appropriation of National Resources

In the 1970s, great economists in the metropolitan centers were giving advice to poor developing countries—advice that was at no risk to them. They kept telling the developing countries that the only way out of their extreme poverty was "growth." Regions like Latin America and the countries in Latin America, because of their proximity to metropolitan centers, like the US, became also the first guinea pigs and victims of such advice. For example, the gigantic appetite of North Americans for hamburgers created a big demand for beef. Forests were cleared in the Amazon and in countries like Costa Rica to convert it into pasture lands to grow beef. The banks, the economists, the politicians all came in to promote this type of growth.

The virgin forest land once cleared, its topsoil washed away, the land could not last very long as grazing land. Countries like Costa Rica exported a lot of beef for the hamburgers in the US and timber for the booming construction industry in the US. Economic growth was booming, the exporters and the cattle ranchers were making mega bucks, the banks and the economists were now treating countries like Costa Rica as the "model" for all developing countries. But the rapid clearing of forests for timber and beef for hamburgers has more or less destroyed the natural resource capital base of Costa Rica. No one was counting the cost to Costa Rica, which is now estimated in billions of dollars in terms of resource depletion (degraded land, washed away topsoil, destroyed forests and so on) while Costa Rica's national accounts recorded massive exports and dollar incomes.

Today Costa Rica is a debt-ridden country, with degraded land which has to be worked even harder to repay the debts, and peasant farmers poorer than before, with neither their previous subsistence farming base or incomes from cash crops to fall back on. The destruction of the natural resource capital, the fundamental basis on which millions of people depend for their very survival, has been the most devastating aspect of the purely exploitative market and trade oriented relationship of the North to the South. Yet, both the Brundtland Commission and UNCED (the Rio Summit) insist that only more trade is good and, if you believe, "sustainable."

The problem is how do developing countries with constantly falling commodity prices (they fell by over 20 percent in the 1980s) manage to earn enough in a "sustainable" manner, both economically and in environmental terms. What is actually happening is that with prices plummeting, overall volumes of world trade not expanding, no increase in the volume of global capital available for new investments either—developing countries are into a cycle of "export-led ecological destruction." With the Damocles Sword of mounting debt repayments hanging over their heads, forcing them to export more to simply earn foreign exchange, developing countries are over-exploiting their already fragile agricultural lands, their forest resources, their fishing resources and so on.

Take the example of the growth of the multi-billion dollar prawn export industry, for the limitless consumption of the North, especially in countries like Japan, which is leading to the destruction of the coastlines by the shrimp farming industry. Much of Taiwan's coast is already destroyed, so is Thailand's, and we are now witnessing India going through the same self-destructing cycle, as more and more local governments in the coastal regions give away land for shrimp farming. Intensive shrimp farming requires both overuse of ground water, leading often to the destruction of fresh water sources and salination of soils. The lessons are there from Taiwan, from Thailand, from other countries in Africa and Latin America but those lessons cannot stand in the way of the greed of the Indian middle classes and elite.

Beef and shrimp have been used here as examples in Gandhi's perspective of living, when he says that there is enough for everyone's need but not for everyone's greed. We should recognize "greed" as much as a factor in economics (modern economics does not) as need. "Greed" is the antithesis of need. Yet in order not to run the danger of purely moralistic approaches, to problems of inequality and injustice, globally or within nations, equally important is the understanding of and a perspective on "power and control." This specially when looking at the role of TNCs in the global economy and they as the major contributors to the appropriation of natural resources of South and depletion of natural resource capital in the South.

If one takes agriculture as the basis of growing food, an activity that requires an important and sustainable interaction between human beings and nature, then it is here the major struggles for power and domination between North and South take place. It was no wonder that bio-diversity, central to the future of agriculture and food security, was a major contentious issue at Rio.

The reason is simple, agriculture the world over is slowly coming under the stranglehold of the TNCs. If you begin with seeds, the seed industry of the North attracts an investment of over US$ 50 billion and the commercial seed market of US$ 13 billion is mostly in private hands. The 20 largest pesticide makers control 94 percent of the world's agro-chemical sales. Fertilizer is another major input that is controlled by powerful petro-chemical concerns. It is not accidental that the world's leading chemical concerns are also becoming the world's seeds-men, this because seeds, fertilizers, pesticides and pharmaceuticals have a common ground in intensive research related to genetics and chemicals. The new armaments in this emerging warfare of modern day colonialism upon the agricultural systems and natural ecological resources of the South is bio-technology.

TNC control over economic activity is used with such power and destructive sweep, to not only control crop production and commodity prices, but also dietary habits and life-styles in the South. Cargill, a famous seed TNC, also controls 60 percent of the cereals traded on the world market. In Costa Rica, a major coffee producing country, Unilever, Gill and Dufus and four other multi-commodity dealers help set the prices of coffee beans and then export, process and market them, reaping the bulk of profits on the way to northern breakfast tables. Food multinationals are equally known for undermining traditional food and dietary habits and creating what people in the South call the "five-star hotel culture." The soft drink industry—Coca-Cola and Pepsi—are the more well-known notorious examples, but food multinationals in many countries of Africa, Latin America and now Asia are changing basic food habits. Twenty-five years ago the staple of Lagos was cassava, today it is American-grown wheat, and advertisements in Nigeria exhort Nigerians to turn to the new food. American exporters of wheat have just begun advertisements in India; perhaps people in South India may begin to wonder, can the humble "idli" (a fine example of traditional Indian science and technology) survive?

From land, to food, to dietary habits, there is this growing Northern corporate control over the lives of those in the South. We should add to this growing influence the control they have always had over mineral and other primary resources. TNCs have traditionally been the miners. Six companies control 63 percent of the world's aluminum mining and 54 percent of its smelting. A few more TNCs exercise control over a third of the world's copper and iron ore. It is in such a background, where northern corporate interests exert such life-and-death control over the natural resources of the South that one should look at present-day persistent northern calls for greater free trade and free market control of the resources of the South.

Labor Migration and Exploitation

Finally, it is in taking up issues of labor migration with respect to

South-North relations that we find the worst forms of racism, racist attitudes, use of naked power, domination and hypocrisy revealing themselves. It is all right for the North to talk of the free movement of capital
and goods, and demand from the South, like crude extortionists, that
southern borders be porous for the movement of capital and goods from
the North, but the reverse, of labor, cannot apply. It is not as if hordes of
people will invade the North if the borders are kept open. It is the racism
in the attitude of the North that dehumanizes and reduces migrant labor
from the South in the North to an inhuman existence. Whatever migration
there is from the South to the North is largely due to (like migration from
the villages to the cities in the South) the destruction of livelihood and the
hollowing out of the economies in the South by northern policies, institutions (such as IMF and World Bank) and corporations.

This is a major and important area with respect to South-North relations,
an area which southern elites (though they benefit immensely from the
deposits of their migrant labor) and northern governments treat as a
problem that does not exist. In the process of European integration and the
creation of a single European market, in European countries, however
much they may protest against accusations of creating a "fortress Europe"
in relation to immigration and migrant labor problems, it is definitely a case
of the pure white races protecting themselves against the invasion of the
black, brown and yellow races. The cruelest irony for the people of the
South is that all this should happen in the year of the celebration of the
voyage of Columbus to the Americas, a voyage that 500 years ago inaugurated the genocide of indigenous peoples in the Americas, the creation of
the culture of the superiority of white races over others, leading to apartheid becoming a part of human history.

Following from that genocidal history of the human race, the modern
world after Columbus, Europeans (or European races) today occupy land
several times the land mass of Europe. To expand their access to land and
resources, Europeans occupied northern America, Australia, New Zealand,
considerable portions of Southern Africa and eastern parts of the Soviet
Union. These settlements required the simultaneous displacement, destruction and genocide of the native people of these areas. With respect to
countries of the North, Japan, a non-western northern country, is equally
guilty of such destruction of its indigenous people in its own northern
territories, where the Ainu indigenous people have lived for centuries.
Japan is also very much part of the racism against migrant labor.

The "ecological imperialism that accompanied the biological expansion
of Europe between 900 C.E. and 1900 C.E."[4] is another matter, that we will not
go into here. Charles Darwin, writing in 1839 in the *Voyage of the Beagle*,
said, "Wherever the Europeans had trod, death seems to pursue the aboriginal. We may look to the wide extent of the Americas, Polynesia, the Cape
of Good Hope, and Australia, and we find the same result." While Darwin
records what European expansion did to indigenous people in the lands

they went to, writing around the same period another man of the white race, Charles Lyell in a book, *Principles of Geology*, written in 1832, had said "Yet, if we wield the Sword of Extermination as we advance, we have no reason to repine the havoc committed." Between 1820 and 1930, well over 50 million Europeans migrated, amounting to one-fifth of the entire population of Europe at the beginning of that period. The reasons were not different from that of migration from the South today. Then, in Europe population explosion and a resulting shortage of cultivable land, national rivalries, persecution of minorities (apart from the opening up of maritime travel and so on) resulted in long distance migration.

Contrast all this with the views now emerging in Europe and America with respect to the peoples of the South and what one sees as underlying perspectives in the North of North-South relations.[5] Jacques Attali, a French liberal, a stalwart of the French Socialist Party and head of the European Bank for Reconstruction and Development, in his book, *Millennium: Winners and Losers in the Coming World Order*, writes off the billions of people in the South as "millennial losers." To him America is a "lost continent" and Latin America is sliding into "terminal poverty." Attali says that the people of the South, with no future of their own can only look forward to "migrating from place to place looking for a few drops of what we have in Los Angeles, Berlin or Paris, which for them will be cases of hope, emerald cities of plenty and high tech magic." Attali gives an apocalyptic warning to his race in the North and tells them to expect "a war unlike any seen in modern times, (one that) will resemble the barbarian raids of the seventh and eighth centuries."

A similar perspective is expressed in the U.S. Presidential Commission (1988) an Integrated Long Term Strategy, which says that conflict with the South, "is a form of warfare in which 'the enemy' is more or less omnipresent and unlikely ever to surrender" and goes on to say that, whereas "in the past we have sometimes seen these attacks as a succession of transient and isolated crises, we now have to think of them as a permanent addition to the menu of defense planning problems."

What one must see in the containment of immigration, hardening of migration policies, deliberately allowing a degree of anti-immigrant sentiment to prevail in the North, is part of a larger policy of containment of the South. It is in that very critical sense, labor migration issues and immigrant labor issues in the North are very central to dealing with the North-South problems on the globe today.

Walden Bello of the Philippines, one of the South's most perceptive analysts and commentators of the policies of the North, says, "The truth is that the North has long given up on the post-war liberal belief that the development of the South is in the interest of the North. The perception that the interest of the poor, colored South and the rich, white North may well be irreconcilable is the basis of an emerging consensus among liberals, conservatives and reactionaries in the west. In place of a strategy of development, the New Consensus is putting in place a strategy of containment directed this time not at the Soviet Union but at the South."[6]

To conclude this section on the state of South-North relations, one incontrovertible fact is that South-North relations have reached a nadir in the history of nations.

Collusion within the North in Emaciating the South

Not only is the North unwilling to reduce its use of the global commons. On the contrary, it wants to use more. And in a classic rendition of might over right, it presently has the power to do so. In order to maintain its unsustainable living standards the North seeks to enmesh the South ever more tightly in a world political and economic order dominated by the North—and increasingly with the North by giant global corporations, the 15 largest of which have gross incomes greater than the gross domestic products of over 120 countries.

Ward Morehouse

The predicament of someone from the South, trying to understand the contours of the South-North landscape and how the North controls the South, is similar to that expressed in an African (Ashanti) saying: "A traveler may tell all that he has seen on a journey, but he cannot explain all."

The most significant aspect of the tightening embrace by the North of the South is the collusion of northern governments, TNCs and global institutions dominated by the North. Hitherto it has been hidden and to a degree covert. Here and there, as for example, during the GATT Uruguay Round talks, this covert collusion came to be exposed. But, it is at the Rio Earth Summit and the process leading to it that this collusion, though still hidden from public view, was most active and also achieved its ends. John Vidal, writing in a special supplement of *The Guardian* prepared in association with Oxfam, to mark the Earth Summit in Rio, has shed revealing light on this aspect. He wrote,

When the history of the 1992 Earth Summit is written the hidden story will be how TNCs, together with governments who are in their thrall, worked behind the scenes to *avoid* regulation on the transfer of technological resources to the South, limits on pollution, restrictions on the timber industries, debt reduction, consumption, and the export of hazardous waste. It will also be the story of how the poorer nations tried to demand justice. It should also include the influence of TNCs in last autumn's axing of the only world body overseeing their activities—the UN's Commission on Transnational Corporations.[7]

We shall, in this section of the paper, briefly look at institutions and institutional processes, where northern collusion against the South takes place.

The IMF and the World Bank

Two institutions were set up immediately after World War II by powerful western nations who met at Bretton Woods in 1943 in order to help oversee and design the international economic system in the post-war era. They were the International Monetary Fund (IMF) and the International Bank for Reconstruction and Development (IBRD). Over the past half century, these two institutions have become the key instruments through which the North, that is ex-colonial countries, now exercise control over the newly independent countries (ex-colonies) of the South. The IBRD signifying its new role in the global political economy has now come to be known very appropriately as the World Bank.

These two institutions, while technically multilateral institutions which come within the purview of the UN system, have managed to remain outside and above it. This is primarily because of the powerful backing these institutions have from the western powers, especially the US and which backing is institutionalized in the weighted system of voting rights that they have adopted, rather than the "one member one vote" system.

While all this is history, the logical corollary to the power that a single country, the US, exercises over the IMF, is that the US has not been hesitant to blatantly use the IMF to advance its own economic objectives. The IMF correspondingly has developed the iron fist (Structural Adjustment Program) in the velvet glove (Structural Adjustment Loan Facility) by which countries in the South have been brought to heel. This in any case was the agenda of the Reagan-Bush Administration when it came to power in 1980.

The Structural Adjustment Programs functioned very effectively in collecting the Third World debt, where Northern governments such as the US, by willful manipulation of global multilateral institutions such as the IMF, have ensured that their private financial institutions (banks) have had their loans repaid. Between 1984 and 1990, the net transfer of financial resources from the South to the North was an astonishing $155 billion. This information is mentioned, in case there are people who still do not believe and are looking for reasons for the collusion within the North against the South.

The economic rollback of countries of the South has been an important aspect of the shaping of the intervention of the IMF and World Bank by the Reagan-Bush Administration. This was of course helped by the fall in commodity prices to the lowest point since the 1930s, which in a way was a result of forcing all developing countries into export-led growth. But even in this export-led growth strategy, when countries tried to shift from unprocessed products to value-added products, it was discouraged. Malaysia for example is allowed to export unprocessed products, but if they try to convert their palm oil (a primary product) to margarine (a value-added manufacture) then the European Community slaps on a 20 percent tariff.

The depression of commodity prices by keeping greater competition among primary producers, preventing them from converting their primary produce to value-added products, increasing the indebtedness of countries, leading to greater and greater northern control has made it possible to roll back the economies of the South. In the first part of this paper, comparisons were made as to how the southern economies have been worse off in the beginning of the 1990s, than in the 1960s and 1970s. Yet the IMF (at the behest of its powerful shareholders) goes on merrily pushing Structural Adjustment Programs (appropriately termed SAP) in the South.

These programs have not succeeded anywhere and the IMF is yet to come up with an unqualified success story. On the contrary, Chile, which in the 1970s had only 20 percent of its population in poverty, now has 45 percent of its population pushed into the ranks of the poor. Malnutrition is pervasive and real wages have declined by over 40 percent since the early '70s. Mexico, about which at times the US and the IMF wax eloquent, are silent when asked why more then 50 percent of the population is unemployed or underemployed or why the purchasing power of the minimum wage is only about two-thirds of what it was in the 1970s.

Critical to achieving the rollback of southern economies is the undermining of the development process by the Bank and the Fund, as part of the collusion of these two institutions with powerful Northern (Western) economic interests—both government and private. The undermining of the development process does also mean undermining the sovereignty of the nations of the South. As Moris Miller, formerly Canada's representative on the Executive Board of the World Bank, has pointed out, "The macropolicy advice incorporated in the SALs touches the very core of the development policy process. . . The rate and manner of growth and related societal objectives of the recipient countries are the very stuff of that elusive but important concept called sovereignty."

So, as the IMF and World Bank keep adding to their collection of scalps of developing countries, Brazil, Chile, Argentina, Zambia, Mexico, Philippines *ad nauseum*, they also add up to the undermining of the collective sovereignty of the South. The crowning achievement in this process, which came late in 1991, is India—founder-member of the non-alignment movement, an active voice in advancing the interests of the developing countries and a moderate success in mixed economy (state-cum-private) approaches. It is therefore also no wonder that Indian technocrats (helping in the administering of the medicine of the IMF and WB), the elites of this country, media and academic votaries of the Bank and the Fund, are all now busy looking for new definitions and creating new lexicons to deal with concepts such as "sovereignty."

GATT and the Uruguay Round

GATT, to some extent, can be considered as the third element in the Bretton Woods trinity. It is a kind of truncated International Trade Organization (ITO) which was to be set up at Bretton Woods but never established due to US resistance. GATT which has hitherto remained an obscure institution in global terms has suddenly moved to center stage in the current round of GATT negotiations, termed the Uruguay Round launched in September 1986.

The Uruguay Round is the eighth round in Multi-lateral Trade Negotiations (MTNs) undertaken by the contracting governments to the GATT treaty. It is a very complex process and as Chakravarthi Raghavan, author of *Recolonization—GATT! The Uruguay Round and the Third World*,[8] says in his book, "The Uruguay Round is the most complicated and ambitious of any post-war multilateral negotiations, and is unlike the earlier seven rounds of GATT MTNs which had sought to liberalize international trade in goods mainly through tariff cuts and selective lowering of non-tariff barriers." Analyzing the different interests battling for supremacy through GATT in the world economy, particularly the US, whose economic supremacy is under severe threat, Raghavan states that, "in order to implement radical changes in the framework of world trade and economy, the Northern countries had to find a 'vehicle.' They decided that the vehicle would be GATT. The choice of GATT for launching a new round of 'trade' negotiations, but with new themes and agenda have to be seen in this perspective. *The choice was not by accident*" (emphasis supplied).

We will not be able to go into great detail here regarding the various maneuvers of the industrialized countries and the collusion between the TNCs and Northern government as attempts are made to bring the Uruguay Round to completion. What is extremely important to understand and emphasize, as Ward Morehouse points out, is that "GATT is the scene of what surely must be one of the most audacious and massive power grabs in modern history, as giant multinational corporations—the biggest of which are already larger than most nation states—seek to replace nation states as dominant actors in the global political economy."[9]

What about the South?

The technological revolution in the last few years has left many countries with virtually no prospects: new technology is the preserve of the countries which already have know-how and capital and are able to develop bio-technology, informatics and the other innovations further. Technical progress, accompanied by large-scale investment, accelerated means of communication and supranational economic decision-making, has made the emergence of a worldwide market possible and changed world society into a *global village*. But this gigantic village includes a constantly expanding slum area and has so far been unable to make any arrangements for its waifs and strays.

"A World of Difference—
A New Framework for Development Cooperation in the 1990s."
A Dutch Ministry of Development Cooperation Policy Document.

As we have discussed in the previous sections, the exploitative relations between North and South, the collusion within the North and the role of North-dominated institutions such as the GATT, the IMF and the World Bank have led to a kind of social Darwinism, a philosophy of the "survival of the fittest" dominating the management of human affairs on the globe. The technological vision of the global village excludes the real villages in the Third World, the tribals, the poor and socially and economically weaker populations of the world. How do all these processes converge in the South itself, before we look at ways out of this dehumanizing, technologized, exclusive global village, to a human, all-embracing global village.

Undermining Sovereignty

A crucial aspect of northern (and western) domination of the globe is a rapid undermining of the sovereignty of nation-states in the South. This erosion of sovereignty is a double-edged sword, as far as the vast sections of the population in developing countries, who already barely subsist on the margins, are concerned. Firstly, loss of economic sovereignty increasingly leads to pressures for State withdrawal from basic social development and economic processes on the assumption that markets—domestic and international—will set the pace of economic development. Social infrastructure, health delivery systems, education, services for the more vulnerable sections of the population (the poor, young, women, tribals) deteriorate and begin to collapse. Markets in the South that are also insufficiently developed and international markets are in no position to create the kind of momentum that is required to make up for the vacuum created by State withdrawal. The result is a gradual breakdown in social arrangements and social peace, leading to increasing breakdown of stability, and increasing violence and chaos.

Much of the 1980s can best be described as man-made catastrophes in large parts of the South. In Central America, El Salvador, Nicaragua and Guatemala have been torn by war and violence. There are about a million destitute displaced persons fleeing the violence in these countries. Another million are refugees in the U.S. or Mexico. Many more would follow them if they could. Some 250,000 people have been killed in the violence since the late 1970s. The picture is not different for other regions of the South. Civil conflicts in Liberia uprooted 1.2 million, more than half its population, 2 million southern Sudanese fled their homes in 1988 due to civil war, nearly a quarter of them in Ethiopia which is itself the source of tens of thousands of people in flight. The current global aggregate of uprooted people is 41 million and represents one in every 135 human beings on earth, most of them children and women.[10] The still festering ethnic conflict in Sri Lanka with no end in sight, which escalated to a full-blown conflict after the racial riots of 1983, is analyzed by many in Sri Lanka as one of the consequences of the open economic policies adopted in the early 1980s.

The other side of the double-edged sword of the loss of economic sovereignty is that the state, in the face of increasing social chaos and violence, hardens day by day, beefing up its security apparatus as one way of dealing with the growing violence. The birth of the national security state is very much a product of the global economic process of the 1980s. Military and defense spending increases, mainly to strengthen the security apparatus of the state to deal with internal breakdown of law and order. Police repression, brutality and lawlessness increasingly become the rule of the day and the poor, illiterate defenseless people in the villages and tribal hamlets are once again the victims of state terror. This again is the uniform story from the South in the last decade and in the beginning of this decade. The new-found western concern for human rights in the South refuses to accept this political economy dimension to the growing violation of human rights in Third World countries.

Cooptation of Elites and Playing the Poor against the Poor

The elites of the South do of course bear such substantial responsibility in this sordid global tale that we are forced to recount the bloodied landscape of global relations between rich and poor that we have journeyed through in this paper. The other side of the coin to the collusion of the North in maintaining this grossly unjust and unsustainable global system is the total cooptation of not merely the ruling power elites and the business and financial interests of the South, but also bulk of the middle class, educated people, research institutions and university professors who (day) dream of becoming a part of an exclusive local village.

But, it is the poor who have to finally bear the consequences for the greed of the South's elite in seeking at any cost to have a share in the unjust global spoils system. The poor are often played off against the poor, whether in global terms or within the South. The most telling moral indictment of the times we live in and the morality we accept is the case of the Brazilian elite using hired gunmen (mostly from the poor and unemployed) to shoot and kill street children in Rio, in order "to clear" from the streets "a social menace," as part of preparations to the holding of the Rio Earth Summit.

The contemporary world's twisted vision of the future at the grandiose Earth Summit was laid in those acts of the physical, violent removal of the poorest and the weakest, namely the poor, orphaned street children. Are these the norms that human civilizations nearing the end of the 20th century and entering the 21st century accept? Can we still change the way the globe is progressing and the way human beings define progress? A vision of progress that gives such irrational sanctity, above even human life and nature, to the unholy triad of money, markets and technology.

Is There a Future for South-North Relations?
Is There a Future for the Globe and Global Solidarity?

It took Britain half the resources of the planet to achieve its prosperity; how many planets will a country like India require?

Mahatma Gandhi,
(when asked if after Independence,
India would attain the British standard of living)

We begin by quoting Gandhi, which in the context of Brundtland, UNCED and so on, is finding its way into many articles, scholarly papers, reports and publications. This is a sign, one hopes, of some minimal reorientation in the way human beings think. There is no doubt that in both North and South this shift in thinking has to happen, it is a fundamental requirement for any future for the globe, for justice in relations between South and North, between people in the South, especially between the elite and the marginalized.

There can be no human solidarity, no solidarity with nature, if we are not willing to put limits on our consumption, whether in the North or the South. The North of course has to scale down drastically. Today an average American consumes 50 times what a Haitian consumes. This has to change. The image and reality of America as a wasteful society that is wasting the world must change and on that scale, so also other countries of the North. The South must decide to disentangle itself from its dependency on the North, and while actively part of the global search for a sustainable future, find its own ways also to work out its future. Blind entanglement in the economic web of the North is no guarantee or insurance for a sustainable, just and equitable future for the people of the South.

To move towards such a perspective, to concretely work and actively intervene in shaping the thinking of people, to influence public policy and redirect institutional energies towards processes of human solidarity and not individual greed, is a tremendous effort. But this has to be done. There is a great responsibility for citizens' movements, voluntary groups, religious and other social bodies, particularly in the North but also in the South, in educating and mobilizing people, toward more fundamental human values, away from reducing all human existence to mere markets and money. Only in this process is a new solidarity, a new chapter in South-North relations possible. Only then can we ensure that we have fulfilled our responsibility, in saving planet Earth for future generations.

Notes and References

1. The Netherlands Ministry of Development Cooperation, "A World of Difference—A new framework for development cooperation in the 1990s," Policy Docu-

ment, The Hague, March 1991.

2. World Development Reports, UN Reports, UNEP, World Bank and World Resources Institute.

3. Susan George, "Debt," in *Earth*, a *Guardian* special supplement in cooperation with OXFAM, London, June, 1992.

4. Alfred W. Cosby, *Ecological Imperialism—The Biological Expansion of Europe 900 to 1900 A.D.*, Cambridge University Press, 1986.

5. I am grateful to Walden Bello, Executive Director of the Institute for Food and Development Policy, in providing me this perspective to look at the behavior of the North.

6. Walden Bello, "Structural Adjustment as Counter Revolution," paper delivered at the International Conference on Debt Crisis, Globalization and Social Justice, New Delhi, March 1992.

7. John Vidal, *Guardian* Earth Summit Supplement (see above).

8. Chakravarthi Raghavan, *Recolonization—GATT, The Uruguay Round and the Third World*, Zed Press/TWN, London/Penang, 1990.

9. Ward Morehouse, "Ensnared in the Spider's Web—The Bretton Woods Institutions and the Elusive Quest for Sustainability and Equity in South and North," New Delhi, March 1992 Conference (see above).

10. Erskine Childers and Brian Urquahart, *Towards a More Effective United Nations*, Dag Hammarskjold Foundation, Uppsala, Sweden, 1992.

Part II

The Search for Spirituality

3

The Spirituality of the Brazilian Base Communities

MARIA VIDALE and ROSA ADELA O. SIERRA

"All who believed were together and had
all things in common" (Acts 2:44).

"I thank you, Father, Lord of heaven and earth,
because you have hidden these things from
the wise and the intelligent and have
revealed them to infants" (Matt. 11:25).

A Fundamental Option for the God of Life

In order to understand something of the spirituality of the Ecclesial Base
Communities (EBCs), to "taste" all their beauty and their great intrinsic
power, the best thing to do is to let the people of the Communities speak
for themselves. They never refuse to share, always in an extremely simple
and natural way, whether it has to do with sharing their "house" (often not
much more than a shack, but it is the house), with inviting you to their
"table," or with revealing their own life . . .

So, let's "hear" Mafalda, resident in the Western Zone of the periphery
of Sao Paulo, who introduces herself in this way: "My name is Mafalda
Catarina Pompeo. I am 61 years old and come from a family of Italian
immigrants. I lived in Ermelino Matarazzo 41 years ago, and it was a
struggle. We didn't have anything there, neither doctor nor pharmacy nor
bakery nor butcher shop. We had only one bus an hour to Penha. We were
without lights, water, sewer . . ."

Near Mafalda are Midori, who comes from Japan, and Floripes, originally from Lorena . . . And if we asked all the others present where they

had come from, we would hear them say, with an unmistakable tone of nostalgia and a suspicious brightness in the eyes:

- I come from Alagoas . . .
- My father came from Minas . . .
- I am from Bahia . . .
- I was born in Ceara . . .
- My family has lived in Parana, in Goias and in Sao Paulo . . .

As Frei Carlos Mesters would say, there are many, many Abrahams and Sarahs today, and the easiest place to find them is the EBCs. This is because they "know," more by intuition than rationally, that here in this handful of men and women who recognize themselves as Church people of God, is the blessing and the fulfillment of part of the Promise: "I will make of you a great people . . ." (Genesis 12:2).

It takes a lot of faith and a lot of courage to persist in this journey which began thousands of years ago, which has already moved through the whole planet and has not yet ended, because it is evident that the frontiers of the Promised Land (whose earth is nothing more than that on which we are standing) appear as the frontiers of the Kingdom which is to come. "It was a struggle," Mafalda said, and she went on: "My father was a prisoner of war in Germany, and when the war ended there was no work in Italy. So, we came to Brazil, and went with my mother to work on a plantation where he and the family were enslaved. The work was hard and poorly paid. They had to buy their things at the company store, and never could pay for what they ate. They had to run away at night, with the overseer right behind them . . ."

What Mafalda describes is nothing other than the great battle between Curse and Blessing. There will always be poor and oppressed people, as long as this battle goes on. Jesus himself left no illusions on this point: "The poor you have always with you . . ." (Matt. 26:11). Nevertheless, we should not become discouraged because of this, for the final victory is guaranteed and we shall see "new heavens and a new earth, where justice abides" (2 Peter 3:13). Firmer believers than the disciples of Emmaus, the poor do not turn aside from the path, and when they are persecuted in one city they flee to another (cf. Matt. 10:23). What is important to them is to survive, because they know they are the keepers of the Promise, and they are certain that in all their comings and goings the God of Life walks with them (cf. Isaiah 43:5) and will bring them to a land where "violence shall no more be heard" (Isaiah 60:18), and that He will heal his people forever (Isaiah 60:21).

A Precious Inheritance Received and Transmitted

This faith is the great wealth of the poor of the EBCs. Like everything that comes from God, they received it by grace and by grace they know they must transmit it (cf. Matt. 10:8). And they do it spontaneously, from parents to children, in the simplicity of the home. This time it is Floripes who tells us about it: "I inherited my faith from my mother and my grandfather . . . My grandfather was a widower and lived near us. He kept the chapel, and as a very small child I went with him to the wakes, because I liked to be at his side . . ."

With regard to the chapel (built by the people's initiative and "watched over" by the people), Mafalda gives the same testimony. After remembering that the family found nothing in Ermelino Matarazzo when they arrived there, she adds: "We had the Church, the Chapel of the Black Cross, where the priest came once a month, and the Vincents prayed the tierce every day in the homes."

Those who come to know any place in the interior of this Brazil after a group of immigrants has settled there always find a chapel and the organization of a worshiping community. The mothers themselves (and the grand-mothers) teach the catechism to the children. We who have been "professional missionaries" for so many years experience a profound joy when we see this, and we thank God for it with the same sentiments as Simeon when Mary and Joseph went (to the temple) to present the Child (Luke 2:29-32). All this only confirms that the faith we received at baptism is seed that will grow in any soil that receives it, but also revives the hope that salvation is near and can really reach everyone (Luke 3:6).

Not just by order or command of a church hierarchy which controls their labor and demands a strict accounting, these "natural missionaries" go witnessing to the good news that human life is possible as long as there is community. As soon as they arrive in a place, they are immediately concerned for the building of a house and a chapel. In the intimacy of the home, in the family, children can be born and be welcomed; in the Church all of them, parents and children, seek new courage for the journey, because there life takes on meaning and they understand that "it is worth what it takes."

It is interesting to find how such people, so open to life, "understand" the God of Life and do his will. In their frequent meetings to celebrate and to hear the Word in "Bible groups," the people of the Communities perceive a Presence which is a demand for communion, a Presence which wants them to be brothers and which wants more children, not bosses. It is not an authoritarian or egoistic presence; at the same time that the Father-God seeks more children and keeps those who have been sent on the journey (Jesus said he had come that ALL might have life), the Mother-God caresses those around her, helps them, protects them . . . This message, which all hear but only the children understand, is clearly perceived by the people of the Communities and impels them to ACT, to move, even when this can bring misunderstanding, suffering and struggle not only in society or in the "traditional" Church, but even in their own families.

The testimonies of Helena, Mafalda and Floripes confirm all of this. Floripes says: "As a child and as a youth, I lived an experience of faith in the family. We were very poor, but my parents always said that we should trust God." Trust God does not mean to sit around and wait for something to happen, but to ACT to make things happen. "Today," Helena continues, "I live my faith in the community, taking part in the popular movements there and doing the jobs to be done." The jobs are varied: Mafalda is the moving spirit in a Bible group, visits the sick, cleans the chapel, teaches catechism, organizes parties and takes part in the community work group which gets together each weekend to build a community hall, which will also be a place of worship for the EBC . . . This takes time, however, and Mafalda confesses: "My husband is beginning to think I am away from home a lot. But I said that I would not stop what I was doing because I believe in it and believe God has called me to a mission." Floripes' husband complains too: "because he doesn't understand." But she says she continues to "take part secretly in the meetings" and bring up her children "in the Gospel."

Anthropological Experience of God

The people of the Communities are a people who have come from long journeys, so they arrive pretty dust-covered. They pass by mountains and valleys, view a lot of panoramas, eat a lot of different foods. They have their own ideas about God, but they don't refuse to listen to others, including participating with a certain ease in "ecumenical" services. There is no doubt, however, that the ancient Greek-Judaic heritage which relegates God to the heavens, invisible, untouchable, but inspector and even avenger, has stuck to the clothing and in the heads of the travelers. Zelinda recalls: "When I was a child I did not see God as I see him now. God, for me, was someone very powerful (the image of the boss who put himself in God's place), who punished us when we did something bad and so we had to be afraid of Him. I did not see God as 'somebody' who would touch our hearts in the way it is happening now . . ." It may be for this reason that the people have made and are making so much of intermediaries, especially if they are still alive and accessible, approachable, and above all welcoming. These saints, these devotions are "up-to-date," are carried with the people when they move and not abandoned. If documents are lost, they may become the identity card, the lifeline of linkage to the past and to the distant family when lost in the big cities and relegated to live under viaducts. This could be seen recently in the Community of the Suffering on Center Street in Sao Paulo. The people were coming from work (some of them are trash pickers) and the discussion was already "heating up" while they waited for their turn to take a shower. The sound of the bells of the cathedral suddenly invaded the room, louder and louder, demanding silence and attention. Not everybody paid attention, but one who had done the most foot-stamping suddenly fell silent and knelt down, took off his cap, bowed his head, clasped his hands and entered a world to which the others present had no access.

Pastoral agents of the liberation line do not always look with approval on these attachments and these manifestations of faith. They consider them too alienating and vertical. Those who live with the Communities, however, know very well that the people succeed in articulating (much better than we do) this "vertical," this sacred dimension of their faith, with the "horizontal," the encounter with the brothers and sisters. This is a very familiar practice, lived out naturally, but taken very seriously as a sacred commitment. They are aware of this. When Floripes remembers her mother and her grandfather, she still feels "like a little child" near them because they were "authentic Christians." "My house was very poor," she says, "but everybody sought it out because they knew they would find love and help there." She tells about a specific case. "Once we took in two poor people, a homeless lady and a paralyzed person over a hundred years old who had been a slave. These old people lived with us for three years, until their families learned about them and came to get them." And Floripes concludes: "For me, they (mother and grandfather) witnessed to the Gospel with these deeds."

Floripes is right. The most authentic and "palpable" experience of God can only be the anthropological experience, which passes through the human person and was guaranteed by Jesus himself. Always, or at least since Genesis 1:27 was written, we have known that if we want to discover who God is, or at least what He is like, we must look at the only image of Him which we have and are. When Philip wanted to know more about this mysterious father of Jesus, Jesus was explicit: "He who has seen me has seen the father" (John 14:9).

So that all might understand "how" the Father really is, He told parables and gave examples. Then the miracles happened, "signs" of the Kingdom. Those who were accustomed to being treated as inferiors felt themselves treated as *equal to equal*; those who had been marginalized from human fellowship felt the experience of *welcome*; those who had suffered hunger were invited to *share* what was held in common, and the "blind" who had never seen certain things before finally opened their eyes and discovered the beauty of being in communion.

Inemesia says: "I think it is very important to share what we have with those who don't have anything." She is right. It is really very important, because it makes it possible to experience the God of Life. We think about Cornelia, a laundry woman from the Community of Fatima, moving spirit of a reflection group, who took into her house pregnant women from the interior who came to the city to have their children but could only enter the hospital at the last moment. We think especially of the great thing the Communities of the Diocese of Sao Mateus (Espirito Santo) did when for four months they fed more than 600 landless families camped at the edge of the highway from Sao Mateus to Nova Venecia . . . Midori, who was still a Buddhist when she arrived from Japan and is a Catholic missionary today, confirms this in her testimony, and insists on adding: "Living in the EBCs, the life of community and of the poor slum dwellers, led me to discover the God of Life and gave me faith in the Living God . . ."

New Creatures

If it is true that for the arrival of the Lord in our midst we must prepare straight paths so that "every valley is exalted and every mountain and hill laid low" (Isaiah 40:3), there is nothing better than to live the spirituality of the EBCs. If we want communion among us to be a reality, we must all live as equals, overcoming any and all difficulties by which we would be "unknown" on the day of final encounter with Jesus (Matt. 7:23). This has been clear from the beginning, and the apostle Paul was very explicit in his letter to the Galatians: "All you who have been baptized in Christ have put on Christ. There is neither Jew nor Greek, slave nor free, male nor female, for you are all one in Christ Jesus" (Gal. 3:28). In this way the "new creature" would appear who had left aside "the old things" to enter a "new reality" (2 Cor. 5:17). This appears to have been the real aim of the first apostolic communities, when the ecclesiastical authority was the "diaconate " and there were women among these deacons (Romans 16:1), and when the slave Onesimus was to be received "no more as a slave but . . . as a beloved brother" (Philemon 1:6).

We know that in Jerusalem and in the other communities, this new egalitarian and fraternal relationship began "in the houses" (and not in pyramidal temples, more appropriate as tombs), where the "brothers" (Acts 1:15) met around the Word and the Breaking of Bread. The house is the family place, the place of life, and so it is in the houses that the people of the EBCs have begun to meet again. It is not always possible to have the Breaking of Bread, which depends on the presence of ordained ministers, but the Bible has been given back and the results were not long in coming. In the Street Groups (known also as Bible Circles or Reflection Groups), always in the form of a circle, it is easy to create a friendly relationship which makes people feel at ease. "I am happy" Mafalda told us "because I do what I like to do, because I love my children and my sisters of the group. They were lonely, suffering persons . . . Loneliness and widowhood had turned them into sad and bitter women. Today we are one family, we are a blessing to each other, and our happiness is great."

The husbands do not always understand or feel happy (as they should) about this "opening out" of their wives. It seems that many of them feel this threatens their authority, power; they are afraid they will be deprived of their "servant" who had always been so available and submissive. The husbands of both Mafalda and Floripes reacted in this way. Mafalda was able to handle the situation, but Floripes saw the problem was serious. "My husband did not want me to be independent, and wanted to put an end to my faith. So, we separated." Despite all the resistance, however, "the thing moves," and is as if concentric waves moved outward from the meetings in the homes, usually coordinated by women, until they reached the Church. There also the people feel at ease and the ordained ministers again act as "deacons," sharing decisions and responsibilities with the lay persons, including women.

This is the way the faith received at baptism finally "humanizes," and brings growth in communion and participation, increasingly "revealing" the face of our God. It is convincing testimony, as Midori was convinced when she sought baptism. "What attracted me to Christianity was the total dedication and the sensitivity of some Catholic colleagues." Later, she was "confirmed" in the life of the EBCs.

Like everything which comes from God (and so cannot be ruined), this faith is not "kept" by the new creature, but is shared with all, and is above all carried as "good news" to those who are crying out for liberation. The EBCs like to pray also (and it is good to remember this), but they know that our faith calls for us to be sacramental, sign and reality, and so we cannot stop with the symbolic, the beautiful rituals that are like dreams, because when they come to an end the lights are put out and everything is just like it was before. Conserved. The faith of the EBCs has its beginning of growth in the houses, reaches the neighbors and even the work place, always seeking the appearance of the "new creature" through *new relationships*. "There's no use in just going to church," Inemesia warns us, "unless we live out in our homes, with our neighbors and those we work with, what we have learned . . ."

EBC is a missionary Church!

Commitment to Life

"The king of Egypt said to the Hebrew midwives: 'When you help the Hebrew women to give birth and see them on the birthstool, if it is a boy kill it.' . . . But the midwives feared God and did not do what the king of Egypt had ordered them, and allowed the boys to live" (Exodus 1:15-17).

The people of the Communities, in general, appear to be humble, simple, unpretentious people . . . A few of them, however, come to think they deserve greater decorations because they arrived *alive* through history from a very dangerous journey during which their lives were many times in danger. The fact of their accepting, apparently, abuse and humiliations may have led to the belief that they had fled from the open struggle to give themselves over to a kind of fatalism. . . In the beginning, the theologians of liberation were intrigued with the conformity and the submission of the people to the constituted order, and seeing them so tied to their devotions hurriedly concluded that such behavior could only be the fruit of an alienating religiosity. Only later did they begin to suspect that it might not be alienation, but a form of resistance, a strategy which is the fruit of experience and wisdom, but also of obedience to the God of Life.

It is a fact that in the midst of the journey the "Community which defends Life" (this was the theme of the recent assembly of the Communities of Rio Sono and Lizarda, in the State of Tocantins) learned that "there are seasons and there are seasons" (Eccl. 3:1): there is a time to weep quietly and there is a time to raise one's head and enter the battle. This has been and is being proved by the Christians at the base, engaged in popular movements which struggle for better conditions of life both in the city and in the rural areas . . . Consequently, even when they appear to want nothing, the people of the Communities remain vigilant and alert to the "signs of the times" (Matt. 16:3). "In the work of evangelization," Ana Paula explains, "we try from the first contact with the children to perceive what is going on around us, whether they are the realities of the neighborhood, the city, the world, . . ." a world which the Communities would like to be able to transform into the Kingdom. That is why prayer has a special characteristic: it moves to ACTION, or to "commitment," as the people prefer to say. "I met Father Ticao and Sister Pilar at a celebration," Amalia remembers, "and that Christmas Novena was the beginning of my commitment to the Community."

From the testimony of Cosme, peasant, migrant, metallurgist, we can see how this commitment promotes the growth of faith and makes of the journey an authentic following of Christ, to the full living out of the paschal mystery of passion, death and resurrection. Cosme says: "As a youth and entering adult life, the commitment of the Church to justice intensified and characterized my participation in the Community. Such an evangelical option for the poor, the renewal of biblical reflection incarnate in life and in history, the events of Vatican II, of Medellin and of Puebla . . . broadened the horizons of my faith and helped me to situate it within the popular and labor movements of the '70s and the '80s." "An important fact," Cosme stresses, "came to cement my faith: the martyrdom of the Church in that moment of history." He adds: "The martyrs taught me how to begin with 'faith in Jesus,' and then to move further on in the search for the 'faith of Jesus.'" Cosme, in saying this, shows himself to be one of the many Christians of the EBCs who discovered in the linkage of faith to life the way to grow toward achieving "the stature of the fullness of Christ" (Ephesians 4:13). Cosme believes that the martyrdom of Fathers Rodolfo and Joao Bosco, of Simao Bororo, Gringo, Santo Dias, Margarida Alves, Father Ezequiel, Father Josimo, Verino and so many others, placed the stamp of martyrdom on the spirituality of the EBCs, leading them to fill out, in their flesh, "that which lacked of the tribulations of Christ" (Col. 1:24), so that all might have life and have it in abundance.

Although they are opposed to the shedding of human blood because as Oseia Cursino wrote in a poetic account of a meeting of Communities:

> The earth has already been polluted
> By the evil of Cain,
> Who shed the blood of his brother,
> And God doesn't want that again.

The EBCs do not refuse, in their profoundly christocentric spirituality, to give their own life when they perceive that "the hour has come" (Matt. 26:45), and thus to irrigate the soil of the Kingdom with "fertile blood." (This was the title Cosme gave a poem he wrote when Santo Dias was assassinated. Dias was a metal worker in Sao Paulo and we want to annex that poetry.)

Worship Acceptable to God

The constant connection which the EBCs make between faith and life allows them to offer the father a truly acceptable worship, as was that of Jesus. The newness of the New Covenant also appears in this authentic worship form, where there are no more professional priests offering "things," but there is an entire "consecrated people" offering itself (Exodus 19:6, 1 Peter 2:9).

What God always asked for, from the most ancient times, was a *people* that would call him Father and offer him the praise of his children in communion. This was the heart of the worship that God wanted, but down through history what He got was usually a series of rites and ceremonies full of empty words and lying gestures which poorly disguised the sin of those who offered them, even priests of "the inner circle." It didn't do much good for God to complain in the words of Isaiah: "You turn things upside down. Shall the potter be regarded as the clay?" (29:16). That is to say, the sin which God rejected from the beginning, when Adam and Eve listened to the tempting serpent (Genesis 3:4). Even today, we can see how great a temptation it is for one brother to step on another and try to put himself in God's place, manipulating the sacred in the attempt to dominate everything and everybody.

In their simplicity the EBCs perceived this, and as Cosme says: "To live an experience of authentic faith, I feel it is necessary to be joined to the community which has as its standard the values of the Kingdom which Jesus of Nazareth came to announce and to live." He adds: "I don't see so much need of the eloquence of someone who can expound in Latin or Portuguese or whatever . . . My faith is not fed by theoretical explanations, even if they present logical and well formulated arguments. I feel that faith comes alive in the active participation of the community, in the simplicity of each brother in the EBC, in their hope and in their anguish, in their limitations and in their immense wisdom, in the advance of their revolutionary awareness and in the withdrawal of their moments of alienation. When a brother celebrates his victories or laments his contradictions, I feel a life communion of each and of all. I feel the *profound meaning of the Eucharist* broadened there, and I perceive the Word of God as it becomes Life and Presence . . ." This, we say, is ritual transformed into worship and therefore acceptable to God.

This may be the reason that the celebrations of the EBCs are so beautiful and have such full participation. In these moments, when the Community has met to celebrate, it becomes very clear what is the spirituality that animates them, and how they are trying to make of their own life a constant *spiritual sacrifice* to offer to God. In the celebration, in fact, the EBCs sing the joy of victories obtained; they express their repentance for recognized failures; they present the sufferings and the anguish of all the brothers; and they commit themselves to continue "working" firmly, as Jesus and the Father (John 5:17) for the full victory of the Kingdom . . . Until the FEAST comes, full and definitive!

Translated by L.M. McCoy

FERTILE BLOOD

(The translator has not reproduced the rhyme in which this was written.)

The thirtieth of October
dawned very sad.
Nature wept,
the sun rose weeping.
Even the sorrowful breeze
foresaw tragedy.
A martyr laborer
offered his life.

My brother Santo Dias
embraced Ana Maria.
Kissing his two children
he went off to his work
without knowing that martyrdom
would crown him with glory.
But because of his love of justice,
he did not fear even death.

The police of the establishment
only protect capital.
They live from our sweat
and are against us.
With an assassin bullet
they struck my companion
who, bathed in fertile blood,
fell in front of Sylvania.

Our struggle continues
Santo . . . you are present

living in our heart
on our journey.
Your cry for justice
echoes constantly.
Today your name in history
is a banner before us.

You are the ground wheat
which multiplies the seed.
This is one of the Blesseds
of which Jesus spoke so clearly.
Your blood is like that of Abel
which eternally cries out to God.
You did not lose your life,
you found it eternally.

Cosme, of the Community of
Ermelino Matarazzo Sao Paulo,
January 1991

4

A Living Spirituality Today

ELIZABETH AMOAH

As an African woman, my experiences in the African context have made me aware that life which is complex, complicating, communal, and holistic is the center of everything.

The holistic life has physical and spiritual components and the two are equally important, and spirituality is an expression of life. The title of this paper is an indication that any form of spirituality in modern times should be centered on giving life in its totality. It should be alive, a living and not a dead spirituality. It should give life not only for one or ten generations but life that is for ever and ever and for all generations. It should concern itself with the present and the future. It is all right for some forms of spirituality to prepare people for "Heaven" but it should also be possible to experience "Heaven here on earth."[1]

What Is Spirituality

There are different types of spiritualities; many people from the Third World live in contexts and situations where there are other religions besides Christianity.[2] Within the Christian tradition one can identify different forms of spiritualities. For example, some Christians live out their spiritual lives by living in monastic communities. Such people devote their time to contemplation, prayer, and to charity. Others too, such as some Christians in Africa,[3] claim to have experienced the Holy Spirit and this experience makes them form congregations or groups, devoting their time to praying, fasting, healing spiritually and physically, making of spontaneous songs and sermons and counseling people on all types of day-to-day problems. Telling examples of such groups are the "spiritual churches" in Ghana.

It is not the purpose of this paper to go into details of what spirituality is. For the purpose of analysis, spirituality is briefly described as the result of, and the end to, the life that ensues from personal or corporate encounter and experience with that which restores to all people on earth their lost humanity and sensitizing the powerful and dominant class to use their tools of power and domination in ways that make people live rather than die. It is a dynamic and radical experience with that which Aloysius Pieris[4] describes as the PRESENCE, that which encourages, urges, and sustains people to stand out for the fullness of life. It was an example of such an experience and encounter that the Woman with the Issue of Blood[5] had with Jesus of Nazareth. After coming face to face with Jesus she was very much convinced that if only she could touch Jesus, even if she had to break tradition and disregard public opinion, she would be healed. So she did it and she was healed. It was such an encounter that resulted in the healing of the woman described as having "a spirit of infirmity eighteen years and could in no wise lift herself up."[6] She met Jesus in the synagogue and she was straightened up as a human being. Another telling example of such an encounter is seen in the story of the rich tax collector, Zacchaeus. After inviting Jesus to his house, he openly declared to Jesus and all those around him, "Behold Lord, the half of my goods I give to the poor; and if I have taken anything from any man by false accusation, I restore him four-fold."[7]

Rich tax collector Zacchaeus came face to face with Jesus and he, Zacchaeus, placed his tools of cheating and exploitation of the poor to make them live as human beings.

Being in Touch with the Spirit

The basis of a living spirituality today is preceded by a radical encounter with that which gives life and that which empowers men and women, young and old, rich and poor to be sensitive to, and to get involved with, life-giving activities. The majority of people in the Third World today are experiencing physical and spiritual poverty. There are many unjust and life-denying situations. Coupled with these, they are internationally bound with a world where it seems fashionable these days to spend huge amounts of money and human efforts to destroy both human beings and the environment more efficiently than to build upon life and a world; these literally dictate the type of life to be lived in the Third World through economic marketing policies, and uncontrollable natural disasters[8] which claim hundreds and thousands of lives in some parts of the Third World.

The Spirit was/is on Jesus and it made him proclaim:

> The Spirit of the Lord is upon me, because He has anointed me to preach the Gospel to the poor; he hath sent me to heal the broken-hearted, to preach deliverance to the captives and recovering of sight to the blind, to set at liberty them that are bruised. To preach the acceptable year of the Lord.

The important point here is that Jesus not only proclaimed the above words, he really acted them out. He, of course, withdrew from the crowd sometimes to be able to have the time to pray, fast, meditate and to be in communion with God. All that one is saying is that in order to be able to get involved in life-giving activities, a genuine and true spirituality demands getting in touch with the spirit, the PRESENCE constantly. Otherwise, it becomes an empty and shallow spirituality.

Conversion and Commitment Necessary

We have already mentioned briefly that the Third World is a mosaic of experiences and contexts so that it will be unrealistic to prescribe one form of spirituality for the whole of the Third World. This means then that a living spirituality besides being based on a PRESENCE, a Deepening Guidance, should be meaningful and relevant to the cultural, economic, political, religious and social contexts. In Africa today some women and men express their Christian spirituality through the use of African forms of culture such as music, drums, healing, and so on. Analyses of their prayers, songs, sermons reveal great use of poetic and vivid language which portrays their cultural, social and religious traditions; such a manifestation of Spirituality is concrete and dynamic emerging from the depths of *human* aspirations and *strivings*.

In such situations, the experience which results in spirituality of any form demands a conversion, a type of death, a complete break from a previous way of life. It implies being "born again" into a commitment and dedication to struggles for the present and future living community. And this is why Mary John Mananzan declares:

> To be a Christian today in a land where injustice and oppression abide is a challenge. To be a woman religious in such a situation is doubly so. It calls for a radical rethinking of the meanings of being a Christian and of the imperative of religious commitment. It precipitates a spiritual crisis. It demands a consequent revision of one's way of life, a true conversion, a metanoia.

The *metanoia* that results in the experience with the PRESENCE, or what others describe as "Deepening Guidance," self-conscientizes the individual and this self-conscientization makes it impossible to remain neutral to what is happening around one.

It is a way of life which demands a close and constant contact with that which is experienced as the Presence and the Deepening Guidance and this may be done in several ways such as fasting, praying, singing, contemplating, or meditating as individuals or groups. One is not saying that spirituality simply implies spiritual discipline such as fasting, praying, etc. The spiritual discipline should make it imperative to get involved with and commit oneself to the realities on earth. The life of Jesus of Nazareth as recorded by the Gospel writers will be cited as an example here. The spirit should not concern itself with the use of indigenous forms of worship alone. It must also concern itself with what is happening in the society—poverty, hunger, internal misgovernment, unjust international economic and marketing order which makes the rich richer, and the poor worse off than they were before, the environmental crisis that is destroying creation, traditions and socialization processes which push women and children to the outskirts of society. An authentic and useful spirituality appreciates and respects the spiritualities of others. This makes it easier to team up with others for the struggles in life.[9/10/11]

Inclusive Spirituality

In other words, it must be an open and inclusive spirituality. It should open itself up to and engage itself with people of other religions to bring about the just society needed. In joining hands with people of other spiritualities to bring about the new community, one's spirituality, in most cases, is enriched and renewed. And this is what happened to the disciples traveling to Emmaus.[12] The two disciples walked with a stranger and they found the unexpected Christ. An inclusive spirituality makes one aware that the PRESENCE, the Spirit, the Deepening Guidance does not limit itself to one's religion alone. God is not put in one box and sealed. The Presence, God, should be allowed to work in all situations of life. It is such a spirituality that will, with the help of the Presence, renew the creation that is presently at the edge of destruction.

One specific religion, spirituality or group of people cannot do the task ahead alone. It needs all hands on deck, for as an Akan saying goes: "One person's hand is not enough to stretch across the face of God (*Onipa baako nsa nntomi nnkata Onyame anim*)."

A living spirituality for the fullness of life is urgently needed today. Whatever forms it takes it must be relevant to the spiritual and material needs of people. And such a spirituality has to come through a true conversion, renewal, a rebirth which is preceded by a constant and deep experience with the source of life and power. It results in a deep and sincere commitment to both religious, social, economic, and political realities of today with the aim of making people live today and tomorrow.

Notes

1. See the Lord's Prayer: "Thy will be done on Earth as it is in Heaven."

2. Christians in Africa and Asia live with people, families who belong to religions such as the African Indigenous religions, and Islam, Buddhism, and Hinduism.

3. Christianity in Africa today is going through a dynamic phase. There are thousands of Christian congregations and groups founded and organized by African women and men who put great emphasis and rely on the active Presence and Power of the Holy Spirit.

4. See Aloysius Pieris, *A Cry for Life, The Spirituality of the Third World*.

5. Luke 8:43-48.

6. Luke, Chapter 13.

7. Luke 19:8.

8. For example, constant droughts in Africa and periodic hurricanes in Asia.

9. Mary John Mananzan, "Redefining Religious Commitment in the Philippine Context" in Virginia Fabella, MM, and Sun Ai Lee Park (eds.), *We Dare to Dream: Doing Theology as Asian Women*, (New York: Orbis Books, 1990).

10. Luke 4:18-19.

11. Some people often accuse these churches in Africa of not being involved in the political and economic struggles in their contexts.

12. See Luke, chapter 24.

5

Popular Religions as Support of Identity—Based on the Mexican-American Experience in the United States

VIRGIL ELIZONDO

Introduction

The Mexican-American is one who through birth or acquired nationality is a citizen of the USA while maintaining a deep Mexican heritage. Today there are approximately 16,300,000 Mexican-Americans in the US and the number continues to increase daily. It is a highly complex socio-cultural group that is quite at home in the US without ever fully assimilating the US way of life. It is neither fully "US-American" nor fully "Latin-American." It lived in its present day geographical setting long before Americans migrated westwards and took over the Mexican territories. The group is among the poorest in the US, although a few have made it to the top of the economic ladder. It has been the subject of consistent segregation, exploitation and marginalization throughout its history in the US. The deepest level of the oppression has been the denial of our history, tradition and religious expression. Because our past and our language have been denied by the dominant English-speaking culture of the US, we have been made to feel as if we were an illegitimate people without a right to exist! Today, we are struggling not only to come out of our socio-economic oppression, but equally out of cultural and religious domination. We are doing this by reclaiming the deepest element of our collective identity: the core religious symbols of our people. We are discovering that one of the key factors in the group identity, cohesiveness and continuity is the persistence of our religious symbols which we will explore briefly in this presentation.

Function of Religious Symbols

The popular expressions of the faith function in totally different ways for various peoples and depend on their history and socio-cultural status. For the dominant culture, the popular expressions of the faith serve to legitimize their way of life as God's true way for humanity. They tranquilize the moral conscience and blind people from seeing the injustices which exist in daily life. For a colonized/oppressed/dominated group, they are the ultimate resistance to the attempts of the dominant culture to destroy them as a distinct group either through annihilation or through absorption and total assimilation. They maintain alive the sense of injustice to which the people are subjected in their daily lives.

By popular expressions of the faith I do not refer to the private or individual devotions of a few people but to the ensemble of beliefs, rituals, ceremonies, devotions, and prayers which are commonly practiced by the people at large. It is my contention which is beyond the scope of this paper to develop, but which will be its point of departure, that those expressions of the faith which are celebrated voluntarily by the majority of the people, transmitted from generation to generation by the people themselves and which go on with the church, without it or even in spite of it, express the deepest identity of the people.

They are the ultimate foundation of the people's innermost being and the common expression of the collective soul of the people. They are supremely meaningful for the people who celebrate them and meaningless to the outsider. To the people whose very life-source they are, no explanation is necessary, but to the casual or scientific spectator no explanation will ever express or communicate their true and full meaning. Without them, there might be associations of individuals bound together by common interest (for example, the corporation, the state, etc. . .), but there will never be the experience of being a people.

It is within the context of the tradition of the group that one experiences both a sense of selfhood and a sense of belonging. Furthermore, it is within the tradition that one remains in contact both with one's beginnings through the genealogies and the stories of origins and with one's ultimate end. We are born into them and within them we discover our full and ultimate being. I might enjoy and admire other traditions very much, but I will never be fully at home within them. No matter how much I get into them, I will always have a sense of being other.

From the very beginning, Christianity presented a unique way of universalizing peoples without destroying their localized identity. People would neither have to disappear through assimilation nor be segregated as inferior. The Christian message interwove with the local religious traditions so as to give the people a deeper sense of local identity (a sense of rootedness) while at the same time breaking down the psycho-sociological barriers that kept nationalities separate and apart from each other so as to allow for a truly universal fellowship (a sense of universality). In other words, it affirmed rootedness while destroying ghettoishness. Christianity changed peoples and cultures not by destroying them, but by reinterpreting their core rituals and myths through the foundational ritual and myth of Christianity. Thus, now a Jew could still be a faithful Jew and yet belong fully to the new universal fellowship and equally a Greek or a Roman could still be fully Greek or Roman and equally belong to the new universal group.

Religious Traditions of the Americas

The beginning of the Americas introduces two radically distinct image/myth representations of the Christian tradition. The US was born as a secular enterprise with a deep sense of religious mission. The native religions were eliminated and totally supplanted by a new type of religion. Puritan moralism, Presbyterian righteousness and Methodist social consciousness, coupled with deism and the spirit of rugged individualism combined to provide a sound basis for the new nationalism which would function as the core religion of the land. It was quite different in Latin America where the religion of the old world clashed with that of the new and in their efforts to uproot the native religions, the colonies found themselves totally subsumed into them. Iberian Catholicism, with its emphasis on clerical ritual and the divinely established monarchical nature of all society, conquered physically but itself was absorbed by the pre-Columbian spiritualism with its emphasis on the harmonious unity of opposing tensions: male and female, suffering and happiness self-annihilation and transcendence, individual and group, sacred and profane. In the secular-based culture of the United States, it is the one who succeeds materially who appears to be the upright and righteous person, the good and saintly. In the pre-Columbian/Iberian-Catholic mestizo culture of Mexico it is the one who can endure all the opposing tensions of life and not lose one's interior harmony who appears to be the upright and righteous one.

With the great westward expansion of the US in the 1800s 50 percent of northern Mexico was conquered and taken over by the US. The Mexicans living in that vast region, spanning a territory of over 3500 kilometers from California to Texas, suddenly became aliens in their own land. . . foreigners who never left home. Their entire way of life was despised. The Mexican mestizo was abhorred as a mongrel who was good only for cheap labor. Efforts were instituted to suppress everything Mexican: customs, language and Mexican Catholicism. The fair-skinned/blond Mexicans who remained had the choice of assimilating totally to the White, Anglo-Saxon Protestant culture of the USA or being ostracized as inferior human beings. The dark-skinned had no choice! They were marked as an inferior race destined to be the servants of the "white master race."[1]

Today, social unrest and dire poverty force many people from Mexico to move to the former Mexican territories which politically are part of the US. Newcomers are harassed by the immigration services as illegal intruders, a curious irony since it was the US which originally entered this region illegally and stole it from Mexico. Yet the descendants of the original settlers of this region plus those who have immigrated continue to feel at home, to resist effort of destruction through assimilation and to celebrate their legitimacy as a people.

Mexican-American Religious Symbols

The Mexican-Americans living in that vast borderland between the US and Mexico have not only survived as a unique people but have even maintained good mental health in spite of the countless insults and put-downs suffered throughout its history and even in the present. Anyone who has suffered such a long history of segregation, degradation and exploitation should be a mental wreck.[2] Yet, in spite of their ongoing suffering, not only are the numbers increasing, but in general they are prospering, joyful and healthy thanks to the profound faith of the people as lived and expressed through the common religious practices of the group. I could explore many of them,[3] but I will limit myself to what I consider to be the three sets of related core expressions which mark the ultimate ground, the parameters and the final aspirations of the Mexican-American people: Guadalupe/baptism; dust/water; crucifixion/the "dead" ones. They are the symbols in which the apparently destructive forces of life are subsumed, transcended and united. In them, we experience the ultimate meaning and destiny of our life pilgrimage.

There is no greater and more persistent symbol of Mexican and Mexican-American identity than devotion to Our Lady of Guadalupe. Thousands visit her home at Tepeyac each day and she keeps reappearing daily throughout the Americas in the spontaneous prayers and artistic expressions of the people. In her, the people experience acceptance, dignity, love and protection . . . they dare to affirm life even when all others deny them life. Since her apparition she has been the flag of all the great movements of independence, betterment and liberty.

Were it not for Our Lady of Guadalupe[4] there would be no Mexican or Mexican-American people today. The great Mexican nations had been defeated by the Spanish invasion which came to a violent and bloody climax in 1521. The native peoples who had not been killed no longer wanted to live. Everything of value to them, including their gods, had been destroyed. Nothing was worth living for. With this colossal catastrophe, their entire past became irrelevant. New diseases appeared and together with the trauma of the collective death-wish of the people, the native population decreased enormously.

It was in the brown Virgin of Guadalupe that Mexicanity was born and through her that the people have survived and developed. At the very moment when the pre-Columbian world had come to a drastic end, a totally unsuspected irruption took place in 1531 when, in the ancient site of the goddess Tonanzin, a Mestizo woman appeared to announce a new era for "all the inhabitants of this land." Guadalupe provides the spark which will allow the people to arise out of the realm of death like the phoenix rising out of the ashes of the past, not just a return to the past but the emergence of a spectacular newness.[5] In sharp contrast to the total rupture with the past which was initiated by the conquest-evangelization enterprise, Guadalupe provided the necessary *sense of continuity* which is basic to human existence. Since the apparition took place at Tepeyac, the long venerated site of the goddess Tonanzin, it put people in direct contact with their ancient past and in communion with their own foundational mythology. It validated their ancestry while initiating them into something new. The missioners had said their ancestors had been wrong and that the diabolical past had to be totally eradicated. But the lady who introduced herself as the mother of the true God was now appearing and asking that a temple be built on this sacred site. Out of their own past and in close continuity with it, something truly sacred was now emerging.

Furthermore, she was giving meaning to the present moment in several ways for she was promising them love, defense and protection. At a time when the people had experienced the abandonment of their gods, the mother of the true God was now offering them her personal intervention. At a time when new racial and ethnic divisions were emerging, she was offering the basis of a new unity as the mother of all the inhabitants of the land. At a time when the natives were being instructed and told what to do by the Spaniards, she chose a low-class Indian to be her trusted messenger who was to instruct the Spaniards through the person of the bishop and tell them what to do. Finally, she initiated and proclaimed the new era which was now beginning. Over her womb is the Aztec glyph for the center of the universe. Thus she carries the force which will gradually build up the civilization which will be neither a simple restoration of the past nor simply New Spain but the beginning of something new. The sign of flowers, which she provided as a sign of her authenticity, was for the Indian world the sign which guaranteed that the new life would truly flourish.

Thus in Guadalupe, the ancient beginnings connect with the present moment and point to what is yet to come! The broken pieces of their ancient numinous world are now re-pieced in a totally new way. Out of the chaos, a new world of ultimate meaning is now emerging. The Phoenix had truly come forth not just as a powerful new life, but also as the *numinosum* which would allow them to once again experience the awe and reverence of the sacred, not a sacred which was foreign and opposed to them, but one which ultimately legitimized them in their innermost being both collectively as a people and individually as persons.

The second great religious expression is the baptism of infants. The Lady of Guadalupe had sent the Indian Juan Diego to the church. The Indian world immediately started to go to church and ask for baptism. Yet, they were no longer being uprooted totally from their ancient ways in order to enter into the church which the Lady had sent them. They were entering as they were with their customs, their rituals, their songs, their dances and their pilgrimages. The old Franciscan missioners feared this greatly. Many thought it was a devil's trick to subvert their missionary efforts. But the people kept on coming. They were truly building the new temple the Lady had requested: the living temple of Mexican Christians. It is through baptism that every new-born Mexican enters personally into the temple requested by the Lady. Through baptism the child becomes part of the continuum and is guaranteed life in spite of the social forces against life. The community claims the child as its very own and with pride presents it to the entire people. In the group, the child will receive great affirmation and tenderness. This will give the child a profound sense of existential security. He/she will be able to affirm selfhood in spite of the put-downs and insults of society: they will dare to be who they are and they will be who they are with a great sense of pride!

Because Earth (tierra) has been so sacred to us there can be no heaven without earth—for it is Father Sky and Mother Earth which are the very basis of our life and sustenance; the stealing and massacre of our lands has been so painful and devastating. Without our earth, we feel like lost wanderers in an endless desert waste. Our identity has always been tied to our earth from which we are born and into which those who pass away will return to the womb of mother earth. Our earth is as much our roots as the earth is the natural place for the roots of trees and plants. Without roots, what can survive?

The ashes of the beginning of Lent are curious and mysterious expressions of the Mexican tradition which finds its full socio-religious meaning when coupled with the holy water which is blessed during the Easter Vigil. For people who have been forced to become foreigners in their own land, who have been driven from their properties and who have been pushed around by the powerful like the mighty wind blows the dust around, ashes as a moment of the continuum of the pilgrimage of life become most powerful. They mark the radical acceptance of the moment; actually there is no choice. But this is not the end, for the people do not only come for ashes, throughout the year they come for holy water to sprinkle upon themselves, their children, their homes . . . everything. They are very much aware that our entire world yearns and travails in pain awaiting to be redeemed, a redemption which in Christ has indeed begun but whose rehabilitating effects are yet to take effect in our present day of world injustices. The sprinkling with the waters of the Easter Vigil is a constant call for the regeneration of all of creation. The dust which is sprinkled with the water will be turned into fertile earth and produce in great abundance.

As in the reception of ashes there is an acceptance, in the sprinkling of holy water there is an unquestioned affirmation: the ashes will again become earth; the dust-people will become the fertile earth and the earth will once again be ours. The dust-water binomial symbolizes the great suffering of an uprooted people who refuse to give in to despair but live in the unquestioned hope of the new life that is sure to come.

The final set of religious celebrations which express the core identity of the Mexican-American people is the crucifixion which is celebrated on Good Friday, and The Day of the Dead which is celebrated on November 2. In our ancient, pre-Christian religious forms, it was the great priest Quetzalcoatl who had traveled throughout our lands preaching self-sacrifice and penance as the way to life. Blood and sacrifice had long been regarded as the essence of life and the offering of blood as the only way to perpetuate the cycles of life. In some mysterious way, blood and sacrifice alone were capable of regenerating new life. Furthermore, life on this earth was like a dream and death was the awakening unto the reality of life. Those who went before us were not dead, but fully alive. They were alive in us who remember them and we were alive in them who guaranteed the continuity of life beyond the time and space of this earth.

The Christian message about the death of Jesus as the beginning of new life gave deeper meaning and clarity to our own indigenous beliefs through the vivid imagery of the scourged, crowned-with-thorns, crucified Jesus of Nazareth. Our ancient icons were now assumed by the suffering Jesus. At the same time, the Christian belief in the communion of saints gave a deeper and more exciting meaning to our ancient belief of the continuity of the ancestors. Far from dwelling in some far-off mysterious place, they were now enjoying the eternal and unending fiesta! Our own *mitotes* (Indian word for community-wide feasts) were now seen to be the images and foretaste of the future unending feast in heaven. In this religious *mestizaje*, the elements of our new identity were being forged and shaped.

For a people who have consistently been subjected to injustice, cruelty and early death, the image of the crucified is the supreme symbol of life in spite of the multiple daily threats of death. If there was something good and redemptive in the unjust condemnation and crucifixion of the God-man, then, as senseless and useless as our suffering appears to be, there must be something of ultimate goodness and transcendent value in it. We don't understand it, but in Jesus the God-man who suffered for our salvation, we affirm it and in this very affirmation receive the power to endure it without its destroying us. Even if we are killed, we cannot be destroyed. This is the curious irony of our celebrations of the dead: they appear to be dead, but they are not really dead! For they live not only in God but in our hearts and in our memory. Those whom the world thinks are dead, those who have been killed by society, defy death and are alive in us. In our celebrations of memory, their presence is keenly experienced. Thus what is celebrated as the day of the dead is in effect the celebration of life, a life which not even death can destroy. Society might take our lands away, marginalize us and even kill us, but it cannot destroy us. For we live on in the generations to come and in them we continue to be alive.

Thus Good Friday and the Day of the Dead are two of the greatest affirmations of life of our Mexican-American people. They defy anyone to try to destroy us; we will not only survive, but survive triumphantly! When, we do not know, but that we will, there is no doubt. This is the basis of our security that cannot be comprehended by many of the western sociologists who try to study us. We do not make sense, according to their categories of classification and understanding. But to us, they are the affirmation and celebration of our collective life which goes on in spite of all the odds against it.

Conclusion

The conquest of ancient Mexico by Spain in 1521 and then the conquest of northwest Mexico by the United States in the 1840s forced the native population and their succeeding generations into a split and meaningless existence. It was a mortal collective catastrophe of gigantic death-bearing consequences.[6] Yet the people have survived as a people through the emergence of new religious symbols and the re-interpretation of old ones which have connected the past with the present and projected into the future. The core religious expressions as celebrated and transmitted by the people are the unifying symbols in which the opposing forces of life are brought together into a harmonious tension so as to give the people who participate in them the experience of wholeness. In them and through them, opposites are brought together and push towards a resolution and the people who celebrate them experience an overcoming of the split. Where formerly there was opposition, now there is reconciliation and even greater yet, synthesis. This is precisely what gives joy and meaning to life, indeed makes life possible in any meaningful sense regardless of the situation and it is in the celebration of these festivals of being and memory that the people live on as a people.

Thus it is that today, the ancient celebrations of our ancestors both pre-Christian and Christian are being reclaimed by the people at large. For some time, we felt apologetic about celebrating them and many modern liturgists tried to wipe them out because they felt that they were not in accord with the modern liturgical reforms of the Catholic church. However, today even the Hispanic Protestants are reclaiming these ancient symbols which, even though they have come through the Catholic church, are not the exclusive property of that church.

Today our Good Friday processions through the middle of the cities of the US, or our Guadalupe celebrations on December the 12th and the many other public expressions of our faith are bringing new life not only to us Mexican-Americans who are reclaiming them, but to all the people of the

US who are finding new life and a source of unity and communion in these religious rituals which better than anything else have been able to blend harmoniously—without the elimination of either—the ancient religious traditions of the Americans with the traditions of western Christianity which started to arrive here in 1492. The reclaiming of these symbols and the collective celebrations of the feasts which they stand for is the beginning of the ultimate unity of the peoples of the Americas. Thus it is not only the affirmation of life for the Mexican-Americans, but the Mexican-Americans offering new life to the others who come to share in the greatest treasures we have to offer our sisters and brothers in the US: the unity of heaven and earth through the sacred icons of our people.

Notes

1. R. Acuna, *Occupied America* (San Francisco: Canfield Press, 1972).

2. Roberto Jiminez, "Social Changes/Emotional Health," in *Medical Gazette of South Texas*, Vol. 7, No. 25, June 20, 1985.

3. For a greater discussion of other religious symbols, consult my previous works: *Christianity and Culture* and *La Morenita, Evangelizar of the Americas*, (San Antonio: MACC Publications); *Galilean Journey, The Mexican-American Promise*, (New York: Orbis Books, 1983).

4. For other aspects of Guadalupe, consult my previous articles in *Concilium* No. 122/1977 and No. 188/1983.

5. J. Ruffie, *De La Biologie à la Culture* (Paris: Flammarion, 1976), pp. 247-252.

6. For a full discussion of the violence of the conquest consult: Elizondo-Boff, "1492-1992: The Voice of the Victims," in *Concilium* No. 6/1990, (London: SCM Press; New York: Orbis Books).

6

African Spirituality: A Cry for Life

BERNADETTE MBUY-BEYA

I am the resurrection and the life . . . Whoever believes in me. . . will never die.

John 11:26

Introduction

God created human beings in God's own image and likeness, making of them living and immortal beings, according to the Scriptures. Henceforth, "life" means loving God and observing the law (Deut. 30:19-20). At the same time, every human being is concerned with the task of ensuring his or her own life, and must seek to solve life's problems by whatever means possible.

This quest for solutions to life's problems necessarily leads to new strategies which can be more appropriate than the earlier ones. In this regard, history affirms that traditional African society offered the population a framework and structures which saw to the survival, both spiritual and material, of the entire community.

Confronted now by new pressures, the traditional structures are proving inadequate, a fact which leads to a profound crisis in which the sense of moral values is increasingly lost; goodness, beauty, and gratuity in the gift of self are becoming rare qualities.

The greatest concern of today appears to be the frantic struggle for power in the hope of ensuring one's own survival. As a result, there are the oppressors and the oppressed, but this oppression gives rise to new forms of spirituality. The African elite, for example, is especially attracted by such mystical movements as the Rosicrucians, the Mahicari, the Ayam, the Message of the Grail, and others.

In this paper I shall attempt to show the manner in which Africans have been grounding their spirituality, both in the past and present. In other words, my concern is to know how they protect their life nowadays and how they secure, from the spiritual point of view, their collective survival. To do this, I shall take Christianity as an example of a new spirituality emerging from the crisis which traditional African society is undergoing, and I shall note in particular the charismatic renewal movement.

Traditional African Spirituality

Spirituality is what permits us to make sense of life. Applied to the reality of Africa, this concept implies an idea which is rooted in the socio-cultural universe of the person. For as Bishop Mukeng's Kalond puts it, spirituality is a reality rich in implications. It is at the very center of the life and culture of the individual and of the community. It is life's motor in every aspect, be it technical, psychological, sociological, political, or artistic. Spirituality is a basic dimension of life, the soul of all culture, its essential element.[1]

One cannot speak of life without at the same time speaking of death. These two realities stand in continual opposition, and humans are only human insofar as they can conquer death. The entire structure of traditional society battles to ensure this victory of life over death, through cult, appropriate liturgy, rites, and the political, economic, and social organizations.

All of these strategies are aimed at freeing humankind from everything that promotes death in order to secure immortality. Thus the special importance given to the rites, music and dances associated with birth, initiation (circumcision and excision), marriage, burial and all sorts of reparations (purifications). They are intended to create harmony between the individual and the community thereby guaranteeing the integration of the individual into the traditional society, which is itself connected to the world of the ancestors.

The traditional African societies had developed a civilization which regulated the life of the community. People were progressively introduced to the mysteries of life by a guru-like master. A long preparation made of them men and women capable of discerning good and evil. The art of living and the respect for moral values was at the heart of the initiation.

Modern Africans find themselves uprooted because of the urbanization to which they have been subjected. They live next door to neighbors of other ethnic groups, who have different cultural values, and they are cut off from the traditional milieu which had guaranteed their stability. They are like a great crane which, when removed from its natural habitat, will not reproduce in captivity. They lack points of reference and can even forget the meaning of the important customs which stabilized the moral and spiritual life of the individual.

The Emergence of New Spiritualities

Colonization in Africa brought Western European civilization and the indigenous civilizations into contact. This encounter meant a culture shock for the Africans, which led to the restructuring of their spirituality. New elements were introduced and old elements modified in order to respond appropriately to the new situation. Now about 46 percent of Africa's 589 million people live their spirituality through Christianity.[2]

The encounter with Jesus Christ went hand in hand with the process of colonization. The faith transmitted was packaged in occidental cultural values. And this transmission was not without difficulties due to the indiscriminate abandonment or rejection of African values. This is why some Africans consider Christianity a foreign religion and have resisted its impact.

This situation is the principal cause of the crises and turmoil which explain the stampede of those baptized in the Christian churches towards new sects and the various mystical movements. Many people claim to be Christian, but without hesitation may turn to negative rites (witchcraft, fetishism).

> The Word was the true light that enlightens all men; and he was coming into the world. . . He came to his own domain and his own people did not accept Him. But to all who did accept Him he gave power to become children of God, to all who believe in the name of him who was born not out of human stock or urge of the flesh or will of man but of God himself.
>
> (John 1:9, 11-13)

The quest for inner peace and for liberation finds its answer in the encounter with Jesus Christ, Son of God and Son of Man. Jesus is "the Way, the Truth, and the Life." He is the one in whom every life finds its fullness: "I have come so that they may have life and have it to the full" (John 10:10). By his life and by his death he made of human beings new creatures and freed them to be adopted children of the Father. The teachings of Jesus can be summed up in this way: Love God and love your neighbor. "As the Father has loved me, so I have loved you" (John 15:9).

Our cry for life is answered in the Gospel if at the same time we decide to give our life to Christ and follow in his footsteps. Before going from this world to the father, Jesus left us a testament:

> If you love me you will keep my commandments. I shall ask the Father, and he will give you another Advocate to be with you forever, that spirit of truth whom the world can never receive since it neither sees nor knows him; but you know him, because he is with you, he is in you.
>
> (John 14:15-17)

Thus are all persons called to live according to the Spirit and accept the Spirit's guidance so as to remain faithful to the Lord until the end of time. From this experience of life in the Spirit have been born various spiritual families which live out a particular charisma received from God as a gift to his people. In the Catholic church one can speak of the spiritualities of Ignatius, Merici, Augustine, and others. The persons behind these spiritual families are considered as fathers and mothers who have initiated new life. They serve as role models for their followers.

If all spirituality implies times of silence and prayer during which the individual is recollected to focus on God, the authenticity of any spirituality is confirmed by a commitment to life.

The Gospel at the Heart of Life

In Politics

For a long time the political arena was considered a worldly place where Christian faith had no role to play. In Africa today, priests, pastors, and bishops are mounting the political platform as defenders of truth and of human dignity. But in this regard a conversion is needed if all in the church are to feel concerned by decisions which touch the destiny and history of African peoples.

It is useless to groan over the oppression and misery of the people while those who govern do so with impunity. Faith in Jesus Christ and love of neighbor must lead the Christian to a concrete commitment to the struggle for the liberation of the oppressed and the transformation of the world. African Christians must actively participate in the so-called "national conferences" of their countries, which are intended to unify peoples and free them from the tyranny of those who govern.

In National Development

Agricultural production, health problems, education, and scourges such as alcoholism, drug abuse, and prostitution—are these a central concern for Christians? St. James tells us that a faith without good works is a dead faith (James 2:17). It is wrong to separate the temporal and the spiritual, for man is both body and spirit, one, indivisible.

As we said in defining spirituality, it is the foundation, the core, of all commitment, whether religious, social, economic, or political. The difference between a Christian and anyone else lies precisely in the motivation which underlies all activity.

Africa is not well, for it has trampled its spiritual values; it must pull itself together and accept a serious ascesis if it is to rediscover all its dignity, both human and divine.

The Case of the Charismatic Renewal in Lubumbashi

A people thirsting in anguish for God looks for places where it can quench its thirst. As one place, I have chosen the charismatic renewal in

Lubumbashi, emphasizing in particular the feminine experience in this area.[3]

Christians of the Archdiocese of Lubumbashi[4] have known this new spiritual experience for more than fifteen years. It has a special character in that it has allowed both men and women to be responsible for prayer groups.

My aim here is not to treat in entirety this new spiritual experience. I shall try rather to grasp its feminine dimension in order to offer a specific contribution. Moreover, I shall not attempt here to present the full range of feminine experience in the charismatic renewal of the Archdiocese of Lubumbashi. My remarks have to do only with the city of Lubumbashi itself.

Twenty-two charismatic groups have been officially counted in Lubumbashi. Their group leaders are known as "shepherds" and "shepherdesses." Outside of these groups there exist others whose activities are beyond the control of the church hierarchy. These are the groups of the late Abbe Mukulu Mwamba, of Abbe Alimasi, as well as of Abbe Kasongo, which have evolved in opposition to the others, which had originated as a result of retreats preached in May 1974, by Father Philippe Verhaehen, a Benedictine monk of St. André (Bruges), who is one of the principal leaders of the charismatic renewal in Belgium. It was in 1975 that the Archbishop of Lubumbashi authorized charismatic retreats in his diocese.

These groups sprang up, in some ways, as an answer to the collective anxiety of Christians created by the conflict between church and state at that time, both locally and across the country. Their evolution, however, underwent a critical period around 1978, as a result of confusion sown in the groups by "easy ecumenism" and their marginalization in relation to the basic Christian communities. Certain of these groups at this time drew attention for their fetishistic practices, characterized by punishments and public denunciations of witches, all of which provoked psychological and moral dreams in the families concerned.

In the face of this grave disorder affecting the future of the church, the hierarchy saw as its duty to regulate the prayer groups.

The Shaba region of the Republic of Zaire has a population of 1,301,800 inhabitants of whom 912,600 are urban and 389,200 are rural (Boute, J. and De Saint Moulin, L., in BESCO, Kinshasa, 1982).

The following extracts sum up the essentials of a few of these directives:

- "It is important that the groups of the charismatic renewal, even if they are not usually an outgrowth of the pastoral ministry of the parishes, be in explicit communion with them." In the same vein, it is asked that parishes be open to these groups, welcome them, and take part in their activities.

- The parish priest is called upon to be the guarantor of doctrine in the groups and to provide a link of unity with the church. He must enlighten and participate actively in the discernment of spirits. He will also bring, and especially to the prayer groups, "the sacramental dimension of Christian prayer, principally in the Eucharist and the sacrament of penance."

- The prayer groups must not see in ecumenism a negating of the differences between the churches. Rather, they must admire through it God's action in each church and encourage all persons to remain faithful to their own Christian tradition. No person should underestimate the suffering and the divisions which reflect the infirmity and sinfulness of humankind.

- Those responsible for the prayer groups must not overemphasize the spirit of evil while claiming to possess some power to thwart it. This power is the privilege of God alone. Moreover, "to strike a person to drive out the spirit of evil is an aberration which cannot be justified, either by Scripture or by the faith-experience of the church."[5]

The Feminine Experience of God

After this brief sketch of the history of charismatic renewal in the Archdiocese of Lubumbashi, we move on to the experience of two shepherdesses. They are Mama Regine and Mama Anto. Note that in Swahili "Mama" is the word for "Mother," a title applied to any adult woman.

Mama Regine

The Person

Shepherdess Regine Citamba was born on New Year's Day 1935. Married in May 1953, she is the mother of ten children. She comes from a family of practicing Catholics and her father was a teacher.

Her special encounter with God happened when she was seven years old, on the occasion of her first communion. This encounter was encouraged by the careful preparation she had had, and the stress laid on the importance of the body and blood of Jesus Christ.

"I felt the presence of the Lord in me, and I never stopped speaking to him. I carried God," she says. From that day on, Mama Regine continued to experience extraordinary events and from the age of twelve she heard and saw strange things. Fearful, her parents kept all of this secret.

As a thirteen-year-old at boarding school, she heard the psalms recited for the first time and she heard the *Veni Creator Spiritus* sung. She was fascinated to the point that she composed prayers herself and sang the Lord's praises all day. At this period she felt a strong attraction to religious life, but a commanding voice spoke to her in these terms: "You will be my servant in the midst of the world." Mama Regine adds, "I obeyed without understanding."

Her first ten years of marriage were a time of great trial because of the irresponsibility of her husband. "In the course of these ten years, I rooted myself in God. I brought up my children alone and taught them fidelity to the Lord. I taught them to express themselves in complete liberty before the Lord."

After these ten years of suffering, which she considers her "way of the cross," her husband returned home. He recounts his own conversion: "I didn't know what I was doing. I saw my wife and children suffering and I was incapable of changing my behavior. Today my old friends make fun of me and they've all dropped me, but I've retrieved my God and family. Since that day I have been 'present' to my wife and to all that she is living."

In 1969 Mama Regine fell gravely ill. Medical care gave no results. Family members called in a traditional healer who undertook a ritual healing. He left fetishes with her and Mama Regine felt in herself a force which revealed to her the diabolical presence all around. "I received a new grace from God. A force dwelt within me whose activity I simply couldn't control." Surprised herself by this new force, she was denounced to her pastor and she accepted exorcism as a sign of submission to the church. But nothing was changed for her.

The Nature of Her Charism

The charism of Mama Regine is the discernment of spirits. Her experiences began with involuntary manifestations of the Spirit in her when faced with the spirit of evil during family or friendly visits. For example, persons in her company would fall down saying that they were possessed by malefic forces and would ask her to free them. The reactions of these persons followed upon what Mama Regine had been sensing. This consisted, she notes, of a struggle between the force present in her and that present in the person with her. Immediately she begins to pray and to calm the person in delirium by touching.

Ever since, people have flocked from all parts to be freed of impure spirits. Mama Regine always invokes the blessed Trinity and entrusts the person completely to the hands of God.

The Organization of Her Group

Mama Regine's prayer group was formed after July 5, 1979, the day on which she received the outpouring of the Spirit at the hands of the late Mukulu Mwamba. They had just finished a group retreat of forty days. This retreat was, in fact, her very first contact with charismatic renewal.

The group, properly speaking, includes twenty to twenty-five permanent members who make up the core. The group gathers for regular prayer on Wednesdays from 3 to 6 p.m. The meeting begins with songs and prayers of praise. A good length of time is allowed for the reading and explanation of the Word of God, which is followed by testimonies to the activity of God in the lives of the participants. Finally, the *Veni Creator Spiritus* is recited aloud by the entire assembly. Mama Regine pronounces a blessing over the group, which then disperses.

It is worth mentioning that during the prayer session the members remain seated, except during the intercessory prayer, when they kneel, and the *Veni Creator Spiritus*, when they stand, arms raised high. The group meets again on Friday at 2:30 p.m. for a special prayer for the sick of all categories as well as for all those who come to express their distress. All of these people enjoy the full attention of the group and are taken under the wing of the members. Then the group prays for each one individually. The prayer takes place at the home of the shepherdess, which gives it all a family atmosphere and which puts all at ease to express themselves.

Note that women are in the majority in the group, no doubt because of the hour chosen. It includes representatives of every social class, but these differences are neutralized during the prayer meeting. One finds the same phenomenon with all of the shepherdesses.

The Testimonies

The charismatic prayer group finds its definition in the testimonies offered by its members. This is borne out in the primacy accorded to testimonies as evidence of each member's progress in the journey of faith.

Among the many testimonies recorded in Mama Regine's group, here is one which particularly struck us: A family had made a pact with the devil. One day, after hearing of Mama Regine and her prayer for deliverance, they invited her to come and pray at their home. She had her husband come with her. Before the prayer, the shepherdess listened at length to the anguished family, then she began praying, inviting everyone to do likewise. During the prayer she felt the diabolical presence in action in the house; something terrible was happening. She hurt physically. As she prayed she asked that they call the family's oldest daughter. The one who went to get her from her room where she had been studying, returned shouting that the girl was dead!

Mama Regine began a prayer that lasted for seven hours. During this time, no one was able to cry, everyone sang and praised God, even as the girl lay stretched out on the floor in front of them. At a certain moment, Mama Regine took the girl by the hand while calling her by name. The girl opened her eyes and simply got up.

Mama Regine says she understood nothing of all that had happened. She let herself be steered by an inner force which she cannot describe. She acts out of obedience; she senses only what must be done at the right moment.

Mama Anto

The Person

Mama Anto, or Antoinette Mwadi Mukeba, was born on June 13, 1936, and is a divorcee since January 1981. In general, her life has been fraught with suffering. Among other events, let us note the following:

- at twelve years of age she experienced her parents' divorce and the break-up of her family;
- her marriage produced four children, two of whom died of sickle-cell anemia, a son at one year of age and a daughter as a young mother of twenty-two;
- blaming her for the illness of their children and so as to punish her, her husband took another wife;
- the life of prayer that she had chosen to be faithful to the Lord occasioned the divorce, for her husband would abide the presence of the prayer group neither in his house nor in his yard.

Mama Anto comes from a Protestant family. Having discovered the eucharist in the Catholic church at the age of thirteen, she would have to wait a long time to experience holy communion. This day was for her "the blessed day" and from that day she has wanted to consecrate everything entirely to the Lord.

Her life is a veritable way of the cross and she says, "I had the impression that God was abandoning me, but I never despaired in him."

In 1974 her younger sister, Mama Charlotte, also a prayer group shepherdess, supported her and encouraged her to pray without ceasing. At this time she discovered the Lubumbashi Carmel, where the nuns taught her how to pray.

In 1978 she made a charismatic retreat which prepared her to receive the outpouring of the Holy Spirit. As hands were laid on her, one person questioned her: "What do you ask of the spirit of God?" She answered, "Wisdom." And someone else said to her, "The Lord needs you for his work. Are you willing to give your life?" She says she understood nothing of what was happening to her, but something had fundamentally changed within her. She began to pray at length. Now God had become *someone* for her.

The Nature of Her Charism

Mama Anto has the gift of healing. Her earliest experiences date from the year 1979. This is what happened. Friends and also other persons had been coming to confide their problems to her, both physical and moral. She listened to them, then prayed with them. Often she fasted and continued praying alone for these people, because she is very sensitive to the problems of others. A few days later they would come and thank her because one situation or another had improved: a husband had returned home, an alcoholic had given up drinking, the sick had been healed, and so on.

She understands that through all of this, God wanted to use her to heal. But at that time she did not yet dare pray openly at home. She always went to the homes of those who asked for her help.

The Organization of Her Group

Little by little in 1979 there grew up around Mama Anto a group of people looking for a place to pray that was not removed from the reality of life.

Mama Anto has a core group of twenty people, but she receives from 150 to 300 participants at each prayer session. The prayer takes place at her home, in the yard or in the living room. She receives people according to no schedule, but the actual prayer sessions take place from 2 to 6 p.m. for women, and from 8 to 10 p.m., even midnight, for men. The ratio of men to women is about equal.

The format of Mama Anto's session is about the same as Mama Regine's. In other words, the meeting begins with prayers of praise and ends with intercessory prayers, after a Scripture reading and lesson.

Mama Anto's regulars are for the most part the marginalized: *wayambars* (street youths), prostitutes, mistresses, singles looking for spouses, infertile women, practitioners of witchcraft, and others.

The Testimonies

In December 1979, Mama Anto was urgently called to the bedside of a religious sister's father, who was dying of cancer of the liver. The doctors had given him two weeks at the most to live. When Mama Anto entered the hospital room, the man was surrounded by his family and was receiving the sacrament of the sick. Mama Anto laid her hands on the sick man saying, "As I was entering this room I received a message telling me that you wouldn't die because God still needs you to work." Mama Anto had the whole family make a novena including fasting.

The same night the sick man opened his eyes and asked to drink. Before the end of the nine days, the doctors asked the family to take the sick man home to die in better conditions. However, Mama Anto continued to pray and to visit the man, walking almost four miles each day.

A month later the man was reexamined. The X-rays were not consistent. The doctors were perplexed. One of them could give no medical explanation, while the other, a believer, thanks God for the miraculous cure. The fine gentleman in question is now seventy-one years old. He attests that he was reclaimed from the dead to serve God.

The Role of Women in Service of Life

Besides these testimonies concerning shepherdesses who have a particular charism and who have found a new way of being of service to life–physical, moral and spiritual–there are also all the other women who work actively to promote life, many of whom do so quietly, discreetly.

The Nurturant Mother

She gives life. Out of the child that she carries in her womb and whom she brings into the world, she tries to make the beginnings of a man or woman. She initiates the child to speech, to the mother tongue, to life in society and to spiritual and cultural values.

In traditional society, the task of tilling the fields is entrusted to the woman. She holds the secrets of the earth's fertility and develops a spirituality linked to the earth, which is expressed through songs and prayers to God at the beginning of each season.

Protectress of life, she also plays the role of mediatrix in her family and her circle. She joins other women to try and ward off death that comes through war or family conflicts. She helps preserve social order by respecting the traditions which favor life.

Women at the Service of Life in the Church

She bears children for the church by teaching them catechism or preparing them for baptism. She is at the center of inculturation in Africa, for she is able to discover new ways of being church through her involvement in the basic Christian communities.

She may commit herself to God in prayer through the prayer, work and silence of monastic life and in this way she offers a little life, peace and rest to all those who, searching for God, ask for the hospitality of the monastery. Or perhaps she chooses to live in the world as an active presence like leaven in the dough.

Conclusion

As I have shown, the meaning of life in Africa has the possibility of incorporating Christian spirituality. An authentic Christian experience, says Father Engelbert Mveng, must be based on both the Gospel and on African tradition. Thus it can be said that the charismatic renewal is a gift from God and an opportunity for the churches of Africa.

To follow Christ means taking up one's cross and walking behind him. For us in Africa, this means that conversion requires breaking away and making new choices, choices that are not simply imposed according to some preestablished, external standard of behavior. The Word of God has to touch us where we live, to call us to raise our eyes and march towards Him.

The fact that those on the fringe of society, the marginalized, are deserting our churches for groups like Mama Anto's sends a message to the churches regarding both pastoral ministry and liturgical structures.

The cry for life comes from every direction. As one example, let me offer this song from my youth, its author's name long since forgotten.

I Am Human

I am human, who'd dare say I'm not?
Who'd dare say I have no body? Then why do

you let me live like a dog?
Why do you let me die like an animal?

I am human, I am human.
You see my skin, you see my bones, you see my
eyes, you see my body, like yours. . .
I'm asking for life, I'm human.

You see my children and they're hungry,
You see these fields which aren't mine,
You see these people who eat my bread!
I want to earn my bread, I'm human.

O Earth, strange land, who rules you, you my realm?
Tomorrow, my Earth, I want you to be mine.
I'm asking for justice, I'm human.

There's no work for my two hands,
Tomorrow will I take as tool plow or gun?
I need work, I'm human.

You see my heart, but do you hear it?
Your heart which beats, mine which strikes out,
A human heart at the heart of the world.
I need you to love me, I'm human.

And in my heart there rises a song,
A song as violent as a great wind,
A song which ranges far and wide like the wind.
I want my freedom, I am human!

This cry of humanity is universal, it has no color. The authenticity of an intense inner life is confirmed by an attitude and by life choices which make of the world a more livable place for all.

Notes

1. "Spiritualité matrimoniale: cas de la jamaa," in *L'Afrique et ses formes de vie spirituelle*, Actes du Deuxième Colloque International, Kinshasa, 21-27 November 1983.

2. *Britannica Book of the Year*, 1988.

3. Mbuy-Beya, "L'expérience féminine de Dieu dans le Renouveau Charismatique," Communication préparée pour le Colloque de Yaoundé, 4-9 August 1986.

4. The Archdiocese of Lubumbashi covers an area of 79,599 square kilometers and is situated between the twenty-sixth and twenty-eighth degrees longitude East and ninth and twelfth degrees latitude South. It includes thirteen rural collectives

and two cities, Lubumbashi and Likasi; it is in the Shaba region of the Republic of Zaire. It has a population of 1,301,800 inhabitants of whom 912,600 are urban and 389,200 are rural (Boute, J. and De Saint Moulin, L. in BESCO, Kinshasa, 1982).

5. Archdiocese of Lubumbashi, Directives aux groupes de prière du Renouveau Charismatique, stenciled circular, July 10, 1983, pp. 10-12.

Bibliography

1. Bakole wa Ilunga, *Chemin de libération*, Editions de l'Archdiocese de Kananga, 1978.

2. Engelbert Mveng, *L'Afrique dans l'Eglise, Paroles d'un croyant*, l'Harmattan, Paris, 1985.

3. Kabanga Mgr., *Lettre pastorale sur la femme*, Easter, 1989.

4. L'Afrique et ses formes de vie spirituelle, Actes du Deuxième Colloque International de Kinshasa, 21-27 November 1983.

Translated from the French by Brother David Patrick Mahoney, CFX

7

Spirituality and Transformation in Black Theology

DWIGHT N. HOPKINS

The spirituality of Black theology arises out of the transformational experience and traditions found in several stories of the radical commissioning in the Christian Bible, African-American women's spirituality, and the folk faith of Black slaves. Just as the God of freedom incarnated God's self in the birth, life, crucifixion, and resurrection of Jesus the liberator, so too, God's same spirit of freedom incarnates herself amongst poor African-Americans suffering in a living death and crying out in their struggle for a holistic life.

The Biblical Story: A Subversive Spirituality

Based on the Christian scriptures, the African-American church, for whom Black theology speaks, maintains a subversive faith in Jesus Christ's spirit. In particular, Martin Luther King, Jr., stands in this spiritual tradition when he paraphrases Luke 4:18 and proclaims the following:

Jesus said the spirit of the Lord is upon me, because he's anointed me to heal the broken hearted, to preach the gospel to the poor, to bring deliverance to those who are in captivity and to proclaim the acceptable year of the Lord. And I must confess that the spirit of the Lord is upon me.[1]

Here in his biblical interpretation, King stresses two aspects of Black theological spirituality. The first act of Christian spirituality is not correct doctrine, but a freeing service to the poor, the homeless, unemployed, those victims of AIDS and rape, the immigrant stranger, the hungry and those without proper clothing. Christian spirituality means confronting the everyday pain and humiliation that face the faceless in society. It means commitment to and standing with those who suffer. To be compelled by the Spirit, then, the Black church has to root itself, primarily, in poor African-American communities where the Lord's spirit was born and still resides. Christian spirituality greets the Black church in the struggle for freedom of the least of these in society ("the truth will set you free," John 8:32). Indeed, for the spirituality of the eleven o'clock Black church service on Sunday to be authenticated, this Sunday spirituality has to receive God's presence in suffering and struggle in the Monday through Saturday Black ghettos of North America. It is this latter spirit that "will guide you into all the truth" (John 16:13).

Black theological spiritual practice fundamentally means social transformation of demonic structures and systems which hold a boot to the necks of poor Black people in the US. Any talk about the Spirit in the Black church that leaves a satanic systemic spirit in place serves the Devil who breeds capitalism, the second-class status of women, US military presence abroad, and, of course, White supremacy over African-Americans and other people of color. Following the Christian spirit's calling, King began to organize against evil structures and, in the last year of his ministry, declared:

> The dispossessed of this nation, the poor, both White and Negro live in a cruelly unjust society. They must organize a revolution against that injustice, not against the lives of the persons who are their fellow citizens, but against the structures through which the society is refusing to take means which have been called for, and which are at hand, to lift the load of poverty.[2]

King named the spirituality of systemic evil; he called it the capitalist system in the US. This demonic spirituality fostered racism at home and imperialist war abroad. For instance, when questioned about the existence of domestic poverty, King replied: "And when you begin to ask that question, you are raising questions about the economic system, about a broader distribution of wealth." Basically, the anointing to follow Jesus led you "to question the capitalistic economy."[3] And for King, God's transformational spirit moved him to organize the in- breaking of the divine kingdom specifically revealed in "democratic socialism."[4] Thus politics (that is, the act of rearranging power relations in accordance with the spirit of freedom) helps to define the spiritual activity of a Black theology of liberation.

In addition to a liberating spiritual practice, the anointing of "the spirit of the Lord" also commissions us to proclaim the good news of freedom. God's loving freedom has become our freedom because Jesus' victory over oppression has opened up a new world where everlasting life begins now (John 3:16). This spirit calls on Black theology to speak to and for those who have no voices. It calls on Black theology to say the gospel of freedom for a full individual collective life reigns now for the African-American poor (in solidarity with the world's poor). Martin Luther King recognized the prophetic nature of speaking the truth of Christian spiritual anointing: "We are called," King proclaimed, "to speak for the weak, for the voiceless, for the victims of our nation . . . "[5]

The poor have to hear that Jesus' kingdom has won and, therefore, has made them somebody. The somebodiness of the proclaimed gospel is not a mushy feel-good, heathenistic, self-indulgence. It, on the contrary, empowers the poor to realize their true spiritual identity. For the African-American poor in particular, it affirms their African self identity. Part of announcing a liberating spirituality to the Black victims of society, then, is to tell them that their African self or their Black self comes from the grace of God. "Yes," shouted King, "we must stand up and say, 'I'm black and I'm beautiful,' and this self affirmation is the Black man's need, made compelling by the White man's crimes against him."[6] Self-identity language of Blackness and Africans grips the poor and helps them to see, with new eyes, the reality and future possibilities of a new heaven on earth. If the social and language structures of the dominating white society have been subverted by the good news of a new kingdom, then poor Black people no longer feel defined by a White ruling culture. They claim and name themselves in the liberated space created by Jesus' liberating spirit. To say who you are is part of waging war against satanic labels that deny your full humanity. Culture (that is, the act of identifying oneself in accordance with freedom), then, is an important aspect of Black theology's transformative spirituality.

Black Women's Story: Holistic Spirituality of the Body

Christian spirituality and transformation in Black theology are more clearly and readily seen in the biblical practice and proclamation of Martin Luther King, Jr. However, the spiritual basis of Black theology also encompasses African-American sources that are borderline to Christianity and, in some instances, non-Christian. The suggestive and imaginary novels of Toni Morrison overflow with instances of God's liberating spirituality pursuing diverse religious paths; thus broadening Black theology into a complex encounter with the Holy. Specifically, Black women add the liberating dimension of a spirituality of the body.

In Morrison's stories, poor African-American women regard the natural state of their bodies as a sacred temple of self-love, normal physical-emotional expression, and a gift to God's spirit in worship. More exactly, Baby Suggs (a character in *Beloved*[7]) pastors a congregation of poor Black folk out in a section of the woods which they call the Clearing. Here this unordained preacher-woman exhorts her "church" to love the flesh of their bodies and to give full play to their natural appetites for crying, laughter and dance. Put differently, this Christian-conjurer calls on her people to lift up their spirits through their bodies, in liturgy and supplication, to divine spirit.

First, church service begins with Baby Suggs' homily on self-love of the sacred flesh. "Here," preaches Baby Suggs, "in this here place, we flesh;

flesh that weeps, laughs; flesh that dances on bare feet in grass. Love it. Love it hard." Stressing a specific passion for a spiritual love of the body, Suggs preaches within a concrete and historical context of White racism, a context quite familiar to her congregation's collective memory and to their daily dehumanizing relation to Whites. Resuming her spiritual sharing of the body's significance, she reminds her folk that "they" (for example, referencing White cultural and political norms) despise poor Blacks' "eyes" and "the skin on your backs;" "they" do not love black hands; and "they ain't in love with your mouth." Instead, her congregation must love their flesh; stroke their hands and touch other Black folk with them; grace their necks and support their backs; provide strong arms for their shoulders; and love their inside parts. Above all, climaxes Baby Suggs, speaking truth, "hear me now, love your heart. For this is the prize." The heart stands as the ultimate part of the body because God has granted poor Blacks the ability to love each other, as well as all bodies that suffer and endure hatred. But in order to be human, to take God's grace of love, planted spiritually within each heart, and love the rest of humanity, African-Americans have to go down deep in the depths of their Black hearts and love the blackness of their physical being. Self-love (for example, coming to terms with the natural created love of God in human hearts) sets the context for resonating with love of others, even feeling compassionate justice for one's enemies. Thus the natural bodies reflect sacred temples of self-love.

In her church services, moreover, Baby Suggs calls out the spirit through the normal physical emotional expression of her congregation. With sacred authority, she summons forth the children and instructs them to laugh before their parents. And the children's bodies, which they loved, filled the trees with laughter. She then orders the men to step forward and dance before their wives and children. And "groundlife shuddered under their feet" as the trees rang with the sounds of children's laughter. Finally, she designates the women and tells them to cry, for the living and the dead. It began with clear roles for each segment of the folk, but then everything and everybody intertwined and intermixed.

> Women stopped crying and danced; men sat down and cried; children danced, women laughed, children cried until, exhausted and riven, all and each lay about the Clearing damp and gasping for breath. In the silence that followed, Baby Suggs, holy, offered up to them her great big heart.

In holy worship, Baby Suggs offers a transformative spirituality of the individual and communal body. Love of self, granted by God's spirit of love and implanted in the heart, enables one's self-identity of one's spiritual self (that is, a cultural claim) which, in turn, helps one to deal with the "theys" of the world (that is, a political claim), even to the point of understanding the position of one's adversary. In addition, one returns God's spiritual love through a demonstrative display of the body's natural activities of laughing, dancing, and crying. Baby Suggs, therefore, leads Black theology down into a Black spirituality of the natural body and into new places where God's call for life can be heard.

Consequently, in Toni Morrison's novels, African-American women's spirituality moves Black theology into the realm of a holistic divinity whose transformational freedom manifests throughout the Black church and community. God's power of loving the poor through justice and liberation knows no boundaries. As a result, an African-American encounter with God opens its heart and mind, ears and eyes to wider resources in the total Black spiritual experience. Black women's spirituality includes Christian and non-Christian thought and action. Such reflection-practice does theology because it witnesses to God's liberating spirit wherever God chooses to reveal God's Christian and non-Christian self. Black women's spirituality embraces the religion of the institutional church and the non-church. It is religious because an unrestrained divine initiative among humanity expresses itself both within the church institution and, at the same time, within the broader African-American women's community (which, of course, links to the rest of Black folk and, indeed, to all of poor humanity).

Furthermore, out of the soil of poor Black women's spirituality, Black theology discovers new theological language, thought forms, metaphors and categories. Thus the liberating appearance of God's spirit in non-Christian revelations, through story, complements the divine spiritual descent upon the decisive Christian revelation of Jesus the Christ ("The Spirit of the Lord is upon me"). The Christian and non-Christian lives of poor African-American women are authentic theological "birthers" of divine transforming presence. In fact, the uniqueness of women's spiritual experience and story must be taken seriously precisely because a Black theology of liberation receives and participates with an incarnational God who tabernacles with the poor. For Black theology, one of the locations of the poor is the gender- racial-poverty reality of Black women. And while attending to the fight against wicked principalities and powers, we also open ourselves up to the multiple positive, creative and spiritual laughter, tears, dance and thinking of African-American women. Women's spirituality of the body is holistic.

Slave Story: Spirituality of the Folk

From 1619, when European Christians brought twenty Africans to the "New World," until 1865 when the end of the Civil War saw the fall of slavery in the USA, White Christians owned Black folk like a master owning a dog. Yet, enslaved Africans knew that God had given them a heart, a head, a body, and a soul infused with a divine spirituality of survival and liberation. Consequently, out of the heat of slavery, Black folk worked with the Spirit to empower themselves and thus recreate their crushed status into a life of new beings. In other words, spirituality compelled them to keep on, keeping on even when their bodies broke while laboring from "can't see in the morning till can't see at night."

More specifically, ex-slave Cornelius Garner uses the inspiration of a liberating spirituality to describe the absence of the divine presence in White slave masters' churches. In the faith of this former slave, a quiet stillness in White people's worship signified a heretical void which replaced God's word of freedom with a demonic, pro-slavery justification. In the language of the slave folk, Garner remembers:

> De churches whar we went to serve God was 'Pisipal, Catholick, Presberteriens, de same as marsters church only we was off to usselves in a little log cabin in de woods.

> Depreaching us got 'twon't nothing much. Dat ole white preacher jest was telling us slaves to be good to our marrsters. We ain't keer'd a bit 'bout stuff he was telling us 'cause we wanted to sing, pray, and serve God in our own way. You see, 'legion needs a little motion specially if you gwive feel de spirret.[8]

Here for the enslaved, to serve God in your own way requires a movement of "de spirret." And so White preaching "'twon't nothing much" because the Spirit did not present itself. If the divinity does not visit the gathered faithful, then the will of God for freedom and a full humanity remains a dream deferred and a promise postponed. Therefore, white Christians could preach, "slaves, obey your masters," because Whites had never experienced the moving grace of a liberating spirituality.

In contrast, African-Americans, who were enslaved, served God in their own way with complete vibrancy, singing, shouting, and dancing. The movement of the bodies of slave folk imaged the joyous thanks and praise that they offered to God who daily gave them life amidst rags and dirt. Black slave folk "got happy" because the Lord had brought them a mighty long way. And so their physical motion and feeling of "de spirret" in worship meant that the chains of slavery could neither control their bodies or their spirits. Worship itself, then, became a space of defiance and proclamation for an unrestrained life.

Furthermore, slaves' spirit-filled motion suggests a change and transformation from the old to the new; a development from a state of decaying death to the birthing of a revitalized Jubilee. In this radical bringing forth of a liberated life for the underside of history, a virtual war ensues between demonic and divine spirits. Another former slave describes this fierce combat:

> There is a real heaven and hell. The hell is the devil and his angels. They are evil spirits and are ever present with us to tempt and try us. They are at war with the heavenly host and seek to dissuade those who would serve God.[9]

Again, African-American bondsmen and women connected genuine service to God with battling evil spirits of oppression; slaves knew theologically that a real heaven and hell existed. And hell embodied and imbedded itself in specific institutional and systemic evils on earth. Therefore, that which attacked the motion-filled spirit of the poor was an ever-present evil. So our stand with the spiritual life of the oppressed compels us to serve with God's spirit of the "heavenly host." It requires specific acts of daily collective and individual warfare against systemic and personal evil. It means a joy in motion for a spiritual life specifically revealed in actual earthly struggle for liberation of the folk.

Conclusion

Spirituality and transformation in Black theology included real life experiences of a poor and struggling African-American community. For instance, the subversive biblical spirituality of Martin Luther King, Jr., calls on us to name definite systems that cause a living death for society's marginalized, organize to remove these shackling structures, and proclaim the good news of God's free existence for the world's havenots. Furthermore, African-American women's religious experience offers a holistic spirituality for all of the divinely created body. It recognizes the dwelling of God's grace of life in both church and non-church and Christian and non-Christian practices of freedom. In addition, slave spirituality of the folk demands that we serve God through transformational motion. Thus, the spirituality of Black theology participates in the growth of God's new creation in our very midst today. Wherever we discover the spirituality of poor humanity, there we encounter the seeds and signs of God's unfolding liberation of human life.

Notes

1. See "Dr. Martin Luther King, Jr., Speech at Staff Retreat Penn Center, Frogmore, South Carolina, May 23-31, 1967," p. 4 (Author's copy).

2. *The Trumpet of Conscience*, (New York: Harper & Row, 1967), pp. 59-60.

3. See "The President's Address to the Tenth Anniversary Convention of the Southern Christian Leadership Conference, Atlanta, Georgia, August 16, 1967," in *The Rhetoric of Black Power*, (eds.) Robert L. Scott and Wayne Brockriede, (New York: Harper & Row, 1969), p. 162.

4. See Martin Luther King, Jr., *The Trumpet of Conscience*, pp. 59-60; and David J. Garrow, *Bearing the Cross: Martin Luther King, Jr. and the Southern Christian Leadership Conference*, (New York: William Morrow, 1986), pp. 364 and 537.

5. Martin Luther King, Jr., *The Trumpet of Conscience*, (New York: Harper & Row, 1967), p. 25.

6. See "The President's Address to the Tenth Anniversary Convention of the Southern Christian Leadership Conference, Atlanta, Georgia, August 16, 1967," in *The Rhetoric of Black Power*, (eds.) Robert L. Scott and Wayne Brockriede, (New York: Harper & Row, 1969), p. 155.

7. Toni Morrison, *Beloved*, (New York: New American Library, 1987). For a fuller treatment on Baby Suggs and the spirituality of the body, see pp. 87-89.

8. Charles L. Perdue, Jr. *et al.*, *Weevils in the Wheat: Interviews with Virginia Ex-slaves*, (Bloomington, Indiana: Indiana University Press, 1980), p. 100.

9. Clifton H. Johnson, ed., *God Struck Me Dead: Religious Conversion Experiences and Autobiographies of Ex- slaves*, (Philadelphia, Pennsylvania: Pilgrim Press, 1969), p. 14.

Part III

The Theological Response

8

Opening Address

SERGIO TORRES

It is with great joy that I welcome you to the Eighth International Conference of Theology and to the Third General Assembly of the Ecumenical Association of Third World Theologians (EATWOT). We have come a long way and we are here animated by the Spirit of God to share what we have experienced during the past five years, to critically evaluate the work of our association and, if we pass the test, to plan a new stage of another five years.

EATWOT is a network of people who try to read the signs of the times with the eyes of the poor of the Third World. As we are scattered in our regions, every five years some members, representing their regional constituencies, get together at the international conferences for mutual critique and enrichment. Then they go back to their countries to share what they have learned.

The Dramatic Context

It is a happy coincidence on this occasion that we are meeting in Nairobi. It was here in 1975 at the fifth General Assembly of the World Council of Churches that a steering committee was formed to organize the first dialogue with Third World theologians. This first dialogue was held in August 1976 in Dar-es-Salaam, Tanzania, where EATWOT was born.

At the time EATWOT was formed, Third World countries had leverage and political power. At the United Nations and in other international organizations these countries were the majority and exercised power in many important decisions. Third World countries became a real threat to the First World. In our conference in New Delhi in 1981 we named this emerging power the "Irruption of the Third World"!

As we come together this January of 1992, we see many changes in the world in general and in the Third World in particular. After the Gulf War, the United States of America, as the main military force, wants to impose a new international order. With the crisis of the socialist countries, capitalism is triumphant and the free market model of economy is presented as the only alternative. In synthesis, the First World has recovered its leadership, the Second World does not exist anymore and the Third World is divided and almost powerless. In the midst of the crisis of the Third World, Third World theology is also affected. Therefore the relevance and the future of our association has to be seriously discussed. I consider that one of the major tasks of this conference should be to look at the changes that we are facing, to discern anew the signs of the times and to reformulate the role of this association. Our general theological theme, "A Cry for Life: The Spirituality of the Third World," cannot be dealt with in isolation from this concrete and dramatic context.

Other Theologies

Before we enter into our discussion I want to present a few insights about the reality of EATWOT according to my own perception. Let us begin with the minorities in the United States. First, I want to welcome to this assembly the presence of a Native American theologian, George Tinker, who will address us on the theme of spirituality. There are new names and new efforts of coordination among Hispanic theologians for the contextualization of Hispanic theology. I want to underline the development and consistency of Black theology. The history of this particular Third World theology is reflected, among other signs, in the publication in 1990 of the twentieth anniversary edition of the book *A Black Theology of Liberation* by James Cone. The critical reflections of several authors at the end of the book, as well as the personal assessment of Cone, reflect well the interaction with other Third World theologies and the positive role of Black theology in the ongoing dialogue of EATWOT.

In Africa

Let us now look at another region: Africa. EATWOT theologians of this region have taken important steps during the last five years. This has been done in a difficult political, economic and social context. On the one hand, poverty has deepened and there is more political instability and social unrest. On the other hand there is progress in the struggle against apartheid in South Africa, and in other countries people are looking for new forms of democracy and participation. We are proud of EATWOT members who have played a leading role in South Africa in the battle against White racism.

Two major theological events in Africa can be cited. The first was the EATWOT African Conference held in Harare, Zimbabwe, from January 6 to 11, 1991. The theme was "Culture, Religion and Liberation." A total of sixty participants of African countries attended and eight regional pre-conferences were held to prepare for the event. This conference was a breakthrough in Africa and it helped to give identity to African theology. Papers read were of high quality and participants agreed that this was a fruitful conference because it helped to uncover oppressive aspects in African culture and religions, as well as to reinforce the liberation aspects. At the end it was agreed that a critical methodology should be found that would enable people to identify the mechanisms of cultural and religious oppressions in order to help the oppressed in their struggle for liberation.

Another important event in Africa was the creation of the "Circle of Concerned African Women Theologians," an independent project, but created with the support of EATWOT and with the participation of EATWOT women. This is not a new association, but a network of women interested in theology. The circle organized a biennial institute in Ghana in September, 1989, with the participation of fifty-three African women.

In Asia

Asia had two programs during these past five years. One was the Third Asian Theological Conference (ATC III) in continuation with ATC II (1983) and ATC I (1979). This conference was held in Suanbo, Korea, from July 3-8, 1989 and forty people attended. Entitled "An Asian Search for a Liberation Spirituality," it was preceded by a year of preparatory meetings in each country. The main papers from this conference were published by Orbis Books as *Asian Christian Spirituality: Reclaiming Traditions* edited by Virginia Fabella, Peter K.H. Lee and David Kwang-sun Suh.

The other program consisted of two important meetings of Asian women. The first took place in Seoul, Korea, just prior to ATC III. The aim was to examine the manifestation of patriarchy in Asia and the search for an Asian women's hermeneutical principle.

The second meeting was held in Madras, India, in December, 1990, as a follow-up to the Seoul meeting. It is also necessary to remember that during this past five-year period, Asian members edited four books on EATWOT events. As one who has been involved with EATWOT from the beginning, I want to underline the leading role of Asian theologians in the EATWOT family. They are recovering their religious traditions; they are in dialogue with other major religions; they are raising critical questions about Christian theology, and Asian women are playing an important role in theology.

In Latin America

Latin America has been deeply affected by the political and ecclesial situation. In the 1980s the economic situation deteriorated and the crisis of the socialist world has had serious repercussions in this area at all levels. For the Catholic church 1992 should be a year for critical evaluation, repentance and conversion in connection with the quincentenary of the colonization of the continent.

Latin American theologians have been part of the dialogue of EATWOT from the start. They offered their experience and their theological synthesis. Sometimes, however, some of them gave the impression of imposing their theology as the universal Third World theology. This created resistance and was the source of much confrontation and frustration. Today the situation has changed and we are in a new stage. Latin American theology is different from five years ago and Latin American theologians have learned from the cultural and religious traditions of other continents. We can describe the Latin American theology as diversification and pluralism with not just one model of liberation theology. New hermeneutical principles are being formulated in addition to the traditional principles based on economic and political oppression. In this way we can distinguish three major theological tendencies within the framework of liberation theology, sometimes in critical dialogue and even in confrontation with the traditional model. These three theologies are: indigenous theology, African-American theology, and feminist theology. There is also a dialogue between economics and theology, efforts for an eco-theology or geo-justice, reading of the Bible from the perspective of the poor, theology and popular religiosity, theology and cultures, and so on.

EATWOT is leading this process in the continent. There are three programs to implement these concerns. The project "Andean Culture and Theology," based in La Paz, Bolivia, is developing a program for the formulation of an Andean indigenous theology. Another project is called ATABAQUE, which is a reflection group on "Theology and Blackness," based in Sao Paulo, Brazil, conducted by an EATWOT member, Antônio Aparecido da Silva. This group has been working on the formulation of a Black theology of liberation from an Afro-Latin American perspective. Thirdly, some EATWOT women are developing a feminist theological approach from a Latin American point of view.

In relation to this region I want to recall the fifteenth anniversary of the English translation of Gustavo Gutiérrez's book *A Theology of Liberation*, and the gathering of many leading theologians of the world at Maryknoll, New York, in the summer of 1988. Most of the papers were published by Orbis Books in a volume as a tribute to Gustavo. This was an important occasion for reaffirmation of liberation theology and for exploring ways of theologizing both in the Third and in the First Worlds.

Dream Coming True

After I have given this general overview I am conscious that it is only a personal interpretation, incomplete and provisional. Our Executive Secretary will present to us a comprehensive report of the past five years. But I thought it would be helpful for us, and especially for the new members, to start our process here with a common understanding of the reality of EATWOT.

After I finished collecting the data for this presentation I realized the vitality and creativity of the regional work of EATWOT. The four regions have made enormous progress in the process of contextualization of their particular theologies. I dare to say that what was a dream in Dar-es-Salaam is becoming a reality today.

However, at the level of the Executive Committee we recognize our failure to provide more opportunities for intercontinental dialogue, which is the main goal of our association. We had only one intercontinental meeting in New Delhi, organized by the Theological Study Commission. It will be important to discern not only our strength but also our weakness as we plan ahead.

Expectations and Suggestions

As I come to the end, I would like express my own expectations about the work in this conference.

I consider it necessary to look at the present context in the Third World and to raise a prophetic voice in the midst of confusion, discouragement and rampant pragmatism.

I suggest approaching our theological theme with mutual respect and listening. We have learned from the past that among ourselves there are differences and commonalities. An international conference is an opportunity for dialogue and mutual enrichment.

I propose to my fellow male theologians to listen more carefully to their female counterparts and to work together as partners with our EATWOT sisters in a common theological project.

I hope that we will not depart without a concrete program to reinforce our association and to maintain our solidarity with the poor and the oppressed of our countries.

I invite all of us to work with compassion and to practice relationships of friendship and hospitality among ourselves. We need to speak the truth, but with loving care.

My brothers and sisters, in the past five years, EATWOT, as an international forum, has been affected by the crisis of the Third World. If in 1976 we were able to offer a new program for Christians and theologians of the Third World, a similar effort is needed in 1992 when we face dramatic changes in the world and in the churches. I invite you all to accomplish this task, to be accountable to the suffering and to the whole of our peoples and I ask God to bless our deliberations.

9

A Theology of Life: Rebuilding Hope from the Perspective of the South

PABLO RICHARD

The meaning of God and the Gospel is under serious threat from the so-called "new international order," which has a fatal impact on the life of the poor and the life of nature. The dominant system today, which is idolatrous by nature, destroys the faith, the hope, and the utopia of the oppressed and outcast majorities in the Third World. We must save the life of the poor and the life of the cosmos, and in order to do so we must rebuild hope and utopia. Today, more than ever, we need a liberating theology to serve as a theology of life and a theology of hope; a theology that reflects critically in the light of faith on human life in a situation of savage capitalism; and a theology that reflects on hope and utopia from among the poor in a situation in which hope is collapsing and utopias are being destroyed.

After five hundred years of colonialism, whose legacy is the present situation in which our situation is worse than it was at the outset of the conquest, we are becoming more aware of the deep crisis of Western civilization. We have built an irrational, unsustainable, and savage world that is killing people and destroying nature. In response, a new and alternative world is arising in the South and out of the South, a world that represents hope for the 80 percent of humankind that live in the Third World: a hope and a utopia coming from the South for the salvation of the whole world.

Translated from the Spanish by Phillip Berryman.

In this essay I will describe 1) the crisis of savage capitalism in the Third World, 2) the rebuilding of hope and utopia, based on the poor and the outcast, and 3) the response to the crisis of civilization that is arising from the South.

Crisis of Capitalism in the Third World

From Development Capitalism to Savage Capitalism

The major reality challenging liberation theology in the new international order is the massive death of the poor. The starting point for a critical reflection on God as the God of life must be this situation of death and the option for life that is urgently required.

Two facts stand out: first, the failure of "historic socialisms" in the East, and second, the failure of "development capitalism" in the South. While a great deal is being said and written about the first, almost nothing is said about the second. In the Third World, before the fall of historic socialisms, capitalism claimed to be a development capitalism: it sought to have a human face and it attempted to use the entire labor force to serve the life of all. The state was intended to serve the development of the whole nation. Development capitalism rarely attained these goals, but at least it defined itself in relation to them. It sought to win over underdeveloped countries in order to keep them from falling under the influence of socialism.

However, with the fall of historic socialism, the end of the cold war, and the imposition of a new international order, development capitalism has turned into savage capitalism. This savage capitalism "has the field to itself" with no rivals; it is now concentrating its power in the North, and unleashing its aggression against the South.[1]

Savage capitalism has two structural features: it is a capitalism that excludes the majority and a capitalism that destroys nature. This is not merely a tendency or a defect that can be remedied, but it is rather a deep structural perversion that poses a grave threat to human and cosmic life, especially in the so-called Third World. Let us examine each of these features, in order to engage in a theological reflection aimed at preserving life.

Savage capitalism (or "pay-the-foreign-debt economics," which in more refined terminology is called "export economics") is first of all a system that excludes many people. This is a relatively new development that comes on top of the quite familiar phenomenon of extreme poverty. It has resulted in a new concept: that of the excluded, the outcast, those who do not count, the dispensable, those who have no impact on market efficiency, those who can die without leaving a trace, the "non-invited to the neoliberal banquet," those who are not even exploited (since being exploited assumes that one is within a system), those who are powerless.

The First World needs the Third World less and less: it has a decreasing need for our raw materials, for our markets, and especially for our labor force. We may still be of interest for tourism or as toxic dump sites, but it is clearer every day that the First World does not need the vast poor majority of the Third World. The poor are similarly redundant and dispensable within our own regional and local economies. A relatively new process of breakdown and fragmentation of society is underway among these outcasts: social and human relations are breaking down; family, community, and neighborhood are falling apart. The violence of poor against poor, of men against women, and of adults against youth and children is rising. Whole populations are increasingly moving from place to place. In the midst of such great calamity new deadly epidemics are breaking out: cholera, tuberculosis, malaria, and measles. The outcast are often victimized. They are defined as guilty victims who must be sacrificed on the altar of the free market economy. The neoliberal state no longer considers it reasonable to invest in health, education, or other basic services among the excluded since they are no longer important to the system. Thus the poor majority of people are not included in the new definition of the common good and are accordingly ignored by government programs.

The second structural feature of savage capitalism is its tendency to destroy nature and the cosmos. Capitalism cannot avoid destroying nature, for protecting nature entails increasing production costs, raising prices, and thus becoming less competitive in the market. Development capitalism by its very nature is contrary to nature. The destruction of nature is doubly fatal to the poor, since it means destroying the earth, their very basis for survival, and it also means destroying their living space, their culture, and their identity. This situation is particularly tragic for indigenous people.

Theology of Life versus Savage Capitalism

In this situation of death, liberation theology raises questions about the credibility of life: about life for all and the life of nature. More radically, it raises questions about the very credibility of God as the God of life, as the God who creates and saves. Liberation theology responds to that question by taking the radical and absolute option for life, within the situation of death created by capitalism. Within this reality of life and death, liberation theology also critically and systematically reflects on God in order to be able to discern between the God of life and the idols of death. Hence, liberation theology seeks to reestablish and rebuild the meaning of God and of the gospel in society and in the church.

The task is not at all easy, since both religious and political powers impose idols of death as manifestations of the one true God, thereby creating a false, antihuman, and idolatrous spirituality. As a theology of life, liberation theology is increasingly stripping itself of any ideological or political position. What is at stake now is no longer one ideology or theory, one political system or another, but the very life of the majority. Now, theology must go right to the radical issue of life and hence to the very heart of faith and to the reality and very truth of God. The starting point for a theology of life is the truth of life and of God within history under the guidance of a direct and open faith. This goes beyond the idolatrous and dehumanizing uses of ideology. Where there is life, God is present; where there is death, there stands idolatry. Where life is credible, faith also affirms the credibility of God as the God of life. Human life thus becomes a real criterion for discernment and an absolute and universal imperative—in the economic and social realms, of course, but also and especially in the ethical and spiritual realms, in pastoral activity, and in theology.

When liberation theology speaks of life it does so in a universal manner and it deals with an option of life for all of humankind and all of nature. Life is understood concretely to include land, work, house, food, health, education, environment, participation, and celebration. Liberation theology takes on this concrete life as its criterion of rationality: what is rational is that all have life, that all have work, housing, health care, and so forth. Unemployment, hunger, illiteracy are irrational. Life likewise becomes the criterion of truth, goodness, and beauty. The denial of life is denial of truth, goodness, and beauty.[2] These criteria of rationality, truth, and goodness are absolute and universal. They apply in the economic and political sphere and in the cultural, ethical, and spiritual realms. The theology of life takes on the rationality of an economics and politics of life, so as to guarantee the reproduction of human life and of nature. Likewise, the theology of life strives to be coherent with a culture of life, an ethics of life, and a spirituality of life. While the option for life does not yet constitute a development model, it provides us with the rationality and the strength to discern it, define it, and build it. The option for life provides the culture, ethics, and spirituality to enable us to confront savage capitalism and to find and build alternatives.

In the strictly theological field, a theology of life assumes the criterion of life for all people and for the cosmos in defining the very life or essence of God. The well known phrase of St. Irenaeus, "*Gloria Dei vivens homo, gloria autem hominis visio Dei*" (God's glory is the living human being, but the glory of the human being is the vision of God) has by now become a standard reference in theology. God's "glory" here does not mean external homage paid to God, but rather designates God's very life or essence.[3] St. Irenaeus identifies this glory or essence of God as revealed in human life. Land, work, housing, health, and so forth are manifestations of God's glory. In this sense life is not simply an economic, cultural, or ethical matter, but a spiritual matter as well. Hence Irenaeus adds that the glory of the human being is attained in the vision of God. God becomes real in the living human being and the living human being becomes real in the vision of God. This is the God of life who is revealed and known in the reproduction of concrete human life for all and in the reproduction and recreation of nature. It is life that makes it possible for us to know God in the light of faith. What is at stake in our affirmation of life is the very credibility of God. All religious experience on the outskirts of life or opposed to life is essentially mistaken and idolatrous. The only true church is the one that believes in the God of life.

The foregoing entails a radical, all-encompassing critique (economic, political, cultural, ethical, spiritual and theological) of the prevailing capitalist system insofar as it casts aside most people and destroys nature and the cosmos. As a theology of life, liberation theology affirms life against the structures of death and seeks an alternative in which all will have life and nature will be whole. This position entails a deep rethinking of Western civilization itself, which is at the root of the present development of capitalism in its form as a savage capitalism that casts aside the majority and destroys nature.[4]

Rebuilding Hope and Utopia from the World of the Poor and Outcast

The Complete Collapse of Hope

We are experiencing a complete crisis of hope. Today hope is presented as something from the past. Rebuilding hope, with a solid foundation in economic and political alternatives to the current free market economic system, is regarded as an irrational, even subversive, act. The new international order seems to have a deep and structural need to destroy hope; despair is seemingly its life-giving spirit. The hope of all oppressors is being realized: to finally build a society in which the poor no longer have hope. We can likewise see emerging a hope of eliminating liberation theology from the church. The new international order inexorably takes over by destroying all resistance and hope, especially among the poor and outcast majority.

There are many sides to this destruction of hope. It means destroying the spirituality of resistance of the oppressed; it means destroying the political will of peoples; it means delegitimizing any critical theory or any utopia.[5] The crisis of historic socialisms and Marxism is used to destroy hope and to impose unquestioning submission to the new international order. While the crisis of socialism is one thing, it is quite another thing to use that crisis to destroy all hope.[6] Neoliberal economists and theologians today are talking the way we did in the 1970s: "the future belongs to us." In a perverse way, they can take the words of Che Guevara, "The present is a time of struggle, but the future is ours," and apply them to the free market economy. There seems to be a feeling of euphoria of having the future in hand, of living at the end of history,[7] the thousand-year Reign. The free market system itself is presented in messianic tones: all the problems of humankind are finally going to be solved by the free market, science, and technology.

The free market economy holds sway as the only possibility:[8] "market or death," "last judgment market," "total market," "absolute necessary globalization," "outside the market no salvation—and no hope (the hope is the market)." There are no alternatives, not because they might not exist, but because the system has the power to destroy any alternative and to kill all those who ponder them. That is why the process of alternative change was killed in Chile in 1973, in Nicaragua in 1990, in Haiti in 1991; that is why the six Jesuits were killed in November 1989 in El Salvador. From the 1950s to the 1970s development capitalism was accompanied by a culture of hope (one that was common to all ideologies: Christian democrat, social democrat, and socialist); since the 1980s what holds sway is free market capitalism along with a culture of despair founded on the destruction of every hope and every alternative.

The Response of the Poor and the Outcast: Rebuilding hope is a fundamental task for the poor, the outcast, and those who suffer. The option for life and the rebuilding of hope is a radical demand of faith, just as it is the underlying rationality and fundamental mission of liberation theology. If the rebuilding of hope is to be real and not illusory or ideological, it must start from the poor and outcast, it must have an economic and social foundation, and finally it must work out a concrete strategy for becoming a reality. Let us examine these three conditions.

The Agent Who Is To Rebuild Hope: Our starting point is the capacity to resist and the life force of the poorest and the outcast. We must learn from the accumulated experience of the oppressed, especially indigenous people and Afro-Americans who have experienced five hundred years of resistance and hope. We must learn from the experiences of life and organization by those who have been left out of the neoliberal system. We must learn from the people's economy of solidarity in what are called the "informal sectors." We must learn from women, especially the poorest, who have always borne the whole burden of survival and who in this century have emerged as social actors within the current system. We must learn from their wisdom, from the lowly, from those who endure social pain, those who observe and suffer present society from the outside and from below. Alternatives appear when one seeks them; hope arises out of the struggle for life.

Intellectuals and political activists generally do not have such a perspective because they often pursue their own interests, or their reasoning is influenced by the logic or feeling of the prevailing system. Intellectuals are not usually weighed down by the urgency of survival or the burden of the whole social tragedy. Lately, in fact, many such theoreticians and political activists have lost all hope and have ended up adopting the rationality of the neoliberal market economy, succumbing to this system's blackmail that it is the only alternative. Liberation theology proposes a kind of thinking with Spirit, with hope, with utopia, with resistance, with mercy, with compassion, in which the poor and the outcast are to be the agent to rebuild hope. That hope in turn serves to inspire possible alternatives and credible utopias that may then energize and guide activity.

Economic and Social Foundations for Hope: A second matter is to define the economic and social basis for hope. This is not an easy task, since, as we have noted, the free market economy, which is being imposed as the only alternative, has the capacity to destroy all possible alternatives.[9] Moreover, as we have also seen, the crisis of historic socialism is used to delegitimize any effort to find economic, political, and theoretical alternatives to the current international economic order. It is, nevertheless, still possible to build alternatives. The time is not ripe for building an overall alternative or macro-alternative to the prevailing system; it is rather a time for discovering spaces where life and hope become possible and credible and from which major alternatives can emerge. I will only sketch some alternatives that constitute an economic and social foundation for hope.

Today there is a degree of consensus that alternatives to the free market system are arising from civil society. Popular movements, grass roots or alternative movements, constitute the distinguishing feature of that civil society. From an economic standpoint the 1980s were a lost decade, but they were fruitful in generating new social movements, such as the indigenous and Afro-American movements; women's liberation movements; movements of young people and children; ecological movements, movements for alternative agriculture, for people's marketing, for appropriate technology; popular economy movements based on solidarity; movements of shantytown dwellers or of neighborhoods; human rights and solidarity movements (groups of relatives of the disappeared and so forth); alternative or traditional health movements; movements of popular education, artistic and cultural movements; religious and Christian movements, and so forth. All these movements are building a new civil society with new social actors appearing on the scene. A new consensus and awareness is appearing that brings with it a new cultural, ethical, and spiritual dimension.

The new social movements are based on a radical critique of political power and of the bodies that wield such political power (government, parties, and political coalitions), and they critique the manipulation and corruption of that power. The ultimate aim of these social moments is no longer to take political power, but to build a new political power, from below, from the grassroots, one that is truly an alternative to the prevailing political power. What is happening more immediately is a (healthy) "depoliticization" of the popular movement, but in the long run what is emerging is a new political society that is more of the people, more democratic, participatory, and effective. It does not reject the political (which would be a perverse depoliticization) but searches for a new way of engaging in and thinking about politics. People are becoming aware of the cultural, ethical, and spiritual power of these popular movements. Of course, social movements have a basic economic and social dimension, but the power of those movements lies also (and often primarily) in their cultural, ethical, and spiritual side. The power of culture and the spiritual dimension to transform history is being discovered as never before. The new consciousness now emerging from civil and alternative society has dimensions not only of class but also of ethnicity and culture (through the participation of indigenous people and blacks), of nation (defense of sovereignty), of generations (youth), of gender (women), and of the environment (about which I will speak below).

In the near future the alternatives that emerge from the new civil society will not be an overall alternative to the free market economy. The all-encompassing scope of market is such that it is very difficult to create an overall macro-structural economic alternative to it. Hence it is not a matter of creating an alternative to the market, but basically of creating an alternative to the *logic* of the market—an alternative to the perverse rationality of the market, and an alternative to the culture, the ethics, and the destructive spirituality of the market (in theology we call it market idolatry). This resistance within the market is not merely ideological or superstructural, as it is embodied in the spaces of life within social movements: in agriculture, the economy, technology, the health and education systems. These systems are not governed by the competitive laws of the market, but by the logic of solidarity and by the new consensus and awareness present in social movements. Resistance arises in those spaces of life, of development, and of the creation of community, where everyone truly participates, and where an economic growth compatible with the preservation of nature is taking place.

The New Strategies of Hope

Building alternatives requires the creation of new strategies and methods of action that can make hope credible. Such methods and strategies must be different from those used in the past by traditional social and political organizations. In this new period social movements are roundly rejecting methods that are "top-down," vanguard-led, manipulative, and focused on superstructures. Today—to invoke an image—people are pursuing the strategy of spiders and ants. Spiders spin webs, and the power of ants lies in their numbers and their coordinated activity. Today it is not great structures with top-down power that are being built, but rather webs where everyone is enmeshed, interconnected, interdependent.

We speak not so much of political power in the singular, but of popular powers (Native American power, Black power, youth power, cultural power, women's power, solidarity power). All these powers are being connected and combined in order to form a new power on the national, regional, and international levels. Local power, communal power, and community power are now more esteemed than ever before. There is an effort to find new forms of coordination and of linking, in which culture, symbols, and myths acquire greater importance. New peaceful strategies are emerging to pressure the market and the state. It is generally agreed that the state must "modernize" if the term is understood to mean primarily being de-bureaucratized and de-militarized. Yet, contrary to certain neo-liberal theories that seek to dismantle the state, and contrary to certain radical theories that see only an enemy in the state, the new strategy proposes, rather, a state committed to defining the life of the poor majority and defending nature. Pressuring the state and, at some point, its possibility to govern forms part of a strategy of building alternatives.

The Role of Liberation Theology in the Rebuilding of Hope and Utopia

Liberation theology is being renewed through the experience of the poor and the outcast in building alternatives to the new international order and in developing strategies that make life and hope possible and credible. Liberation theology strives to rebuild the life of the poor, to strengthen their spirituality of resistance, their yearning for change, their critical thinking, and their utopia. Liberation theology seeks to offer encouragement to the alternative civil society that is emerging in the new popular movements; it seeks to be part of the new consensus and the new awareness arising out of those movements as it takes on all the cultural, ethical and spiritual force driving them; and it assumes a shared responsibility for achieving their objectives. Everything that we have said thus far has to do with the space and the logic that drives the renewal of liberation theology in the new international order. Within this space and with this logic liberation theology, from its own perspective, strives to rebuild the hope and the utopia of the poor and the excluded.

We have said that the grassroots peoples' movements are rediscovering the cultural, ethical, and spiritual power that drives them. Likewise, we have said that the alternative that we seek is not so much an alternative to the free market economy as such, but rather an alternative to *market logic*. In this respect cultural, ethical, and spiritual resistance is especially important. This situation opens greater space for liberation theology and makes it more necessary than ever. In the area of culture, we must deal with the challenge of the inculturation of the gospel or evangelization from within cultures. This issue became central in 1992 in the context of the five-hundred-year anniversary and of the Fourth Conference of the Bishops at Santo Domingo. A great deal has been said and written on this issue, but I think we are still at the beginning, especially when we consider that such an inculturation of the gospel takes place within the new social movements and alternative civil society as a response to the crisis of Western civilization.

In the realm of ethics, liberation theology seeks to make a clear distinction between life ethics and market ethics. In life ethics, human life is an absolute value. The good and the true is that all have life: work, land, food, housing, health, education, and the environment are fundamental ethical imperatives. This ethic of life stands against the market ethic, in which the basic ethical values are profit and earnings, efficiency and power, and likewise against an ethic of law in which private property and respect for contracts hold sway as an absolute, even over human life itself.

If liberation theology has a vast field in which to develop and an urgent contribution to make in the cultural and ethical realm, it is especially on the spiritual terrain that liberation theology develops in its own proper and specific way. Obviously, I am not referring to that abstract, alienating, and ultimately idolatrous spiritual dimension created by the dominant system itself. I have in mind that profound and necessary spiritual dimension that drives the new civil society and the alternative social movements. This is the spiritual dimension that is present in the option for life and in the rebuilding of hope. Liberation theology has always developed a spirituality that is liberating in ongoing history; now it is simply reformulating that spirituality in the context of the new international order.

Liberation theology arises out of the experience of God in the world of the poor and outcast, and proclaims God as the God of life against the idols of death. That is why it is a liberating and anti-idolatrous theology. Liberation theology is not feared because it speaks of liberation or politics, but rather because it speaks about God from the standpoint of the poor as a God of life and hope. The church itself fears liberation theology for the same reasons. The church has never been afraid of politics, but it is afraid of being confronted with the living God, with the gospel of life, with the following of Jesus. This spirituality is what is most specific to liberation theology; therein lies its power and its capacity for rebuilding hope.

Within this basic formulation, which is both traditional and ever relevant, I would like to highlight a pressing task for liberation theology: the rebuilding of utopia. Liberation theology has always been utopian insofar as it is a theology that believes in the God of life. Today more than ever, however, it must be utopian within the new international order that radically destroys any utopia. The free market economy regards itself as a perfect society seeking to find the answer to all problems. The new international order contains a kind of messianism. It demands that everyone believe in it and submit to it so as to save all human beings. The reality, however, is that only a very few are invited to this neoliberal banquet and the party is being held on an earth that is increasingly devastated each day. The system asserts its own perfection and saving messianism, while leaving out many and destroying everything on earth. Life for all and the preservation of nature do not fit in this neoliberal market economy. Indeed, life for all and life for the cosmos is a utopia that could destroy the free market. As one of its philosophers, Karl Popper, says: "Those who want to build the Kingdom of heaven on earth, turn the earth into a hell." Nevertheless, life for all and the preservation of the cosmos (anticipation of God's reign on the earth) is the utopia of the poor and of the outcast. It is this utopia that liberation theology seeks to rebuild and to establish.

What is the foundation of the utopia that liberation theology seeks to rebuild? It is clearly our faith in the God of life as a transcendent God. The dimension of transcendence is essential in all utopian thought. The transcendent is what is beyond a limit (as the imminent is what stands on this side of a limit). The biblical tradition, the tradition that liberation theology assumes, presents such transcendence in two stages. Initially, it is oppression that constitutes the barrier beyond which the transcendent is defined. God assures fullness of life beyond oppression and hence is transcendent. Oppression sets a limit to human life. God does not accept that barrier and breaks it. In this sense the transcendent God is the liberating God, the God who breaks the chains of oppression, the God of exodus, the God of justice, the God of life.

At a second stage of biblical revelation, the barrier defining the transcendent is no longer oppression but death. God assures that there is life beyond death and is thereby transcendent. The best expression of transcendence as life beyond oppression is found in Isaiah 65; transcendence as life beyond death is found in Revelation 21. In both cases transcendence is symbolized as "heavens and new earth": in the first case, as a world without oppression; and in the second, as a world without death. In both cases, however, and throughout the Bible, this life beyond oppression and death is always in this world, in this history. The transcendent is not beyond history, but beyond the oppression and death within this history. Our faith in the transcendent God is thus the basis for the utopian dimension of liberation theology. This utopia is grounded in God and depends on God, but it is embodied in history and it is what guides our action and our thinking. Liberation theology rebuilds the utopian dimension of faith within the historic praxis of liberation.

Liberation Theology as Theology of the South: A Response and an Alternative to the Crisis of Western Civilization

North-South Confrontation and the Crisis of the West

Geographically the term "South" designates the impoverished peoples of Latin America, Africa, and Asia, but in symbolic terms it likewise designates all the poor and the outcast of the rich countries throughout the world. The "North" designates the power centers that are basically located in the richest and most industrialized countries, but it likewise designates all the rich and powerful who maintain, enjoy, or manage those power centers. In numerical terms the North represents 20 percent of the world population (about one billion people) and the South represents the remaining 80 percent (about four billion people). From an economic standpoint we can represent north and south the with the following statistics published by the United Nations Development Plan:[10] the North, the richest 20 percent of humankind receives 82.7 percent of the world's income; the South, the poorest 80 percent of humankind receives 17.3 percent of the world's income. A breakdown of these figures shows:

World Population	World Income
Richest 20%	82.70%
Second 20%	11.00%
Third 20%	2.30%
Fourth 20%	1.90%
Poorest 20%	1.41%

Furthermore, the richest 20 percent of humankind controls 81.2 percent of world trade, 94.6 percent of loans, 80.6 percent of domestic savings, and 80.5 percent of investment. It is very clear who is rich around the world and who is poor, and it is even clearer that there is a tremendous gap between rich and poor. Indeed, the richest among the poor (the second 20 percent that receives 11.7 percent of income) are quite poor when compared to the richest of the rich.

Moreover, the 25 percent of humankind that live in the richest countries consume 70 percent of the world's energy, 75 percent of its metals, 85 percent of its lumber, and 60 percent of its food. If the whole world were to consume what the rich consume, the world would explode. The present international "order" works only by maintaining inequality. In order to be able to maintain this international order, an international elite has been formed, and it controls economic, financial, military, and cultural power and the major transnational media. Likewise, there is emerging a kind of worldwide parallel state—or rather an international dictatorship—made up of the governments of the group of the seven most industrialized countries. The international "order" is maintained around the world through the 900 billion dollars that is invested in the arms race every year. In addition, this power structure is maintained "through the individual support of millions of uncoordinated citizens led by magnetic (charismatic) personalities who through the media manipulate emotions and control reason" (Brzezinski, quoted by Gorostiaga, p. 48).

Thus, it is very clear who is the North and who is the South. In the wake of the fall of historic socialisms and the end of the cold war and the East-West conflict, however, the international confrontation between North and South—the North's aggression against the South, the North's wars and interventions in the South—is becoming ever more blatant. This aggression of North against South is planned and structural. Its aim is to destroy the sovereignty of the poor countries of the South—that sovereignty that is absolutely necessary as the basis for building democracy. The agenda for war and intervention is being extended day by day: the battle against terrorism, against drugs, against human rights violations, and most recently, to impose democracy, security, and peace, to overcome hunger, and to halt migration. That agenda is used to justify every violation of international law and the right of peoples to self-determination. Indeed, some are even talking about "flexible sovereignties" (flexible so that they can be violated by the Northern powers).

This whole system of North-South domination is justified ideologically by economic neoliberalism and religious neoconservatism, along with all the "modern" ideologies that are racist, chauvinist, colonialist, and authoritarian in character. In condemning liberation theology and taking centralistic, authoritarian, and ethnocentric stances, many churches also put themselves on the side of the North in the North-South contradiction. All this lopsidedness, all this inequality, all this aggression by the North against the South, all this human destruction and destruction of nature, all this destruction of values and of legality, is unquestionably leading not only to a crisis of the capitalist system, but more profoundly to a crisis of civilization, a deep crisis in "Western Christian civilization"—indeed a crisis of modernity itself, which arose with the industrial revolution, the Enlightenment, the French Revolution, and the present technological and technetronic revolution.

The South's Response to the Crisis of the West

In this context of North-South confrontation and the crisis of civilization, there is emerging in the South and out of the South (from the 80 percent of humankind that makes it up) a new response that is its own: a movement, a consensus, a convergence, an alliance, an agenda, a strategy, and above all a new awareness. The South exists and has its own theology. The South refuses to accept its own death and destruction. The South refuses to allow itself to be run over and treated unequally. The South refuses to surrender the sovereignty of its peoples or to forego democracy. The South has a culture, an ethic, a spirituality, and an identity. The South wants to live and to live in abundance. The South wants the whole world (including the North) to have life and the cosmos to be recreated and saved in its entirety. This is the context in which liberation theology is seeking to redefine itself as the theology of the South. Let us examine this point more closely.

In the South there is arising a new way of combining the various expressions of the oppressed people: work (the working class, both the part that is integrated and the part that is excluded), culture (race, ethnic groups: Indians, Blacks, Mestizos), gender (women), generation (young people, who are not simply the "hope of tomorrow" but true actors even now), sovereignty (nations), and nature (the cosmos, the land). We can likewise include with the same degree of universality the spirit (spirituality, religion) as an essential and quasi-universal dimension in the identity of the South. Solidarity between social and alternative movements is growing, along with a new consciousness, one marked by this alliance of labor-culture-gender-generation-sovereignty-nature-spirit. The movement of North-South confrontation becomes specific in the confrontation of labor with capital, of Black peoples and Indian cultures against racism and colonial ethnocentrism, of women against a patriarchal system, of young people against authoritarianism, of poor nations against the intervention and arrogance of the Western powers, of nature against a system of development that is inexorably destroying it, and a movement of the spirit against a materialistic, consumerist, perverse, and idolatrous system.

From its origins in Hellenistic and Greco-Latin civilization, passing through colonial Christendom and into its modern liberal development, Western civilization has been based on a distinction between soul and body; it has asserted that the soul must have dominion over the body—ultimately showing contempt for the body.[11] The soul is regarded as the realm of the spiritual and of encounter with God, and the body is regarded as the material realm and the site of sin. It is rational and natural that the soul should have dominion over the body: the soul dominates the body, as reason dominates the appetite, as form dominates matter, as the perfect dominates the imperfect (see the well known chapter 1.3 of Aristotle's Treatise on Politics). The most important point is that this domination of soul over body is taken as the model or social paradigm for the dominion of master over slave, of man over woman, of adult over child, and of the human being over animals and nature. This was the theoretical framework for Western conquest. Juan Ginés de Sepúlveda, one of its most noted intellectual champions, wrote:

> Being slaves by nature, the barbarians, uncultured and inhuman, refuse to accept the domination by those who are more prudent, powerful and perfect than themselves, a domination which would bring them very great benefits, and it is in addition right, by natural law, that matter should obey form, the body the soul, appetite reason, brute beasts human beings, the wife her husband, children a father, the imperfect the perfect, the worse the better, for the universal good of all things.[12]

Ginés de Sepúlveda uses this framework to legitimize the domination of Spaniards over the Indians, whom he calls "tiny men" (homunculi).

The new awareness arising in the South, out of the non-Western world, seeks precisely to subvert this Hellenistic-Western- colonial framework. A movement in history combining the workers' movement, the women's movement, that of young people, of Indians, of Blacks, the movement of the liberation of the body and of nature is now emerging. The most interesting feature is that in this historic movement a new awareness is being born, an awareness that regards this liberation movement as a spiritual movement within history. There is also an awareness of what is rational, what is natural, what is perfect, and what is best. In this awakening of the oppressed in the South, in this movement of the liberation of the body, of workers, of women, of young people, of Indians and Blacks and of nature, a profound redefinition of what is truly spiritual, rational, natural, and perfect is taking place.

Thus, we have a very deep revolution of rationality itself, of natural law, and of the spiritual sense. Spirituality is not the result of a "soul" dominating the body, but rather spirituality is what drives the body in its assertion of life over death. Likewise, spirituality does not come through a patriarchal system, through an authoritarian system, through dominant Western culture, through a system that is anti-nature. Quite the contrary: the perfect, the rational, the spiritual is now the liberation of the body, the liberation of nature, the liberation of women, the liberation of youth, the liberation of indigenous and Black people, in order to build a world in which all may have life.

Liberation Theology as Theology of the South: Rescuing Hope, Utopia and the Spirit

Liberation theology assumes in its entirety this new awareness, this re-definition of what is natural, rational, and spiritual. Furthermore, liberation theology asserts that this conception of what is truly spiritual is what is most genuinely and originally inspired in the whole Judeo-Christian tradition. Hellenistic- colonial-Western-liberal Christendom subverted this original inspiration of Christianity and transformed it into its opposite. Christianity did not evangelize the Hellenistic world, but instead the philosophy of the latter "evangelized" Christianity. Aristotle replaced Jesus (explicitly so in Juan Ginés de Sepúlveda). In original Christian thought the distinction-opposition is not between body and soul but between life and death. The human being is a living body animated by the spirit. The spiritual is the tendency toward life, in the body and in the soul. What stands opposed to the spiritual is not the bodily but the carnal. The flesh is not identified with the body but with the tendency toward death in every human being, body and soul. In the human being (body and soul) there are two tendencies: one toward life, which is the spiritual tendency, and the other toward death, which is the carnal tendency. The Holy Spirit guides us spiritually toward life, in body and in soul; sin guides us carnally toward death, in body and in soul. In original Christianity, salvation is not salvation of the soul, but salvation of the human being from death in body and soul. The soul is not saved from the body, as it was in Hellenistic philosophy, but rather the human being (body and soul) is saved from death. That is precisely faith in the resurrection (cf. Rom. 8 and 1 Cor. 15).

With its fundamentalist and spiritualistic theology, the new international order has brought about a deep and structural crisis of spirituality in the world. The crisis of civilization that we are experiencing also raises the issue of radically reformulating the meaning of the spiritual. Modern spiritualisms are simply the supreme expression of the idolatrous spirit of a materialistic, consumeristic, patriarchal, and warmongering system that destroys life and hope. I have already said above that we discover the meaning of the spiritual in affirming concrete human life; out of the hopes and utopias of the poor; out of liberation movements of Indians, Blacks, women, and young people; out of the life of nature and of the cosmos. I also said that this meaning of the spiritual is consonant with the meaning of the Spirit in biblical tradition. It is a fundamental task of liberation theology to rescue the meaning of the spiritual in the process of rescuing the meaning of life and of hope, in continuity with biblical and church traditions of the earliest times.

In this context, with this spiritual sense and with this biblical faith, theology also poses the question of the meaning of God. It does not do so in a falsely abstract and universal way, but rather poses the question of the meaning of God in the crisis of civilization prompted by the new international order; the meaning of God at the heart of a savage capitalism that excludes the majority and destroys nature. It raises the question of the meaning of God out of the South, from within this 80 percent of humankind condemned to dire poverty and to being outcast. It raises the question of the meaning of God out of the spiritual meaning of human life, the spiritual meaning of the life of the Indian, the Black, the woman, the young person, and nature.

Liberation theology seeks to rescue the meaning of life and of the spiritual—and the very meaning of God—not only in society but also in the church itself. I have said that the church is afraid of liberation theology not because it speaks of liberation, but because it speaks of God. Our greatest fear as church is to confront the living God, the transcendent God in history, the God of life, who becomes present and whose self-revelation occurs in the reproduction of life and in the rebuilding of hope. Nothing is more disturbing than to speak of God out of the poor and oppressed, the Indian or the woman, young people or nature. This meaning of God is disturbing because it is this very meaning of God that we find in the biblical tradition. This meaning of God is challenging because it announces a God transcendent in history who destroys all oppression, who destroys death itself within history, and therefore threatens all the idols of the system. Liberation theology is by its essence anti-idolatrous and destructive of all false spirituality. It stands opposed to the idolatrous fundamentalisms of the system that are so tempting to the church. In this sense we still need a great deal of liberation theology to nourish our spirituality so that we may continue to believe in the God of Life in the midst of the world and within the church.

Notes

1. Cf. F. Hinkelammert, "La crisis del socialismo y el Tercer Mundo," *Pasos* No. 30 (July-August 1990).

2. The classic discussion "Quid est verum, bonum, et pulchrum?" (What is the true, the good, and the beautiful?) is relevant here.

3. The word "glory" in Hebrew *kabod*, designates God's "weight" or "essence": cf Ex. 33:8; Ps. 113:4.

4. Franz Hinkelammert says: "An alternative can take shape only on the basis

of an affirmation of life in the face of this celebration of death. The affirmation of life, however, cannot be a simple romantic affirmation. . . It means a rethinking of Western civilization that will entail moving beyond it. The starting point for reconstituting it must be the life of all those who have been excluded from life by this very civilization." In "La lógica de la expulsión del mercado capitalista mundial y el proyecto de liberación." *Pasos*, special issue 3/1992, p. 10.

5. Helio Gallardo, "Radicalidad de la Teoría y sujeto popular en América Latina," *Pasos*, special issue 3/1992, p. 30.

6. Helio Gallardo, "Cinco mitos en torno a la crisis del socialismo histórico," *Pasos* No. 31, September-October 1990.

7. Francis Fukuyama, "The End of History?" in *The National Interest*, Summer 1988.

8. For what follows, Franz Hinkelammert, "Capitalismo sin alternativas? Sobre la sociedad que sostiene que no hay alternativa para ella," *Pasos* No. 37 (September-October 1991) and *Pasos*, Special issue 3/92, "La lógica. . ."

9. Cf. Franz Hinkelammert, "Capitalismo sin alternativas?" *Pasos* No. 37 (September-October 1991).

10. UNDP Report: *Human Development 1992*. Cited and commented on by Xavier Gorostiaga, "Está la respuesta en los países del sur?," *Envío* (Nic.) Nov. 1992. In the following section we are utilizing this article.

11. Cf. P. Richard: *La Fuerza Espiritual de la Iglesia de los Pobres*, San José (DEI) 1988, 2nd. ed., pp. 99 ff. Also my article in *Concilium* (1990/6), pp. 59-67: "1492: The Violence of God and the Future of Christianity."

12. Cf. art. in *Concilium*, p. 62.

10

A Cry for Life from Latin America

IVONE GEBARA

It is an extremely difficult task to speak of spirituality today. Earlier, especially a few years ago, it seemed to be so easy. At the time there seemed to be a certain consensus among Christians on this subject, more so when one considered the great spiritual currents within the church. It was even relatively easy soon after the documents of Medellín in 1968 and of Puebla in 1979 to speak of the spirituality of the poor and then also of liberation spirituality together with liberation theology.

Nevertheless, the situation has changed very rapidly during this past decade and we have once again started our pilgrimage in search of a new spirituality to articulate and to put together as it were, the broken pieces of our life. The socio-economic system that continues to thrive on the lives of human beings has not yet taken even a step towards change for the better despite the great struggles and courageous endeavors of the Latino-American and other peoples.

Today, life appears to be fragmented into pieces, seemingly without coherence or unity. One takes up one fragment, then leaves it behind to move on to another. We absolutize at times one aspect, at other times another. We tend to relativize things that do not come within our immediate horizon and our lives, as we go through life with heavy and loaded hearts. Yes, our hearts are heavy, saddled as they are with so many different sorrows and burdens and it is evidently our burdened hearts that yearn for solace, tenderness, strength and meaning.

One laborious day dawns, and yet another. We wait! for what? the rain? the train? the bus? the next year? revolution? justice? God? Time seems to be dragging on, especially for the poor. Nothing seems to be on time for them, except of course the unexpected or unwanted catastrophe! There is impatience and restlessness deep down within us, try as we may to cover it up, conditioned as we are by society to put on a calm front. Our bodies are so weary as we set to work early each morning to trudge through the daily routine and our hearts continue to murmur unceasingly, "My soul thirsts for God, the God of my life."

The voices of people rise, yes, they rise above this din as they cry, "O my God, come to my aid, help me, give me your hand." Oh! why? why such suffering? why all this? countless sighs, ceaseless mourning, the cries smothered within their breasts. Yes, the cries of those who long for something better. Something that one does not know, perhaps, even how to name! It could be nourishment and food, or it could be a house or even just a drink to quench the thirst. Could it be good health? or justice? and yet again could it be love that one is yearning after? Yes, it is all these and more, much more. It is something we call "spirituality."

One day a friend of mine who had read some of my writings told me that I was a pessimist or almost one as regards the evolution of society and church in Latin America. He said that I showed little of the signs of the Kingdom and of hope for the poor. I listened to his words but I found it difficult to accept his remark. For to me it is extremely important to capture the cries of people for life and make myself one with them. Besides, I find myself becoming more and more skeptical of and dissatisfied and disgusted with the unrealistic discourses of certain theologians and social scientists who continue to maintain that despite everything the situation is changing for the better. To me, this appears to be an intellectual fantasy.

I feel that most theologians are too dry and formal. They do not attempt to be poetic enough in their theologizing. They often speak of wishful thinking and aspirations as if they were actual reality. What is horrifying is that they would dare to do the same when speaking of the poor and their lives. By doing this, they make simple, gullible people more anxious and frustrated in the measure that these people do not find in their lives that which these theologians preach about so vehemently.

Theology, for me, is simply a discourse on "that which is not yet," but arising from that which is already lived and experienced by various groups of people. To do " poetic theology" is to do theology in such a way that the discourse remains only a "Word" that would maintain the movements of the waters of life—"the waters that give significance," which embracing our existence would keep us always moving forward. It is undoubtedly the energizing presence of hope which revitalizes us through and through and yet does not provide exact answers to our quest, making no pretext of absolute objectivity. Gustavo Gutiérrez in his book *We Drink from Our Own Wells* says that all theology is a spiritual experience and encounter with the Spirit, hence spirituality.

In like manner, my reflection on spirituality is my way of doing theology: a way marked by the fact that I am a woman who loves to cook, mixing together various ingredients and seasonings to obtain a good flavor, sometimes strong, sometimes mellow and at other times hot. Is this not a

symbolic expression of the historical life of human beings on earth? I wish to develop the following three points:
- The deafening noises in the world and spirituality.
- The ever increasing garbage of the world and spirituality.
- Through the desert open out new pathways.

The Deafening Noises in the World and Spirituality

To speak of noise is in some way to situate oneself away from the countryside: that is in the city, the place of noise, deafeningly strident with the ever increasing traffic, the tooting of horns, a vibrant mixture of noise, of music, of cries. My reflection then is from the city alone, for were I to speak of the countryside, other experiences would arise within me, the question of spirituality being equally present in all the diverse corners of the world.

Could we pause to ask ourselves what spirituality has to do with noise? At first glance nothing at all, for the general tendency of those in search of spirituality is to flee the world and strive to find oneself and the absolute in silence, in prayer and in quietude. I, too, love silence because above all else it permits me to recall better so many souvenirs and yearnings, it helps me to reflect deeply on challenging problems at hand, it helps me to rest and also because my formation has made me love silence and be at ease with it. But the question lies beyond this level. Here, when I speak of noise, I refer to those deafening noises that are the product of our consumer society, and sold to or imposed on people at large, more specially on the poor. This noise paralyzes all thought, keeps on beating ceaselessly at the ear-drums, alienates the person and rends one's heart apart, away from one's self. This is the noise that is being boomed out from all kinds of factories, by loud and noisy music. It is these and other such intoxicating noises that do great harm to people. Yes, sonorous pollutions among so many other pollutions! Visual, corporal, material, environmental . . .

Then there is this noise, particularly of ideas that come to cloud our minds, us pastoral workers. I speak analogically of this noise, yet it is intense and always present. We produce plenty of ideas on every possible thing. It is said that a well-informed person is worth two. So, we keep on selling and buying ideas and opinions to such an extent that in the end we become intoxicated and never arrive at being the well-informed persons we wanted to be. And more than that, we have lost ourselves in this haze of floating ideas. We are supplied with information of all sorts, sometimes true, sometimes false, at other times more or less true, so that ultimately we do not know for sure which is true. Each tries to make the other believe that one version is the truth. Little bits of truths that rip the body and mind apart, that lead to the disintegration of that desire for unity among us. Who can save us from this noise of senseless sounds and ideas? How can we withstand all this noise which creates such emptiness and dissatisfaction with us? Could we really speak of spirituality in the midst of such noise?

The search for a remedy is not a refusal of progress or the denial of great human achievements. But, it certainly is a struggle against the destruction of that which is human. Human progress can never be made into an idol. And the anti-human orientations of progress are idolatrous and need to be combated. Hence, in such a context, finding new pathways is a serious challenge for the future millennia. There may be many and varied paths, not merely one. No more can one speak of special centers for the production and propagation of spirituality for everybody, nor even for the Christian community. We live at a time when the spiritual understanding of existence—the understanding that gives depth, orientation, perspectives for life is found more and more through relationships among different persons and groups that have come together for multiple reasons. Moreover, the meaning of human life or human existence can no more be found right away at the first go or be given once and for all for all times. On the contrary, it is always made and remade, continually evolving, conditioned as it is by so many unforeseen elements that weave into the fabric of life, being always influenced by new encounters, friendships and events.

The time has now dawned when Christian intellectuals, theologians, religious, leaders of the church can no longer lay down spiritual directives for the poor. For the poor have their own openings, their own understanding of spirituality which often do not coincide with those of our cultural and intellectual world. There may be some sort of communication between these two different worlds; yet we cannot forget that too often we have pretended and believed that we were the people who gave the poor the key to the meaning in life, that is to say "spirituality." Was it not so even when we proclaimed that our option for the poor and our solidarity with them was the beginning of our path to a truly evangelical spirituality bringing about also solidarity among the poor themselves?

I would like to cite here an example from my own life experience. I live among the common people of Camaragibe, about 15 kilometers from the city of Recife. Unemployment, under-employment, non-availability of work is the economic plight of the majority of the population here. Precarious living conditions are something that they are used to. All sorts of disputes and fighting, dangling of blood-stained knives, together with innumerable cries, form part of the day-to-day violence among these people. I ask myself, "Where can I find the unifying element in their lives?" I find it impossible to answer this question with assurance. These things have touched me deeply, and I would now like to share with you the insights I have drawn from such experiences.

Neither unity nor meaning in life comes uniquely from the institutional church, nor from discourses on liberation. It does not come either from pastoral workers or their apostolic activity, though undoubtedly they do good work indeed. I firmly believe that it is the daily struggle for life and the desire to survive that brings the poor together. And, in this struggle there is the " samba," the drum, the local coffee shop, the Sundays with beer or "living water," as they call it. There is also the beach, a football match or other such games. What about the conversations in the marketplace with neighbors, and various religious services, as also so many other encounters and activities, both big and small, all of which form part of their daily life, giving it meaning? The poor may cry out from their misery, yet they also know how to laugh at it. They have plenty of humor, which is not lost on their own existential situation so full of suffering. They seem to brave and even defy death; yes, they would even dare to dance with death.

Our intellectual world is an analytical world of duality and categories. We make class differences, distinctions between the work of God and that of idols, between the one whom we call God and false gods. Nevertheless, idolatry is nothing but the outcome of human creation which could in the end destroy the human being as well. So one has to be very careful and discerning to be able to name and situate clearly these idols and not to create at the same time a distorted God who is far beyond life and above human reach.

We speak much of unity, but we never arrive at living it. We say that life is a blending of many realities, but we stick to our dual positions.

When we speak of something being private I believe we really speak of places or things that are set apart and supervised, places where the unexpected and unplanned have no entry, or even places where the un-customary and the unusual that are outside the established law or order are not accepted. Ultimately it is evident that there is a basic fear of freedom and its consequences, which brings insecurity.

To look for spirituality in the midst of noise is to believe on the one hand in the vitality of life found among the poor, and on the other to free spirituality from its monastic prison. What I mean here is that often we have identified spirituality with a style of life linked to that of monks, religious, the clergy, or even that of the active laity. We find it difficult to come out of this traditional prison which has penetrated deep into our flesh, to perceive the beauty in diversity and the depth of meaning that is so close to us, quite within our reach. This prison in which we are closed makes us withdraw from simple people, though ever so often we may be moving physically among them, at times willing to help them to regain their rights.

We are so used to reciting certain prayers, to certain types of music, works of art and buildings, that to us they appear to be the only things capable of bringing us closer to the absolute, the transcendent Being. Perhaps they remind us of the image of the absolute. But let us not forget that it is only one image, the one to which we are accustomed. What about those other possible images found among the people? Images, if we would but open our eyes, would reveal to us a better and deeper understanding of the mystery of transcendence. Transcendence is always above and beyond our images and words, and we need to accept this truth concretely, not limiting it to mere theory. Transcendence should touch the innermost depths of our being, bringing about real change in our human relationships and in our attitudes and in the way we understand ourselves. I shall develop this further in the next section.

The Ever Increasing Garbage of the World and Spirituality

We are flooded by garbage, yes, garbage from atomic wastes down to the daily refuse found on our roads and in our homes. Certainly we are great producers of garbage and of all sorts of rubbish. Yet, the type of garbage produced depends on one's social class. It is very easy to place people by the garbage they produce. Generally, the rich are the greatest producers of garbage. Are they not the ones who produce atomic wastes? The empty tin cans from used tinned foods? The waste matter that destroys the ozone layer, and other refuse and waste so detrimental to life? Nevertheless, they are the ones who live very hygienic lives. Their homes, offices, gardens, clubs and temples are spotless and well kept. Never would they believe that they are at the same time the greatest producers of garbage. For them, dirt comes from others, the poor, the slum-dwellers, those poorly nourished vagrant people who loiter on the streets. These are the people who make the cities dirty and ugly with the badly built houses which come up like mushrooms, without any planning, without roads, without beauty and above all without respecting the proximity of elegant residential areas and tourist sectors. Are they not the ones who upset traffic by jumping in between the vehicles to beg for a little money? Are they not responsible for making the roads dirty and cause untold trouble and inconvenience to others by their way of living? Do they not smell so bad that no one could come near them? Is it not from their areas devoid of water and proper sanitation that all sorts of epidemics rise and spread through the land? Undoubtedly the poor are also producers of household refuse that threaten the rich.

The rich produce plenty of garbage but their healthy and well-kept world makes them believe that it is not they but others that produce garbage. On the contrary, the poor live among garbage, and at times they may find food from garbage heaps. Their greatness lies in this: that they know they are submerged in dirt, and desire to come out of it. What I say here is nothing new. Many articles and books have been written on the miserable plight of the poor. But my questions concern spirituality and its connection to dirt, to garbage. Do these people who live in slums, these who live in the periphery of cities, or the countryside, these who breathe in the wretched smell of the dumping grounds, do they live without spirituality? Since they do not fit into our categories of spirituality, how should we situate them? Does the Spirit live far from them? Or, by any chance, is the Spirit present among them as an invisible support in their daily struggles for life? Either the Transcendent One has abandoned them or she is there present among them according to their own way, a way of being that we fail to grasp. Is she not vibrantly present in their strivings for a better life and happiness?

The rich and also religious, because of their way of life, could afford to buy any amount of books. They are able to have retreats, spiritual renewals and aggiornamento. They have the means to travel to distant and famous monasteries in Tibet, in well-known places for spirituality, for sabbatical years or for thirty- or forty-day retreats of discernment, profession, and so forth. Yes, they all have possibilities to escape from external noise in sound-proof rooms and do transcendental meditation. These people of goodwill are big consumers of such spirituality, easily found in the supermarkets of spirituality, with all sorts of types being available to suit different tastes. These things are not accessible of course to the disinherited ones of this world. Yes, the spirituality of these privileged people seems to be guaranteed by the same market forces in their varied religious activities which, in a way, continue to perpetuate the same old traditions by which they hold that the Spirit always blows in the same direction and place, permitting one to see clearly God's plan, God's will and place.

In general, many would think of spirituality in this manner. Yet taking into consideration the lives of the poor and the challenges of our historical era, I would dare to say that the Spirit, Creator of life, is very much active among certain types of garbage and from within cries for life, for life in fullness. Our traditions have locked up the Spirit in the " pure and clean," in the midst of incense and hymns of the glory of God in "dignified" places, understood to be so according to our stereotype, occidental theology. I suspect that by this attitude we have missed much of that which is beautiful; we the so-called professionals in religion, a caste set apart as it were, rooted to and conditioned by our rigid religious traditions! We need to realize that the Spirit's creative and re-creative power manifests itself in joy, peace, justice, solidarity, mercy, and is found and felt in so many different ways and places that we never dreamt of. Above all, is it not being arrogant to limit the Spirit to one particular place only, as if the Spirit's power could be a material thing, an idea or even a theory?

It is to be emphasized that there is an immense richness far above and beyond our occidental models of spirituality and we fail to fathom it. Life continues, recreates itself; the new-born is eagerly awaited despite poverty. One takes a chance with the future against all odds and incertitudes! It is then one finds the joy of living and it certainly is one form of spirituality of the base, without any idealizing of the poor or theoretical elaboration. I realize the importance of temporality and of finding meaning in simple day-to-day life. But we need also to understand the need for change and appreciate differences. It is here that we find meaning though we may not speak of it. Above all, it must be noted that the potential for a true and valid change in the quality of life is also found there.

I find it equally important to situate oneself fully in the reality of daily life with its uncertainties and precariousness if one is to touch at the very heart strings of the meaning of existence. Existence is an irruption of life within us, a temporary irruption nevertheless, which can be lost at any moment with the passage of time, our sojourn on earth being but temporary. It is simply because of this that we must be open to receive that which is temporary, that which is passing in all its multiple expressions with all its vulnerability. We must love that which is temporary as a component part of our being and comprehend the meaning within, capture the deepest meaning of flesh, blood, earth, far beyond that which is given to us by official theology or by canon law.

Spirituality in that which is provisional, that which is fleeting, is an expression of faith in life. It is a search for confidence and hope, so necessary to live today so as to achieve a better tomorrow for all. And, this hope lived within passing reality is the spirituality of large masses of people who hardly have any certitude of survival. Theirs is a day-to-day spirituality with no long terms, for it is experienced in the constant struggle for life.

The garbage found in the world of the poor shows vividly how vulnerable life is. It also speaks of our inability to dominate and reduce the poor to objects of our possession. Besides, it demonstrates our failure to grasp the revolutionary potential within it and the openings for building a different and better future. The garbage of the poor may some day lead to a life of abundance—the life that comes from the Spirit who breathes wherever she wills.

The poor somehow manage to eke out a living. They drink, they cry, they sing, they pray, they also experience silence, they create mythical beings, invisible protectors who help them in their daily struggles and so they keep on hoping. All this is spirituality, so related to their lives, their aspirations, those who always hope and struggle to continue to live. Yes, the spirituality of those who say in the words of a Brazilian song "Live and do not be ashamed to be happy . . . so sing and sing with the joy of being an eternal apprentice."

Through the Desert Open New Pathways

Why do we search for new pathways? And why go looking for them in the desert like the ancient monks? This desert from which open new paths is not that of the monks. It is the desert in which we find ourselves, the desert I have described above, the desert of stones and bricks, of huge cities, these dirty and noisy deserts where the polluted air entering through our nostrils causes harm to our lungs. We cannot flee from here, it is our home, it is where our parents work and also where we are engaged ourselves. This is the heritage we hope to leave for the future generations. It is here that we have laid to rest the bodies of those whom we love, yes, the bodies of those who have contributed to our history, of those who before us have dreamt dreams, have planted flowers, trees, and have shed many tears and much sweat. It is from this desert, full of significance, that must spring forth mercy, tenderness and solidarity, the concrete expressions of human love. It is from the renewed love of the mangled, broken, wounded and glorified life, this life that is ever present in the desert, that new significance and meaning will be born, that new alternatives will emerge. There is a struggle to which we are all called and that is to find new strategies for collective action. For this, we need to be patient and know how to keep on hoping against all odds and be attentive to spot out the course of the new paths to true liberation.

It is from today's realities, from our own dreams and also from that which is unforeseen that that "life in abundance" we are thirsting after will emerge, from among our midst.

The present world situation makes the poor appear absolutely power-less to change the "stones into bread," to throw far, far away the garbage that they produce themselves and also that which is being dumped on them. To those who live constantly under the fear of not being able to make ends meet and at the butt end of economic and political games of the powerful, faith in the " unexpected" seems to be the only "capital." In this sense, they and we have to build up this faith in the "hidden face" within and beyond events. It means to believe that the life within us stretches itself far beyond us into the future. It is also that tomorrow that brings new hopes.

The God of life, the absolute mystery or in simple terms *life* itself in which we have our being, within which we move and find nourishment, is worthy of deep respect and does not require much to show tenderness, sharing, and justice.

It was certainly life and enthusiasm for life in fullness that was mani-fested in Jesus. The pain and sorrow that he experienced at seeing life despised and minimized led to the birth of a movement that was open to accept the marginalized of his time, as had been foretold by the prophets of the Old Testament.

The urgency of the times calls for a return to a great simplicity that would permit us to look upon life that surrounds us with all its beauty and ugliness, with all its comedy and tragedy, in all its sweetness and bitterness as having potential for global change.

This spirituality is like the wholesome food found in the home, that simple food that one relishes so much because it does us immense good. It is the spirituality of being attentive to the other, of mutual support, of sharing of joys and sorrows, of sharing of problems and search for solu-tions. At the moment these little things are important until the so-called "big things" come our way. I know my suggestion appears simplistic to many who would wish to lead clear and effective action to bring about rapid revolutionary change.

I confess my own poverty. I am one among those millions who digest the "little book" of life with sweetness in the mouth but bitterness in the stomach (Apoc. 10:10), without clear answers to multiple questions that overwhelm me and which vibrate like the "warm" blood within our veins.

Conclusion

Spirituality is part and parcel of the human adventure. It is the foundation on which human life rests, whether we are aware of it or not. This spirituality is found wherever there is solidarity, trust, hope and the joy of living.

Spirituality, which I also call "vitality" (life), is today a universal movement cutting across cultures, races, classes, even though these are important elements in life. It is the spirituality of those who stretch out their hands to save life, to foster it and respect it and help it to bloom and grow despite the loud and deafening noises and the garbage produced by the elite of our society. It is the spirituality of those who sing, "Life is beautiful, is beautiful, is beautiful," in the words of the Brazilian song.

To recapture the beauty of life is to find once again new pathways and roads to bring about justice in our societies, to recommence yet again a global struggle for valid global change for the better.

11

Spirituality and Native American Personhood: Sovereignty and Solidarity

GEORGE E. TINKER

There are aboriginal peoples, indigenous peoples, in North America today. I treasure this opportunity to share something of our struggle and of a theology that is emerging out of that struggle. I also hope to challenge you to hear the voices of indigenous peoples in this world as those among the most oppressed, both by the powerful nations and by the so-called developing nations.

We are, if you will, a Fourth World, even as we find ourselves at home here in a conference of Third World theologians. As Fourth World peoples, we share with our Third World relatives the hunger, poverty, and repression which have been the continuing common experience of those over-powered by the expansionism of European adventurers and their mission-aries five hundred years ago. What distinguishes Fourth World indigenous peoples from Third World peoples, however, are the particular repercus-sions of conquest and genocide as they affected our distinctive indigenous cultures. While the immediately obvious effects of conquest and genocide seem similar for Third and Fourth World peoples, poverty, unemployment, disease, high infant mortality, and low adult longevity there are deeper, more hidden but no less deadly effects of colonialism, which make an impact on Third and Fourth World peoples in dramatically different ways. These effects are especially felt in the indigenous Fourth World spiritual experience, and we see our struggle for liberation within the context of this distinctive spirituality. This is often overlooked in Third World liberation theology models of social change, which often remain inappropriate and ineffective in the struggle of indigenous peoples for their right to self-determination. In fact, the themes of much liberation theology derive from the very modes of discourse of the western academy, against which indigenous peoples have struggled for centuries. These modes of discourse, whether theological, legal, political, or economic or even the so-called social sciences, have structured colonial, neo-colonial, and now Marxist regimes which, in the name of development, modernization or even solidarity, inflict spiritual genocide on Fourth World peoples. It is from this perspective that I want to share with you how an indigenous understanding of the spiritual is integral to the salvation of Native American peoples, quite apart from the struggle toward liberation envisioned by many Latin American theologians. I would like to begin by drawing both some contrasts and some affinities between Third World theology and what might define a Fourth World Native American theology.

Gustavo Gutiérrez, the foremost thinker on liberation theology, argues four important points: (1) namely, liberation theology should focus on the non-person rather than on the non-believer; (2) it is an historical project that sees God as revealed in history; (3) it makes a revolutionary socialist choice on behalf of the poor; and (4) it emerges out of the praxis of the people. The latter emphasis on praxis is perhaps the most enduring and pervasive gift of liberation theology. For reasons I hope to articulate clearly, however, a Native American theology must find the emphasis on the historical unsuitable for us, and I will begin with a much different understanding of Gutiérrez's category of the non-person. Moreover, Native American culture and spirituality will imply different political solutions from those currently imposed by the socialist paradigm. I trust that my critique will be received as a collegial attempt at constructive dialogue leading to mutual understanding and solidarity between Third and Fourth World peoples and an advance for the cause of genuine liberation.

Personhood and Genocide

In an early *Concilium* essay, Gutiérrez describes the meaning of his category of the non-person in language that strongly distinguishes liberation theology from the rest of modern theology:

> Much contemporary theology seems to start from the challenge of the *non-believer*. He questions our *religious world* and faces it with a demand for profound purification and renewal . . . This challenge in a continent like Latin America does not come primarily from the man who does not believe, but from the *man who is not a man*, who is not recognized as such by the existing social order: he is in the ranks of the poor, the exploited; he is the man who is systematically and legally despoiled of his being as a man, who scarcely knows that he is a man. His challenge is not aimed first at our religious world, but at our *economic, social, political and cultural world*; therefore it is an

appeal for the revolutionary transformation; of the very basis of a dehumanizing society. . . What is implied in telling this man who is not a man that he is a son of God?[1]

While these words frame the experience of oppression suffered by indigenous and Third World peoples alike, they fail to highlight the particularities of indigenous peoples' suffering of non-personhood. The very affirmation of Third World "non-persons" continues what has been, in praxis, a disaffirmation of indigenous people for five hundred years now in the Americas. While he avoids the language of explicit political programs,[2] Gutiérrez, like other Latin American theologians, explicitly identifies the preferential option for the poor with socialist and even Marxist solutions that analyze the poor in terms of social class structure[3] and overlooks the crucial point that indigenous peoples experience their very personhood in terms of their relationship to the land. By reducing the non-person to a class of people that share certain universal attributes, other sometimes more telling attributes become non-functional and non-important in the minds of those engaged in the analysis.[4]

Native American peoples resist categorization in terms of class structure. Instead, we insist on being recognized as " peoples," even nations with a claim to national sovereignty based on ancient title to their land. Whether we be classed as "working class" or " the poor," such classification continues the erosion of the group's cultural integrity and national agenda. As much as capitalist economic structures, including the church (missionaries) and the academia (like anthropologists), have reduced Native American peoples to non-personhood, so too the Marxist agenda fails finally to recognize our distinct personhood. Reducing our nationness to classness imposes upon us a particular culture of poverty and especially a culture of labor.[5] It begs the question as to whether indigenous peoples desire production in the modern economic sense in the first place. To put the means of production into the hands of the poor eventually makes the poor exploiters of indigenous peoples and their natural resources. Finally, it runs the serious risk of violating the very spiritual values that hold an indigenous cultural group together as a people.

This failure to recognize the distinct personhood of Native American peoples has a history—as long as the history of European colonialism and missionary outreach in the Americas. In particular, it should be noted that it was the church's failure to recognize the personhood of Native Americans that proved to be the most devastating. Such is the case from Motolinia and Mendiota in the South to Jaka Eliot in the north. While colonial armies were engaged in direct genocidal destruction of American Indian tribes, the missionaries were from the beginning equally complicitous in acts of genocide. However well intentioned, the missionaries were of a piece with the colonial conquest. Less direct than the military (yet always accompanied by them), the missionaries consistently confused the gospel of Jesus

Christ with the gospel of European cultural values and social structures. As a result they engaged in what can only be called the cultural genocide of Indian peoples, all in the service of conquest and the expansion of capitalist economies.

Even those missionary heroes who are most revered in modern memory, from Las Casas in the south to Eliot in the north, conspired with the political power of the colonial oppressors to deprive Indian peoples of their cultures, to destroy native economies, and to reduce culturally integral communities to subservient dependence—all for the sake of the "gospel," and with the best of intentions. (It was, after all, Las Casas who invented the *reduction* paradigm for missionary work among Indian peoples as a way of more gently exploiting Indian labor on behalf of the king.) The consistent failure of the missionaries of all denominations who came to evangelize our Native American tribes was precisely that they failed to notice, let alone acknowledge, our personhood. They saw our cultures and our social structures as inadequate and needing to be replaced with what they called a "Christian civilization." Even as they argued liberally for the humanity of Indian people, they denied our personhood.

Much of liberation theology and socialist movements in general can promise no better than the continued cultural genocide of indigenous peoples. From an American Indian perspective, the problem with modern liberation theology, as with Marxist political movements, is that class analysis gets in the way of recognizing cultural discreteness and even peopleness. Small but culturally integral communities stand to be swallowed up by the vision of a classless society, of an international workers' movement or of a burgeoning majority of Third World urban poor. That too is cultural genocide and signifies that we are yet non-persons, even in the light of the gospel of liberation.

God and History

In *The Power of the Poor in History* Gutiérrez begins by expounding on God's revelation and proclamation in history, arguing that God reveals God's self in history.[6] I want to argue that this is not only not a self-evident truth, but that a culturally integral Native American theology, rooted in our indigenous spiritual traditions, must begin with a confession that is both dramatically disparate from and exclusive of Gutiérrez's starting point. Essentially, a Native American theology must argue out of Native American spiritual experience and praxis that God reveals God's self in creation, in space or place and not in time. The western European (nineteenth century) sense of history as a linear temporal process means that those who heard the gospel first have and always maintain a critical advantage over those of us who hear it later and that we have to rely on those who heard it first to give us a full interpretation. In a historical structure of existence, certain people carry the message and hold all the wisdom. They know better and more than later converts.[7] For better or worse, this has been our consistent experience with the gospel as it has been preached to us by the missionaries of all the denominations, just as it has been our experience with the political visions proclaimed to us by the revolutionaries. This impetus, no doubt, is the reason Gutiérrez must trace the historical intellectual development of all humankind from Kant to Hegel, to Marx, to Freud and finally to Marcuse. (See *The Theology of Liberation*, pp. 30f.)

The problem, from Las Casas to Marx, is the assumption of a hegemonic trajectory through history which fails to recognize cultural discreteness. Even with the best of intentions, solutions to the suffering of oppressed peoples are proposed as exclusive programs not allowing for a diversity of possibilities. We must never forget that Las Casas, the hero of the 1992 quincentenary, was just as much given over to the conquest of Native Americans as were Cortés and Pizzaro. He only hoped to do it more gently and less violently. He accomplished much of his goal in his creation of the so-called reduction missionary system, used so effectively and destructively by later generations of European Jesuits and Franciscans and also Protestants in both the northern and southern hemispheres. The missionaries of all denominations consistently express their historical commitment to the progressive conquest of Christianity and what they identified as the culture of Christianity.

Whatever the conqueror's commitment, to evangelization and conversion or to military subjugation and destruction, it was necessary to make the conquest decisive at military, political, economic, social, legal and religious levels.[8] Just as the conquest had to be decisive, so too must the revolution be decisive. There can be no room for peoples who consider themselves distinct economically, politically, socially and culturally to find their own revolution or liberation. A prime example of this was the situation of the Miskito Indians in Nicaragua during the Sandinista revolution. Summarily relocated from their coastal territories where they had self-sustaining local economies due to high altitude communal coffee plantations, Miskito peoples were forced to labor as culturally amorphous workers with no regard to the abject cultural dislocation they had suffered. Once they had been a people; then they were reduced to a class whose peopleness could not be a factor. The pre-determined trajectory of historical dialectic allows no culturally disparate options, at least not cultural options that are decidedly disparate.

Whether in its capitalist or socialist guise then, history and temporality reign supreme in the West. On the other hand, Native American spirituality, values, social and political structures, even ethics, are rooted not in some temporal notion of history but in spatiality. This is perhaps the most dramatic (and largely unnoticed) cultural difference between Native American thought processes and the western intellectual tradition. The latter is firmly rooted in the priority of temporal metaphors and thought processes. Native Americans think inherently spatially and not temporally.

(See Selvia, *God Is Red* and *Metaphysics of Modern Existence*.) The question is not whether time or space is missing in one culture or the other, but which metaphoric base functions as the ordinary and which is the subordinate. Of course Native Americans have a temporal awareness, but it is subordinate to our sense of spatiality. Likewise, the western tradition has a spatial awareness, but it lacks the priority of the temporal. Hence, progress, history, development, evolution, and process become key notions that invade all academic discourse in the West, from science and economics to philosophy and theology. History thus becomes the quintessential western intellectual device and gives rise to structures of cognition and modes of discourse that pay dutiful homage to temporality.

If Marxist thinking and the notion of a historical dialectic were finally proven correct, then American Indian people and all indigenous peoples would surely be doomed. Our cultures and value systems, our spirituality and even our social structures, must soon give way to an emergent socialist structure that would impose a notion of the good on all people regardless of ethnicity or culture.

Culture, Discourse and Spirituality

All of this has much to do with my assigned topic of spirituality. Without understanding the spatiality of Native American existence, one cannot understand Native American spiritual traditions. Spatiality and spiritual traditions are keys to understanding the continuing threat to Indian personhood and the specter of cultural genocide (economic, political, intellectual and religious) that constantly hovers over our heads.

One could argue with Native American peoples that we must learn to compromise with the "real world," that to pursue our own cultural affectations is to swim upstream against the current of the modern socio-economic world system. When rightists and capitalists of any shade make the argument, I am clear that they are arguing the self-interest or prerogatives of those who own the system. When Third or Fourth World peoples make the argument, I am curious at how readily some of us concede the primacy of western categories of discourse. How easily we internalize the assumption that Euro-American philosophical, theological, economic, social, spiritual and political systems are necessarily definitive of any and all conceivable "real" worlds. We Native Americans are just arrogant enough in the midst of our oppression and poverty to think that our perception of the world is just as adequate, and perhaps more satisfying and certainly more egalitarian than the West's. In order to sense something of the power of our culturally integrated structures of cognition, a beginning understanding of Native American spirituality is a necessary starting point, for all of existence is spiritual for us. That is our universal starting point, even though we represent a multitude of related cultures, in actuality, with a great variety of tribal ceremonial structures expressing that sense of spirituality.

If the primary metaphor of existence for Native Americans is spatial and not temporal, this goes a long way toward explaining what nearly everyone already knows, that American Indian spirituality and American Indian existence in general are deeply rooted in the land. It explains why the history of our conquest and removal from our lands was so culturally and genocidally destructive to our tribes. There is, however, a more subtle level to this sense of spatiality and land-rootedness. It shows up in nearly all aspects of our existence, in our ceremonial structures, our symbols, our architecture, and in the symbolic parameters of a tribe's universe. In my own tribe, for instance, the old villages were always laid out in two halves, dividing the peoples into Hunka and Tzi Sho, an Earth Division and a Sky Division. This reflected the fundamental manifestation (revelation?) of Wakonta, the Sacred Mystery, Creator, God(?) to the people. Since Wakonta is an unknowable Mystery, Wakonta had to make itself known to people. It did so as a duality, as Wakonta Above and Wakonta Below (Wakonta Monshita and Wakonta Udseta), as Grandfather (Itsiko) and Grandmother (Iko), as Sky and Earth. We should not think here of the oppositional dualism of good and evil that we have learned to identify as typical Western (Eastern) dualism. Native American duality is a necessary reciprocity, not oppositional. They are different manifestations of the *same* Wakonta, not of two Wakontas, even though they carry personality specificity just as traditional Christian trinitarian doctrine would assert. While they are manifestations of the same Wakonta, they are different manifestations, both of which are necessary in order to have some balanced understanding of the otherness that is the Sacred Mystery. Indeed, Wakonta has manifested itself in a great many other ways, all of which help our people to better understand the Mystery, our world, ourselves and our place in the world.

The architectural geography of our spirituality was played out even further in a variety of ways. Most significantly, we were what anthropologists call an exogamous kinship system. Individuals were required by social mores to marry outside of their own division, meaning that every child and every person is both Hunka and Tzi Sho, even though she or he belongs structurally to only one division. While this functions politically to give the village group cohesion, it functions at a much more deeply spiritual level that still pertains for a great many Indian people today. Namely, each individual recognizes herself or himself as a combination of qualities that reflect both sky and earth, spirit and matter, peace and war, male and female, and we struggle individually and communally to hold those qualities in balance with each other.

This is not the only spatial symbolic paradigm of existence that determines Native American individuality and community. The fundamental symbol of plains Indian existence is the circle, a polyvalent symbol signifying the family, the clan, the tribe, and eventually all of creation. As a creation symbol, the importance of the circle is its genuine egalitarianness. There is no way to make the circle hierarchical. Because it has no beginning and no end, all in the circle are of equal value. No relative is valued more than any other. A chief is not valued above the people; nor are two-legged valued above the animal nations, the birds, or even trees and rocks. In its form as a medicine wheel, with two lines forming a cross inscribed vertically and horizontally across its whole, the circle can symbolize the four directions of the earth and, more importantly, the four manifestations of Wakonta that come to us from those directions. At the same time, those four directions symbolize the four cardinal virtues of a tribe, the four sacred colors of ceremonial life, the sacred powers of four animal nations, and the four nations of two-leggeds that walk the earth (Black, Red, Yellow and White). That is, in our conception of the universe, all human beings walk ideally in egalitarian balance. Moreover, Native American egalitarian proclivities are worked out in this spatial symbol in ways that go far beyond the classless egalitarianness of socialism. In one of the polyvalent layers of meaning, those four directions hold together in the same egalitarian balance the four nations of two-leggeds, four-leggeds, wingeds, and living-moving things. In this rendition human beings lose their status of primacy and "dominion." Implicitly and explicitly, American Indians are driven by their culture and spirituality to recognize the personhood of all "things" in creation. If temporality and historicity lend themselves implicitly to hierarchical structures because someone with a greater investment of time may know more of the body of temporally codified knowledge, spatiality lends itself to the egalitarian. All have relatively similar access to the immediacy of the spatially present.

This sense of the egalitarian plays itself out in Native American life precisely where one might expect Indian culture to be challenged, namely, in ceremonial aspects around hunting and harvest. The key to understanding hunting and harvest practices is the principle of reciprocity, whereby the hunter or harvester engages in some action reciprocal to the act of harvest itself. Native American tribes, as is well known, had and many still have extensive hunting ceremonies, ceremonies that begin before the hunters leave the village, continue on the hunt itself, reach a climactic point when the animal is killed and do not conclude until the hunters all undergo purification rites prior to re-entry into the village with their hard-earned cache of meat and hides. While these ceremonies include aspects of prayer for a successful hunt, the more dominant theme is the one of reciprocity. Namely, the hunter is participating in a mythic activity which has its origin in mythological stories in which human beings were given permission by the animal nations to hunt themselves for food. The resulting covenant, however, calls on human beings to assume responsibilities over against the perpetration of violence among four-legged relatives. Prayers for the animals must be offered, even prayers to the animals, asking their immediate permission to be taken for food. Moreover, some reciprocal offering is almost always made, as the hunter sprinkles tobacco around the slain animal or corn pollen on its closed eyelids, depending on tribal tradition. Agricultural harvest calls for similar ceremonial attention and reciprocity. Nothing is taken from the earth without prayer and offering. When the tree is cut down for the Sun Dance, for instance, something must be offered, returned to the spirit world, for the life of that tree. The people not only ask its permission but ask for its cooperation and help during the four days of the dance itself. These animals, crops, trees, and medicines are relatives and must be treated with respect if they are to be genuinely efficacious for the people.

Lakota peoples, one of hundreds of distinct Native American peoples in North America, have a short prayer that captures the general cultural and spiritual sentiment of all native Americans. *Mitakuye ouyasin*, they pray, "For all my relatives." In this prayer relatives are understood to include not just tribal members but all two-leggeds, and not just two-leggeds but indeed all the "createds" of the world: the four leggeds, the wingeds, and all the living-moving things, the trees and rocks, mountains and rivers, fish and snakes, and so on. It is for this reason, then, that not even an animal or tree is harmed without appropriate spiritual reciprocity in the American Indian world. In the act of hunting or in harvesting, ceremonial acts of reciprocity must be preformed in order to maintain the balance and harmony of the world in the midst of perpetrating an act of violence. To act without such responsibility is to introduce imbalance and disharmony into the world. All the created of the world are our relatives and command our respect as fellow createds.

Creation, Justice, Peace

I want to suggest that a Native American theology coupled with a Native American reading of the gospel might provide the theological imagination to generate a more immediate and attainable vision of a just and peaceful world. What we lack yet today is a creative and powerful theological foundation for the justice we desire. All our churches take seriously to some extent the scriptural demands for justice, yet none of them has a persuasive and satisfying means for arguing or achieving those goals. While God revealing God's self in history holds out some promise for achieving justice and peace in some eventual future movement, the historical/temporal impetus must necessarily delay any full realization of the *basileia* of God.

As a world of discourse that is primarily spatial, a Native American theology must begin with the Native American praxis of a spirituality that is rooted first of all in creation. I consistently argued in the WCC "Justice, Peace and the Integrity of Creation" process that it should have been titled, "Creation, Justice, Peace." Such a theological prioritizing of creation on my part is far more than a prioritizing of environmental concerns. Rather it functions to provide a spiritual and theological foundation for justice. Respect for creation must necessarily result in justice, just as genuine justice necessarily is the achievement of peace.

I start with a particular understanding of the *basileia tou theou,* the *basileia* (or kingdom) of God,[9] a concept so central to the preaching of Jesus in the gospels. While Euro-cultural scholars have offered consistently temporal interpretations of this metaphor, any American Indian interpretation must build on a spatial understanding rooted in creation. Western scholars consistently want to ask the question "when?" of the *basileia* and disallow any query about the "where" of the *basileia.* While Native Americans know little about either kings or kingdoms, only a spatial response to the question "where" begins to make any sense at all of the metaphor. Whatever the *basileia* is, it must be a place. Certainly, the verb *engizein* allows for and even predicates a primary meaning of spatial nearness, and in Luke 17:20 Jesus instructs the Pharisees that the *basileia* is " in your midst" (*entos humas*), that is, already spatially present.

My own interpretation treats the *basileia* as a metaphor for creation. Indeed, the metaphor is not used in the Old Testament at all, but the image of God as king occurs almost always in contexts that refer to God's act in creation. If the metaphor has to do with God's hegemony, where else is God actually to reign if not in the entirety of the place that God has created? To assume any less is to lapse again into a triumphalistic mode that permits human beings, the church or governments, to decide who is and who is not privileged and to determine the process by which one might become so privileged.[10]

American Indian spirituality sees as its fundamental goal the achievement of harmony and balance in all of creation. We do see the hegemony of the Mystery (God?) in the whole of existence, but we see ourselves as participants in that whole, doing our part to help maintain harmony and balance. After all, we see ourselves as merely a part of creation and not somehow apart from creation free to use it up at will, a mistake that was and is endemic in both the First and Second Worlds, and has been recklessly imposed on the rest of us in the name of development. While our spirituality is enormously complex in this regard, maybe it is enough in this context to say that we are pressed by our spirituality to understand the *basileia* as the place that is all of the real world, creation. Thus *no one* can be left out of the *basileia.* In the spirit of the prayer *Mitakuye ouyasin,* we all belong. The question is whether I will recognize God's hegemony over myself and all of creation. Will I live faithfully in relationship to God and creation?

In Mark 1:15, Jesus' first audience is told that because the *basileia* is near they are to "be repenting and be 'faithing' in the gospel." If, as many scholars since Jeremias have argued, the Hebrew/Aramaic word *shub,* to turn or return, is the underlying notion that Mark has translated as repentance, then the call to repentance becomes a call to return to a proper relationship not only with the Creator but also with the rest of creation. I understand the call to repentance as a call to be liberated from our human perceived need to be God, and instead to assume our rightful place in the world as humble two-leggeds in the circle of creation with all the other created.

This understanding of *basileia* and repentance, I want to argue, can become a powerful impetus for justice first of all, and finally for peace. What I am arguing is not some value-neutral creation theology of Matthew Fox, some new-age spirituality of feel-good individualism. Rather it is an ultimate expression of a "theology of community" that must generate a consistent interest in justice and peace. Namely, if I image myself as a vital part of a community, indeed as a part of many communities, it becomes more difficult for me to act in ways that are destructive of the community.

If we image ourselves as fellow-createds, mere participants in the whole of creation, functioning out of respect for and reciprocity with all of creation, then our relationships with each other as two-leggeds must also be grounded in respect and reciprocity. As fellow-createds, acknowledging God's hegemony over all, there can no longer be any rationale for exploitation and oppression. The desire for or even the perceived necessity for exerting social, political, economic or spiritual control over each other must give way to mutual respect, not just for individuals but for our culturally integral communities.

This understanding of *basileia* would mandate new social and political structures, genuinely different from those created by either of the dominant Euro-cultural philosophical-political structures of capitalism or Marxism. The competition generated by western, Euro-cultural individualism, temporality and paradigms of history and progress must give way to the communal notion of inter-relatedness and reciprocity.

The pervasive nature of the social transformation that might be involved as a result of such a theology may become apparent in the singular challenge that it represents to the reified status of the "nation state" ideology of virtually all modern political theory. By what divine right does any immigrant political entity under the guise of a nation state assume explicit sovereignty over conquered and colonized indigenous populations? The challenge of indigenous peoples is a socio-economic and political challenge as much as it is a spiritual one.

In the wake of JPIC it should be clearly noted again that the theological priority of creation is not simply a priority for environmental concern, but rather, creation is a firm foundation for justice and a vision for peace. If we can begin with an affirmation of God as Creator and ourselves as created, then perhaps there is hope for a spiritual transformation that can bring us all closer to recognizing the kingdom of God in our midst (Luke 17:21). Then perhaps we can acknowledge our humanness in new and more significant ways, understanding that confession precedes return, and that both become the base for living in harmony and balance with God and all creation. Besides confession of our individual humanness, this means confessing the humanness of our churches, the humanness of our theologies, and the

humanness of the world economic and political order in which we participate. Then it is possible to make our repentance, to return, to go back from
whence we came, that is, to go back to the Creator in whom we like all of
creation "live and move and have our being" (Acts 17:28). We must go back
to a proper relationship with the Creator in which we confess our human
inclination to put ourselves in the Creator's place and renew our understanding of ourselves and our institutions as mere creatures. We must go
back to a recognition of ourselves as a part of, and integrally related to, all
of creation.

The American Indian understanding of creation as sacred, of Grandmother earth, as the source of all life, goes far beyond the notion of such
Western counter-institutions as the Sierra Club or Greenpeace. It embraces
far more than concern for harp seals or a couple of ice-bound whales. It
embraces all of life from trees and rocks to international relations. And this
knowledge informs all of the community's activity, from hunting to dancing and even to writing grant proposals or administering government
agencies. It especially concerns itself with the way we all live together.
Perforce, it has to do with issues of justice and fairness and ultimately with
peace. If we believe we are all relatives in this world, then we must live
together differently than we have. Justice and peace, in this context, emerge
almost naturally out of a self-imaging that sees the self only as part of the
whole, as a part of an ever-expanding community that begins with family
and tribe but is finally inclusive of all human beings and of all of creation.
All in this world are relatives, and we will live together out of respect for
each other, working toward the good of each other. Respect for creation,
for instance, must result in an ongoing concern for economic balance and
resistance to economic injustices that leave many poor and oppressed while
their white American or European relatives or even Japanese relatives live
in wealth at the expense of others.

American Indian people have experienced and continue to experience
endless oppression as a result of what some would call the barbaric invasion of America. On the other hand, we certainly suspect that the oppression we have experienced is intimately linked to the way the immigrants
pray and how they understand creation and their relationship to creation
and Creator. Moreover, we suspect that the greed that motivated the
displacement of all indigenous peoples from their lands of spiritual rootedness is the same greed that threatens the destruction of the earth and the
continued oppression of so many people. Whether it is the stories the
immigrants tell or the theologies they develop to interpret those stories,
something appears wrong to Indian people. But not only do Indians
continue to tell the stories, sing the songs, speak the prayers, and perform
the ceremonies that root themselves deeply in Grandmother, the earth, they
are actually audacious enough to think that their stories and their ways of
reverencing creation will some day win over the immigrant conquerors and

transform them. Optimism and enduring patience seem to run in the life blood of Native American peoples.

Notes

1. "Liberation, Theology and Proclamation," in *The Mystical and Political Dimension of the Christian Faith, Concilium: Religion in the Seventies*, Vol. 6, edited by Gutiérrez and Claude Geffré, (New York: Herder and Herder, 1974), p. 69.

2. See Gutiérrez's essay, "Theology and the Social Sciences," reprinted as Appendix II in Paul E. Sigmund, *Liberation Theology at the Crossroads: Democracy or Revolution*, (New York: Oxford, 1990), pp. 214-225.

3. See Gutiérrez, *Praxis de Liberación y Fe Christiana* (San Antonio: Mexican American Cultural Center, 1974), p. 19. Cf., José Míguez Bonino, *Doing Theology in a Revolutionary Situation*, (Philadelphia: Fortress, 1975), esp. pp. 85-97, 147ff.; Hugo Assmann, *Theology for a Nomad Church*, (Maryknoll: Orbis Books, 1976); and Juan Luis Segundo, *The Liberation of Theology*, (Maryknoll: Orbis Books, 1976), esp. p. 115. His later denials to the contrary, this Gutiérrez clearly says in his 1971 *A Theology of Liberation* (Maryknoll: Orbis, 1973), pp. 26f.: "Attempts to bring about changes within the existing order have proven futile. This analysis of the situation is at the level of scientific rationality. Only a radical from the status quo, that is, a profound transformation of the private property system, access to power of the exploited class and a social revolution that would break this dependence would allow for the change to a new society, a socialist society."

4. Segundo is most explicit in this regard when he argues for the sacrifice of "minority" freedoms for the sake of improving the well-being of the "masses": "minority aspects (for example, freedom of thought, freedom of religion, freedom for Christian political actions) seem to be systematically overvalued in comparison with factors that are more revolutionary because they affect great human masses at one extreme of the process, such as in conditions of dire poverty, ignorance, disease and death" (*The Liberation of Theology*, p. 89). Gutiérrez, for his part, in his recitation of dependency theory, argues to expand the analysis beyond that of a confrontation between natives to an analysis of class struggle. "But only class analysis will enable us to see what is really involved in the opposition between oppressed countries and dominant peoples" (p. 87). Both levels of his analysis, however, begin with assumptions about the validity of the native state. Moreover, class analysis will not analyze or treat significantly small culturally integrous communities except as a part of a larger, more amorphous class grouping.

5. The North American Catholic bishops fell into a similar pattern in their epistle on the economy, suggesting the right to have a job as an immediate basic human right. See G. Tinker, "Does All People Include Native Peoples?" in Charles Lutz, *God, Goods and the Common Good*, (Minneapolis: Augsburg, 1987).

6. *The Power of the Poor in History*, translated by Robert R. Barr, (Maryknoll, Orbis Books, 1983), pp. 3ff.

7. Elizondo, in distinguishing between the "old" churches of the First World and the young churches of the Third World, says of the old churches, "They are encumbered by centuries of traditions of seeing themselves as THE Church, and their missionaries carried their model of Church to many parts of the world as if it were the one and only model of the Church. This myopia was simply the product of the interiorized culture of the Church seeing itself through the optic of the empire or the optic of the sociological model of the monarchy." Virgil Elizondo, "Conditions

and Criteria for Authentic Inter-Cultural Theological Dialogue," in *Concilium* 171: *Different Theologies, Common Responsibility: Babel or Pentecost?* edited by Claude Geffré, Gustavo Gutiérrez and Elizondo, (Edinburgh: Clark, 1984), p. 21.

8. Robert Williams, *The American Indian in Western Legal Thought*.

9. I use the Greek word *basileia* as a way of avoiding the unnecessarily sexist language of the usual English translation. Of course, the metaphor itself makes little sense to Native American peoples when it is literally translated. The praxis of our existence allows for no experiential knowledge about kings, queens or other monarchical rulers.

10. I use the word privilege here not only in an economic, social and political sense, but specifically in a soteriological sense. We dare not pretend that these two categories are unrelated in western theology. Certainly they were thoroughly intertwined in the missionary evangelization of Native American peoples.

Response from Latin America

ANA MARÍA TEPEDINO

In this moment I humbly want to be the voice of Black women and men, Indian women and men, as well as white women and men in Latin America. Indian, Black people and women have been oppressed and marginalized. But we resist; we keep on living and hoping. We women ask how? Black people ask the same question. After centuries of suffering we keep on living, suffering but laughing because life is a celebration. When I spoke with Eleazae, our Zapotec brother yesterday, he posed the same question.

What strength sustains this attitude? Where does it come from? Well, it's something very strong which comes from deep inside and this strength is spirituality. Spirituality is what keeps us living and giving hope and meaning of life.

That's a commonality we people from Third World have been experiencing—a cry for life, a scream for life. Concerning George's reflection, two aspects impressed me:

1) The importance of theology of creation for a broader understanding of justice and peace. The *basileia tou theou* as the entirety of creation and the consequences toward the relations between persons, and between persons and creation.

2) The importance of the circle as a symbol of Indians' existence, because of its egalitarianness. This is a consequence of the theology of creation. We are all relatives and must be respected as "fellow-createds." For us women, Blacks and Indians, who have been suffering from hierarchy in the church and society, the circle as a model of relationship is very important.

The Gospel of the Colonizers

As you know, the Gospel brought by the Portuguese and Spanish to Latin America was not good news to the indigenous people. They came as conquerors in order to establish the *basileia* for theology in the "new world." As for religion, the church became the vehicle for the crown of Portugal and Spain (social, political, and economic power). Christian conquerors (with some very important exceptions) didn't respect the peoples which lived in the *Tierra Grande*, but simply intended to dominate these people, affirming

133

that they possessed the only true faith in God, the only way to salvation, and thus provoking an alienation of their own faith, denying diversity and pluralism, and insisting on their own understanding of religions, society, economics, and politics as the best for the new world.

This attitude leads to a denial of the religious expression of the indigenous populations. So, although the Christian churches proclaimed the God of life, often they have been the instruments of death to the conquered peoples.

The colonizers valued themselves as the saved and superior human beings. Their religion, behavior, culture became the controlling pattern, the dominant culture. The same process was suffered by the Black people who came to Latin America and the Caribbean. They were viewed as pagan, uncivilized, inferior objects, incapable of intelligent thought and action. Women have been marginalized and oppressed in every way economically, socially, politically, racially and sexually. Since colonization continues even today, we have been raped and robbed of our dignity. Well, the theology of liberation helped us to speak our own word and to make our voices heard.

We from Latin America have an auto-critical attitude towards some aspects of the theology of liberation. Furthermore, we cannot speak of a theology of liberation but of theologies of liberation. Theology of liberation is the interpretation of the life we live, at least one part of life, the lives of the poor in general. Now we understand that this is not sufficient. The poor have many faces: Indian women, Blacks and other persons are challenging the theology of liberation. But we must recognize that we can do this today because of the very theology of liberation.

We, Indians, Blacks and women are taking the word and we are challenging theology of liberation hermeneutical patterns. We feel that the hermeneutic approach of Indians, Blacks and women should be considered and incorporated.

There are problems which are still without solutions. For women the theology of liberation is patriarchal, and for Indians there is no real communication between the theology of liberation and Indian theology. Marxist analysis is insufficient in the face of the complexity of reality. So, we have internal criticism which is deeper than seen from the outside because we are seeing it from the inside. And I can also affirm that George's view is not adequate. There are many critical works about Gustavo Gutiérrez's writings, and it is necessary to make a complete reading of this work. We need a serious and well founded critique.

Spirituality Lived Daily

Now I want to consider the spirituality of Latin America. Our spirituality, which maintains our fight for better living conditions, is lived in everyday life. A woman from a basic Christian community (BCC) said in a meeting: "I am fighting not for myself, but for my sons, daughters and grandchildren, because I want a better life for them."

Fighting for better life means struggling for bread, for jobs, for education, transportation, housing, day-care centers, better salaries, because existence is spiritual for us. God is in the midst of these fights. After all, God cannot stand for less than a full life for any of God's children.

The small fights co-exist with the bigger fight to transform society, transform the world of death into the world of life. But our models were broken and the people are discouraged, disappointed, in distress, tired. Again, as they did many times in the past, they seek inner strength: spirituality.

Experience of Blacks, Indians, Women

I have some friends who tell me about their experience: they are Black and have been raised in the Catholic faith, and they believe in God, in Jesus and in the Holy Spirit. These last few years, with the appearance of Black movements, their consciences have been aroused about their roots, and they begin to have a double way of relationship to God, but little by little they are integrating the two ways in a new way of living spirituality. The Black spirituality is matriarchal, and the priesthood of women is another way of working religiously; they create community and they influence the spirituality of a part of society.

Indians' experience is similar in a certain way. They have always lived their root spirituality but clandestinely; this helped them to keep on living and hoping. But now this hidden spirituality is becoming visible, although they don't allow outsiders to meet their parents or participate in their rituals.

Women in general, since colonization to our day, have been living sustained by their spirituality. The divine is an integral part of life: I would say it's natural to them, and they communicate with God/Jesus/Mary/the saints in all the moments of joy and of distress. And this attitude empowers them to fight for a better life. Even when, historically, they have been through a process of "romanization" of faith, they kept their own spirituality, and although they had to practice a "more clerical spirituality," their own sprituality re-appeared in the BCCs.

In the BCCs we try to change the church's hierarchal model into a more democratic "circular" model. These men and women make the experience of becoming persons by beginning to speak their word and by participating in the celebrations and in the life of the community. Latin American people are very religious and God is found in all moments of their life. Popular spirituality is lived in the midst of the struggles, in the small signs of life which enable us to "feast" life. We cannot understand Latin American spirituality without the "fiesta," the gracious moment when we communicate with God who is "graciousness" and without the "martyrdom" of so many persons, as life offered graciously because of the engagement in favor of the poor, in the struggle for justice and life.

Response from South Africa

TAKATSO MOFOKENG

It is indeed a great privilege for me, as an African from South Africa, to respond to this highly valuable and challenging paper by George Tinker. This paper is, to my mind, a radical expression ("radical" meaning going to the roots) of the Native American spirituality that challenges us to engage in an honest and equally radical response, also as our expression of our radical African Christian spirituality. We shall attempt, even though in a preliminary way, to do that in a spirit of love and solidarity.

Defining black spirituality as our whole being and our whole life, that is, the way we walk, talk, laugh, cry, struggle and celebrate, the way we worship and pray, the way we sing and do theology, the way we work and rest as well as the way we do theology and create culture, we shall proceed to address the following issues.

The Context That Bases and Defines Our Spirituality

Objectively, we black South Africans are a colonized and subjugated people whose land has been conquered. Our culture is also colonized and subjugated. The same goes for our religion. Ironically, we live in a painful paradox of having been Christianized by our colonizers and dispossessors. In other words, we have been coerced, albeit partially, into the ideological universe of our subjugators. In cases where that insertion into the world of ideas, thought forms and spiritual experience of our conquerors has succeeded, our absorption has only given us the status of being perpetual junior partners in the perception, definition, development and articulation of that universe of ideas and emotionality. In other words, those of us who have succumbed to that coercion exist and operate as junior Christians in the Christian community that is dominated by their oppressors.

Subjectively, brothers and sisters, we black South African Christians are Africans who are presently engaged in an all-encompassing struggle for liberation that will hopefully culminate in our regaining the material basis of our existence, our land, our identity and the uncontested right for self-definition and articulation even in Christian terms. This comprehensive struggle that I have referred to forms and informs our spirituality. This struggle also encompasses the struggle to be Christian in our own way and to be theological in our own way, not in absolute isolation, but in solidarity and dialogue with other suffering and struggling people of Africa and the entire Third World. It is within this context that I wish to respond to the presentation of brother and comrade George Tinker.

Inseparability of the Struggle for Identity and Subjectivity for Self-understanding and Articulation and the Paradox of Our Situation

I agree with George about the right of each struggling people to identify and define itself according to its self-understanding and also that such people need adequate means for that, and that such means should not be imposed nor regarded as absolute and perfect. They should be judged in terms of whether they promote or deny and reduce our humanity and our purpose in life; in other words, whether they enhance or deform our spirituality. I also agree with George that categories and paradigms derived from the North have acquired a hegemonic and dominating tendency like their formulators and that it will be a contradiction in terms to struggle against their formulators while excluding them from our field of struggle as if they could be innocent or neutral. Having said that, I think that our struggle, that is, our critical view of such paradigms and concepts, does give us the freedom and power to be in dialogue with them and to use them if necessary and advisable. As far as Marxist tools of analysis in particular are concerned, and as far as the Marxist utopian project is concerned, we have acknowledged, and that goes for Gustavo Gutiérrez also, both their usefulness as well as their inadequacy. We have criticized them, in particular, for inadequacy in understanding the significance of culture and religion, and hence they cannot be regarded as a comprehensive definition of what it means to be human for us. I agree with George that his experience and perception of human identity also emphasizes their inadequacies. The same goes for the capitalist paradigm. To us Africans our identity and humanity lies in land, nature and people and our religious universe.

On the inadequacy of the class concept in defining people in society and with a national consciousness I do not think that one should make a choice between class and nationality as if the two are mutually exclusive. The concept of class is an analytical concept that enables people who exist on the fringes of a highly developed modern capitalist society, as Tinker's people do, to understand the dynamics and mechanisms of production and power distribution and utility in that society. This is an area that cannot be adequately covered by the nationality concept. It is not able to comprehend and define adequately the operations of a pervasive material and immaterial culture in such societies as the United States. On the other hand, the nationality concept enables all classes in society to comprehend and explain the loyalty of a particular cultural group (one that cuts across all class structure of society) to one another. This contemporary reality seems to be hidden to the class concept. In an effort to achieve a comprehensive view of social reality, the two concepts should, therefore, be used together and simultaneously, because of their mutual complementarity.

Logically, this critical consciousness and appropriation of everything foreign should hold where we come to a foreign religion and its means of self-articulation. The Christian religion and the Bible have come from "outside" and encroached on the hegemonic sphere of Native American religion or way of life and challenged its legitimacy. We can imagine, as we have experienced in our African context, that the confrontation that inevitably ensued was gradually and partially negotiated away and a state of relative harmony achieved. We are not told, however, that was indeed the case and how it happened. We are not told how and whether the Bible, the religion and culture of the Bible were critically appropriated.

We cannot, just as it happens in this paper, quietly identify the concept of *God* with the reign of God which we find in the Bible before finding out and explaining which God we are dealing with. This is a crucial issue. Modern scholarship has shown that there is a variety of traditions as well as differing trajectories of people and communities of the Bible, and that one needs to make a conscious, informed and critical choice before one speaks of God and the reign of God. We should be able to say which God we are dealing with—God of the oppressors or God of the oppressed and the poor.

In exploring the usefulness of creation as a theological framework, all Africans will acknowledge spiritual existence as the primary definition of existence, and they experience existing in community with nature and a God who is not far off. As such, any separation between African humans and nature leaves Africans feeling incomplete and unfulfilled; hence the unacceptability of any duality in perceiving and talking about human nature and existence. This oneness lies at the root of our struggle for land in our country.

We therefore also share the view that a theology done within the context of creation could yield a viable and sustainable ecological perception and program.

12

The Jesus of Faith: A Christological Contribution to an Ecumenical Third World Spirituality

GEORGE SOARES PRABHU

This paper attempts to spell out some of the problems which arise when one attempts to determine the role of Jesus in an ecumenical Christian spirituality that will respond effectively to the Third World's cry for life. It does this in two parts. The first part provides a historical and hermeneutical survey of the christological discussion in the early church and the New Testament to make us aware of some of the problems implicit in an attempt to construct an ecumenical Christian theology for the Third World; the second offers a meditation on the "Jesus of faith" as a basis for christological reflection. The whole paper is not meant to offer a finished christology but stimulate christological reflection. Like so much in Third World theology today, it poses more questions than it answers.

A Hermeneutical Prologue

How does one engage in "Christ-talk" in a way that will be responsive both to the cry for life which emerges in many different voices and in many different tones throughout the Third World today, and be acceptable to Christians as Christians, (perhaps even as "anonymous" Christians) and not merely to some particular churches or sects among them? To do this, one cannot, then, simply take over the considerable volume of christological writing (some of it quite excellent) current in theological circles today, however much it may derive inspiration and insight from it.[1] Jesus, the giver of life, in our Third World situation of anguish and of death, must be sought afresh by confronting Christian tradition with contemporary Third World experience.

Early Christian Tradition

The Christian tradition with which contemporary Third World experience must interact cannot be the classical christological tradition of the early church, from which most modern christologies derive, and which finds its normative expression in conciliar formulae, notably that of Chalcedon. For this christology, however "correct" it might be, represents a narrow culturally conditioned, and even politically motivated development which exploits only a very small fraction of the christological potential that the New Testament offers. The dogmatic christology of the post-apostolic Hellenistic church, to which we are all heirs, developed along a single line which took off from the logos-christology of John, itself a rare though not wholly unrepresentative growth in the complex jungle of New Testament theology.[2] It eventually crystallized in the formulae of Nicea (325 c.e.), Ephesus (431 c.e.) and Chalcedon (451 c.e.), which became the normative "dogmas" for succeeding ages.

Many factors prompted this unilinear and, I believe, ultimately impoverishing development, which has led to the progressive alienation of Jesus from the world, by robbing him of his individuality as a human being: "he became," as the church historian W.H.C. Frend has said, "man but not a man."[3] The logos theology of John obviously offered an easy entry into Hellenistic philosophical thinking, so that it was natural that it should be taken up by the church Fathers theologizing in a Hellenistic world,[4] and developed in terms of the then current neo-Platonic philosophical categories of "nature" (*physis*), "substance" (*ousia*), "subsistence" (*hypostasis*) and "person" (*prosopon*), however imprecisely and ambiguously these were then understood. Christ-talk in the early church adopted one particular philosophical idiom, but within it proceeded to develop an endless series of aggressively competing models, each more intricate than the one before.[5]

But when, with the conversion of Constantine in 312 c.e., the prophetic religion of Jesus became (paradoxically) the legitimizing ideology of the Roman Empire,[6] then the imperial unity required an end to theological dissension and some kind of uniformity of belief. It was, partly at least, because of such concerns for "imperial integration" that the Council of Nicea, the first ecumenical council[7] was convoked by Constantine in 325, and largely managed by him. Indeed the fateful *homoousios* (consubstantial), the crucial expression of the Nicene Creed, which became the "most disputed word of the fourth century," was probably inserted into the baptismal credo of Syro-Palestinian provenance which the council had adopted as its consensus formula, at the behest of the emperor.[8]

This imperial venture in theology did not, of course, bring an end to the christological controversies of the early church. These continued with unabated vigor all through the fourth century, pitting the Antiochenes and their *dya hypostaseis* (two subsistences), which gave full importance to the humanity of Jesus, since this alone could offer "a perfect pattern of virtue and redemption to humankind" against the Alexandrians and their *mia physis* (one nature), which stressed his divinity, so that eucharistic participation in the body of the true Word of God would provide "an antidote to the corruption of death."[9] A brilliant if somewhat patchwork synthesis was eventually reached at Chalcedon in 451. This affirmed faith in "one and the same Christ, Son, Lord, Only Begotten, made known in two natures [which exist] without confusion, without change, without division, without separation . . . concurring into one person (*prosopon*) and one subsistence (*hypostasis*) not parted into two persons but one and the same Son, and Only begotten, the divine Logos, the Lord Jesus Christ."[10] But this did not put an end to the controversy. The formula became, indeed, the norm for all christological development in the Latin West, much of the Greek and some of the Syriac East; but it provoked fresh controversies, even more violent than before in Egypt and Syria, creating new divisions which have yet to be healed.[11] "It settled very little in the East," Jaroslav Pelikan suggests, providing the terms for subsequent controversies, "rather than the solution for past ones."[12]

I suggest three conclusions be drawn from this rapid survey of the christological controversies of the early church from which the traditional christology of our Christian churches has emerged:

1) Any attempt to encapsulate the mystery of Jesus into a formula, however intricate, subtle and complex, is bound to be inadequate, theologically and pastorally. The mystery of Jesus cannot be conceptualized, delimited, defined, or packaged into neat philosophical categories, and attempts to do this lead only to the alienation of Jesus from life. A different kind of analysis (one which will focus on the life-giving "mystery" of Jesus and not on the conceptual "mechanism" which pretends to explain him), and a different mode of expression (metaphorical not ontological) are needed if we are to understand the significance of Jesus for Third World *spirituality* of liberation and dialogue today.

2) No christological formula has in fact been accepted as normative by Christians as a whole. Nicea was rejected by the Arians, Ephesus by the Nestorians, Chalcedon by the Monophysites, not to speak of innumerable other barely remembered sects with unpronounceable names, squabbling with quite extraordinary ferocity over obscure points of doctrine. It would be easy, of course, to discount all these as "heretics" living in a state of stubborn error and unworthy of serious attention, except to be taken out and burnt at the stake. But distinctions of "orthodoxy" and "heresy" depend on one's point of view;[13] and accusations of heresy (usually mutual) do not negate the fact that all who profess faith in Jesus, no matter how they articulate this faith (whether as Arians, or as Nestorians or as Monophysites, or as Roman Catholics, or Anglicans or Protestants) are authentic Christians, whose understanding of Jesus is an integral and indispensable part of the ecumenical Christian tradition. A theology which pretends to

be ecumenical cannot limit itself to the christological conceptions of one or the other church, or group of churches, no matter how important they might be for the moment.

3) This christological development, in which religious passion was so strongly contaminated by ecclesiastical rivalry and political ambition, and where theological argument was so frequently supplemented by mob violence and court intrigue,[14] took place within the compass of a single cultural tradition, what Raimundo Panikkar has called "the Mediterranean world and its cultural colonies,"[15] or as Karl Rahner more accurately describes it, the Hellenistic church.[16] Even the so-called oriental churches were Hellenistic in their theology even if Semitic in their language. The christologies of the Copts or the Syrians were different and opposite variants of Roman or Byzantine christology. For even in these "oriental" churches (which are not East but West, looked at from India or China or Japan!) theological discussion was pursued in the Greek categories, because these areas had already been absorbed into the Hellenistic world. Possibly the common people would have maintained links with their traditional culture and religions (as in India today, where the veneer of westernization of the so-called "educated classes" is paper thin), but the theologians (as also in India) were brought up to theologize in the dominant Hellenistic idiom. Christian theology is much less catholic than it imagines itself to be.

It is only with the end of the Vasco da Gama-age that non-Hellenistic theologies begin hesitatingly to appear. EATWOT has been a powerful midwife for these in the harsh Egypt of our North-dominated theological culture, where barrenness and infant mortality among non-establishment theologies is high. Because the Christian churches, by and large, are still far too dominated by the Northern ecclesiastical policies and academic forms, Third World theologies (except for Latin American liberation theology which has taken off and become, I believe, the most significant theology in the Christian world today) have yet to acquire a life and configuration of their own. Any useful christological contribution to a *Third World* spirituality will obviously have to break out of such northern domination. If it is to do this, it will not be able to draw on the christological tradition of the early church, which is Hellenistic, sectarian, and flawed by unacknowledged political biases, but will have to reach behind it to the New Testament, from which all Christian theology ultimately derives.

The New Testament

The New Testament too is, of course, culturally conditioned. It is largely a Hellenistic text with a Semitic (Aramaic) substratum. But, unlike the christological formulae of the early Christian tradition, the New Testament is a privileged text, accepted as sacred and normative by all Christian denominations. The New Testament is this because it expresses (it is believed) the faith-experience of the "apostolic church," that is, of the

Christian community at the privileged moment of its beginnings. It is, as it were, the constitution of the church, embodying (as the constitution of a nation state does) the salient features of the specific identity it assumed at the moment of its birth. A Christian community will remain to itself (that is, will be Christian) only as long as it remains true to the foundational experience of Jesus (understood both as object and subject) which brought it into being. But this originary experience (the faith experience of the apostolic community) is precisely what the New Testament embodies. For the New Testament is, by definition, made up of just those writings in which the community sees its originary faith experience authentically expressed.[17] The New Testament is thus the unique textual source for a genuinely ecumenical Christian theology.

The foundational experience of Jesus which is the basis of the whole Christian tradition is expressed in the New Testament in a variety of ways. For each New Testament writing has a christology (one might even say is a christology) which interprets and articulates Jesus' experience in response to the specific needs of its community. Since community settings differ and evolve, christologies are strikingly varied. They use a variety of *titles* drawn from various cultural backgrounds (Hebrew and Greek) to express the significance of Jesus (Son of God, Son of man, the eschatological Prophet); they compare Jesus to various Old Testament *types* to indicate his saving function (Jesus is the new Moses, the new Israel, the new Elisha, the new Solomon); and, rarely, they use concepts derived from Hellenistic Judaism or Hellenism to attempt a description of his being (the wisdom christology of Matthew and of Paul, the logos christology of John). By and large these christologies are largely functional, not (like the christologies of the post apostolic tradition) ontological. They are concerned more with describing the significance of Jesus (his role in saving history) rather than with explaining the structure of his being.[18]

Attempts have been made to organize the various New Testament christologies into a linear sequence, showing the development in christological thinking as Christianity grows out of its Palestinian homeland and enters the Hellenistic Jewish diaspora (Paul) and eventually the Gentile Hellenistic world (John). Raymond Brown has spelled out this development in terms of the progressive retrojection of the "Christological moment," that is the moment when Jesus was believed to have become the Christ.[19] Christological speculation was sparked off by the Easter-experience, however this is conceived. It was this that first awakened the followers of Jesus to his true significance. But then their understanding of Jesus as the Christ developed, it is suggested, gradually, and several stages can be noted in this development:

1) The first followers of Jesus were Palestinian Jews; they shared the standard messianic expectations of their people.[20] They believed that the risen Jesus would return shortly as the victorious political Messiah of the kind expected by their people. Jesus was not yet the Christ even after his

resurrection (he had not yet fulfilled Jewish messianic expectations), but he would return as the Christ in the near future. In Acts 3:19-21 Peter urges his Jewish listeners to repent so that "times of refreshing may come from the Lord and that he may send the Christ who has been appointed for you, Jesus who must remain in heaven until the time comes for God to restore everything he promised long ago." If the people repent, Peter claims, the risen Jesus will soon return as the triumphant Messiah. The christology implied in this curious and very ancient text (a fragment of an early Jewish Christian credal formula which Luke has incorporated into his description of Peter's speech) is thus a *future christology* whose christological moment is the Parousia.[21]

2) This future christology soon becomes a *present christology*. In the earliest formulae used in Christian preaching, as these have been preserved for us in the letters of Paul (Romans 1:3-4) or in the speeches of Peter and Paul reported in the Acts (Acts 2:32-36; 5:31; 13:32-33) Jesus becomes the Christ (the Son of God invested by the Spirit) at the Resurrection. Obviously he is a Christ very different from the one awaited in popular messianic expectation. He is now, in the Hellenistic Jewish Christianity of Paul, the heavenly Lord enthroned in heaven, ruling over his people through the power of his spirit, experienced by them in the cult. The political messiah of Judaism has been spiritualized. The kingdom of Jesus is not of this world; he liberates not from earthly oppression but from sin; his peace is "heavenly peace," tranquility of soul. The spiritualism of Greek thinking with its dichotomy of matter and spirit has begun to infect the holistic earthy spirituality of the Palestinian Christianity.

3) In subsequent moments of the tradition the christological moment is pushed further and further back into the pre-Easter life of Jesus. In the gospel of Mark, Jesus is already the Christ in his pre-Easter earthly existence, because he is anointed by the Spirit as "Son of God" or Messiah at his baptism (Mark 1:11-13). In the infancy narratives of Matthew (1:18) and Luke (1:35) he is the "Son of God" invested with the Spirit from the moment of his conception. A present christology thus becomes an increasingly *past christology*, as the christological moment is pushed back from Jesus' resurrection, to the beginning of his public ministry, and, last of all, to his conception. From the first moment of his existence (but not before, there is no suggestion of pre-existence in the synoptic Gospels) Jesus is the Christ. New understandings of messiahship are demanded by this retrojection of the christological moment. Jesus is the suffering Messiah who realizes his sonship in his death on the cross in Mark (15:39); he is incarnate Wisdom who exercises his messianic office by teaching the will of God in Matthew (11:28-30; 23:34). The title can be applied to Jesus only by doing violence to its original content!

4) The content is again radically transformed in John (for the Messiah in Jewish thinking is never divine) when, in the largely Gentile church for which he is writing, he presents Jesus as the pre-existent, divine Messiah,

the incarnation of the logos, the word made flesh: "the word became flesh and made his dwelling among us" (John 1:14). Past christology has become the *pre-existence christology* we are familiar with. Such pre-existence christology is, I believe, first found in John, though there may have been intimations of it earlier.[22] It is possible of course that there are references to pre-existence in the hymns quoted by Paul in Philippians 2:6-11 and Colossians 1:15-20. But this is not at all certain. For neither the Adam-christology of Philippians, nor the cosmic (or wisdom) christology of Colossians necessarily implies pre-existence. The hymn in Philippians interprets Jesus as the new Adam, like him in the image of God, but who unlike Adam does not grasp at divinity. The hymn in Colossians portrays Jesus in terms of Wisdom, the attribute of God associated with creation and salvation, which Hellenistic Judaism personifies, without making it a person distinct from God (Prov. 8:27-30; Wis. 8:4-6; Sir. 51:23-27). The exalted Christ is seen as the supreme manifestation of divine wisdom, the crown of creation and of saving history. "Jesus," as J.D.G. Dunn says, "is to be seen as the wise activity of God, as the expression and embodiment of God's wisdom more fully than any previous manifestation of the same wisdom whether in creation or in covenant."[23]

This rather simplified overview of the development of New Testament christology gives us a feel for the richness and complexity and relativity of the christological thinking in the New Testament, and suggests a number of lessons:

1) We realize how strongly *contextual* the christology of the New Testament is. New Testament Christology "evolves" under the influence of its environment. As long as the first Christians remained predominantly Jewish (whether in Palestine or in the Diaspora) they subscribed to its radical monotheism, and could not possibly have conceived of theology which would have made Jesus in any way divine. Palestinian Judaism looked for a future political Messiah (Acts 3:19-20) or saw Jesus as the eschatological prophet (Q). The most that Hellenistic Judaism (also radically monotheistic) would concede was the spirit christology of Matthew and Luke, according to which Jesus is conceived by the Spirit of a virgin, analogously to the conception of great figures in the Hebrew Bible from barren women; or the Wisdom (or cosmic) christology of Paul (1 Cor. 8:6; Col. 1:15-20) and possibly Matthew (Matt. 11:2-19; 11:28-30; 23:34) which sees Jesus as the supreme manifestation of God's wisdom. A divine, incarnate Jesus first appears in the Hellenistic and sectarian community of John. New Testament christology shows, to quote the provocative title of a recent work on the subject a movement "from Jewish Prophet to Gentile God."[24]

2) This scheme of an evolving christology, while it is useful for pointing out how New Testament christologies have changed with the changing context of the early church, must not be taken too literally. We must not suppose that New Testament christology evolved in the sense that it underwent a simple progression from the simple to the complex, or the

imperfect to the perfect, so that its earlier forms were rendered obsolete by later ones. The earlier christologies of the New Testament were not provisional christologies waiting to be superseded by others. The appearance of the logos christology of John does not make Mark's interpretation of Jesus as the suffering servant, or Q's interpretation of him as the eschatological prophet, irrelevant. These earlier christologies have been complemented by Johannine christology, not surpassed or "fulfilled" by it as non-Christian religions are sometimes said to be "fulfilled" (and therefore surpassed) by the coming of Christianity. The New Testament shows *a pluralism of christologies* (corresponding to the pluralism of theologies in a multi-religious world), in which each adds a new dimension to the christological whole, a new insight into the mystery of Christ, a new configuring of the gestalt of Jesus. The many christologies of the New Testament offer glimpses from various angles into the ineffable mystery of Christ, just as the various religious traditions of humankind offer glimpses from different standpoints into the inexhaustible and incomprehensible mystery of God.

3) Unlike traditional dogmatic christology, which is exclusive and works for the imposition of a single, "orthodox" christological model, New Testament christology is inclusive and pluriform. Every community evolves its own understanding of Jesus responding to its own cry for life. And because life changes christologies change too. The New Testament preserves all these different christologies, without opting exclusively for any one among them, because it does not wish to offer us (as dogmatic theology pretends to do) a finished product, to be accepted unquestionably by all. Rather its pluralism indicates a *christological open-endedness*, inviting us to discover our own particular christology, that is, the specific significance of Jesus for our situation in the Third World today. The New Testament, then, does not offer us a specific model for our christology, for its christological models are, historically and culturally, quite as conditioned as the christological formulae of early Christian tradition. It makes no more sense today (outside academic circles) to talk of Jesus as "Son of Man" or even "Son of God" or "the Word made flesh" than it would to talk of him (specially in advaitic India) as consubstantial with the Father, or (specially in the postmodern North) as having no human "personhood." Instead the New Testament gives us a model for our christologizing by mediating an encounter with Jesus, and inviting us to articulate his significance for us today in our own local language, just as the New Testament writings did in theirs. To follow Jesus one need not (to answer Panikkar's anguished question) become spiritually a Semite any more than one need become intellectually a Greek.[25]

4) At the heart of all the New Testament christologies lies an *experience of Jesus*, the impact he made on the first followers through his life and teaching, his death and his resurrection.[26] It is this total experience of Jesus, mediated to the New Testament authors through the communities to which they belonged, which was the starting point of their christology, as it has

to be of ours. Because the language of the New Testament is metaphorical, and is made up not of sharply defined concepts (like "nature" or "person") which are tied to a particular philosophical system and unintelligible outside it but of rich symbols (like "Son of God," "bread," "light," "life") which, while emerging from a particular culture are rooted in a common human experience and so can be transposed from one world view to another, the New Testament is able to communicate the experience of Jesus which underlies its many christologies to us. It is this trans-cultural *experience of Jesus* received (and inevitably interpreted by us in and for our situation) that must be the starting point of our christology as it was of theirs.[27]

Christology in the Third World Today

Our christological task, then, is not to repeat or elaborate the formulae of traditional christology (whose metaphysical categories make little sense for us in the Third World today), nor to adopt and adapt one or other christological model from the New Testament (whose christologies are expressly tied to particular communities living in concrete historical situations). Our task is to create new christologies, by confronting the cry for life which resounds in our Third World with our own experience of Jesus. The starting point of our christology is then the dialectic confrontation of our Jesus experience with our Third World situation. A word must be said about each.

The Third World Situation: The Cry for Life

The Third World situation in which our christology is to be elaborated has been correctly presented as a cry for life. This cry for life has, I suggest, three elements, related to the three basic dimensions that shape human life: the economic dimension which grounds our physical existence; the affective dimension which grounds our psychic life; and the symbolic or meaning-giving dimension which finds expression in our religious quest. A human being does not live by "bread alone"; he or she also needs the "word" that will affirm his or her dignity as a free human person, and will disclose what life is all about. Both bread and the word are urgently needed in a Third World marked by its massive economic poverty; its racist, sexist and caste discrimination (which cannot be reduced to merely economic factors, however much Marxists have tried to do this); and its pluriform religiosity, which throws up competing worlds of meaning. Its cry for life is a cry for survival, for recognition, and for meaning. It is a cry for liberation (economic and cultural) and for dialogue. It is within these parameters that Jesus must be interpreted for the Third World.

The Christian Experience of Jesus: The Jesus of Faith

The Jesus we try to interpret as a response to the Third World cry for life is not the "historical Jesus" unearthed for us by historical criticism, whose methods are much less effective, and whose results much less assured than is generally realized.[28] Nor is it the "Christ of faith" presented to us in the dogmatic or liturgical formulae of the churches, which are tied to world-views and ontologies that are not necessarily those shared by Third World Christians today. Instead, it will be what I venture to call "the Jesus of faith,"* that is, the Jesus presented to us in the confessional history of the New Testament, which is not necessarily identical with its critical history.[29] This Jesus is the real Jesus who lived in Palestine, but he is Jesus not simply as he "actually lived" (the *wie es ergenthon gewesen* of positivistic historiography), but as he was encountered and experienced by his first followers. That is why we speak of "Jesus" (not of "Christ"), but the Jesus of "faith" (not of "history"). The Jesus of faith is the Jesus of history as experienced by his faithful followers (and not, for example, as experienced by the religious and political leaders who opposed him). It is a category that lies between the Jesus of history and the Christ of faith, taking off from the Jesus of history and moving towards the interpretative explicitness of the Christ of faith.

Such a starting point avoids the danger of constructing our interpretations of Jesus on the continually shifting results of a supposedly neutral historical critical method, which, in fact, operates with its own unacknowledged biases;[30] and it allows us to build on the whole Jesus experience and not only on those aspects of it which are amenable to historical investigation (like his ministry and his death, but not his incarnation and his resurrection!). Obviously the Jesus of faith has to be continually adjusted to the faith of the community on the one hand, and the critical study of the gospels on the other. It emerges, in fact, in *the dialectic interaction of the critic's Jesus of history and the community's Christ of faith.*

Unlike the Jesus of history, which is the result of critical search for information (and so belongs to the noetic level of speculation), the Jesus of faith is the object of an experience (and belongs to the level of personal encounter). If our christology is not to be an academic exercise which leaves us and our world untouched (as the immensely greater part of Northern theology does) it must start off not from information but from experience. The Jesus we interpret must be a Jesus we "know," not just a Jesus we know about. As Raimundo Panikkar has put it:

> The identity (read "the experience") of Christ we are looking for is not that which comes from accurate historical information, nor even what a philosophical scrutiny of his words and doctrines may yield concerning who he is, but the identity which is found in the encounter with a person, that knowledge which springs up when we really know and love somebody, which is more than, and different from, the results of all examination of the objective data.[31]

But Panikkar's formulation tends to be over-individualistic. The experience of Jesus of faith is not to be confused with the subjective experience of the individual. It is, and in this it differs from that personal experience of enlightenment which is a primary religious category in Asian religions, a *community experience*. The Jesus of faith is the community's Jesus, who is encountered in the living faith of the local Christian community, of which scripture and tradition are constitutive parts, and where faith meets scholarship in a mutually corrective tension. The theologian reads the New Testament not as a neutral scholar, but as a critical believer steeped in a tradition, who has encountered Jesus in the Christian life of his or her community, confronts this experience with the biblical text read critically, and reflects on the implications of this critically corrected Jesus experience for the world in which he lives. All this is done as part of a holistic, organic doubly dialectical process, in which (1) the Jesus of faith emerges through the dialectic interaction of our lived experience of Jesus and the study of the gospel text about him, and (2) a meaningful christology develops through the dialectical encounter between the Jesus of faith and the world in which he is experienced and proclaimed.

The place in which the Jesus of faith is encountered and a Third World christology elaborated is, therefore, not primarily the academy and its search for the Jesus of history, nor merely the church in its worship of the Christ of Faith, but the *community* which is shaped by and gives expression to the experience of Jesus in the totality of its life, its worship, its study and its action. Christological theory presupposes (and is presupposed by) christological faith and *praxis*. That is why Third World christologies cannot be produced in classrooms, nor in theological conferences like ours, but only in Christian communities, where Jesus Christ is encountered, experienced and "lived."

These communities in which Jesus is actively experienced and understood are, I would suggest, not merely communities of professing Christians, like the basic Christian communities of the Christian Third World (in Latin America, the Philippines, and parts of Africa); but also (in the massive non-Christian Third World, elsewhere in Asia and Africa) communities of those who profess basic human values (freedom, love and justice), which ultimately are what Jesus proclaimed, lived by, and died for. For is not Christianity after all ultimately a "true humanism," in which Jesus tells us what the human person in the nexus of its relationships with God, fellow humans and the cosmos should aspire to be? Such basic human communities will, I believe, carry the christological quest a great step forward. For Jesus, as Mahatma Gandhi has said, "belongs not only to Christianity, but to the entire world."[32] Incomparable christological insights into his significance for the suffering world have been given, not least by Mahatma Gandhi himself;[33] by non-Christian social activities like Baba Amte, winner of the Magsaysay award, whose impressive work for the rehabilitation of lepers was inspired, he confesses, by his reading of the gospel;[34] or even by a notorious pop-guru like the Osho Rajneesh, whose eight books on Jesus, though they always trumpet the Osho's own tantric-advaita, abound in extraordinary creative insights (unavailable elsewhere) into what Jesus means today.[35] A great wealth of christological material lies untapped in the christological insight and the christological praxis of such "outsiders" who, like the centurion in Matthew 8:5-13, have come to know Jesus, even though they are not numbered among his followers; or in the "precursors" of Jesus (like Nachiketas of the *Katha-Upanishad!*) which a discerning Christian can find in extra-biblical religious texts. It is here that dialogue enters into the christological process.

Such dialogue, and the Third World christology it nourishes, will focus on the "mystery" of Jesus, not on the "mechanisms" that have been put forward to explain this mystery. By "mystery" is meant the person of Jesus, or the events in his confessional history (like his incarnation, the cross, the resurrection) in as much as these are enduring sources of significance for the person who seeks to "understand" them. "Mechanisms" are the models that have been proposed to explain the mystery, like the two natures in one person of Chalcedon or the popular understanding of the resurrection as the reunion of the soul of Jesus to his resuscitated body. Mysteries mediate significance; mechanisms offer explanations. Mysteries are therefore articulated in metaphors (like "Son of God," "the Word made Flesh"); mechanisms are articulated in precisely defined concepts that depend on specific ontologies. Mysteries unite, for all Christians assent to and find life in Jesus as savior, and believe in his incarnation, cross, resurrection, however differently they may understand them; mechanisms (as the history of theology amply shows) divide, because they are tied to specific culturally conditioned world views. The incarnation would be understood very differently in the non-dualistic Indian world from the way it has been understood in the dualistic Greek one, or is understood in the post-enlightenment secular world. The resurrection was understood as the emergence of a shade from the world of the dead (*sheol*) into the world of the living (the new heavens and the new earth) in the Palestinian world of Jesus; it was reconceptualized as the reunion of an "immortal soul" surviving in "heaven" after the dissolution of the body, with a recreated earthly body in the Hellenistic world of the post-apostolic church. Mysteries endure but mechanisms change. Mysteries belong to what Schillebeeckx has called "theologies of Jesus," which focus on the significance of Jesus of Nazareth; mechanisms belong to what he calls "christologies," which propose models to explain the divinity of Christ.[36] A christology which hopes to contribute to a spirituality that is both Third World and ecumenical, relevant to Third World concerns and acceptable across denominational groups, cannot afford to get lost in the "network of metaphysical clouds"[37] that invest mechanisms, but must focus on the mystery of Jesus. It is after all the mystery that counts. For while mechanisms as provisional models may satisfy the human craving for intellectual clarity, it is the mystery that gives life and endures.

Traditional christology has moved from mystery to mechanism. In a postmodern situation which is suspicious of mechanisms, and in a Third World which has learned at its expense how quickly preoccupation with "explanation" blunts the prophetic edge of the "Word," Third World theology would usefully adopt an alternative process, a "hermeneutical circle," which moves from experience/praxis to mystery and back to experience. It is in terms of such a hermeneutics of the mystery of Jesus presented in the gospels that the following christological meditation on the Jesus of faith has been attempted, as a possible way towards a Third World christology, but here (as in so much of Third World theologizing), there really is no way. The way, as the poet has said, is made by going.

A Meditation on the Jesus of Faith

Every religious tradition begins with an originary experience of the Absolute Mystery that we name God. The Christian tradition too begins with Jesus' experience of God. What we call an experience of God is not an insight into the "being" of God or into the ontological structure of reality. For God is not to be thought of as a "being" out there, standing over and against us, to whom we relate as we might relate to other human beings. God is not someone we can "objectify," measure, gather information about, study. God is the absolute mystery in whom we have our being.

The Experience of God

God is, therefore, as all religious traditions tell us, absolutely transcendent, irreducible to any created category, always beyond name and form. To see God, says the Bible, is to die. The Tao that can be known is not the real Tao. Kiteme, the Luo diviner tells the missionary, "is totally different and apart from humankind and apart from all creation." The Buddha when questioned about the existence of God answers with a smile.

We cannot therefore properly speak of God, but may only invoke him. His name, it has been said, is justified only in the vocative. For God is not a "he" or a "she" or an "it" but an I, indeed *the* "I." God is the I-am, the I-am-who-am, the *aham*. God is therefore not the one spoken about; rather the one who speaks. God is the I who speaks and each of us is a spoken thou of God. Every one of us is the "thou art" uttered by the "I am."

As such, God is not only utterly transcendent but wholly immanent as well. God is origin and the goal of the cosmos and of history (Isa. 1:1). God must not be thought of as distinct from the universe as the crypto dualism (the standing temptation) of our Christian myth invites us to do. Neither is he wholly identical with it, as the monism, which is the standing temptation of oriental religion, supposes. God and the universe are not one; nor are they two. For whatever metaphor we adopt (creator-creature, whole-part, soul-body), God cannot be enumerated side by side with the world.

When we speak about "God" we are not therefore speaking of a being distinct from, other than the world. We are speaking of "the ground of our being," the infinite horizon of our self transcending existence, the ultimate meaning of life, the absolute value. Any statement about God is always a statement about the world.

An experience of God is therefore not so much an insight into the ontological structure of reality; it is an insight into the meaning of life; telling us what life is all about, offering us a guide for living, showing us the way (*hodos, tao, marga*). Theologians of course will offer us mechanisms to explain the experience, and construct elaborate metaphysical edifices using the conceptual bricks they have at hand. These may or may not be useful but they are not to be confounded with the experience they are attempting to explain, which can allow for other alternative mechanisms. The experience is an immediate contact with the reality of experience, so that the distinction between the experiencing subject and the object experienced disappears. It needs no demonstration, no argument, no explanation. The explanation is not the mechanism.

The God-Experience of Jesus

Jesus experienced God as unconditional love. He did this, probably, at his baptism by John, at a moment when, in a great act of solidarity he identified himself with sinful Israel (Mark 1:9-11). The experience irrupted into his life, shattering (as all such call experiences do) the ordinary patterns of existence, and impelling him to adopt the life of an itinerant charismatic preacher who announced in word and deed (in miracle and in parable, in table fellowship with outcasts and in aphoristic teaching), the imminent coming of the Kingdom of God, that is of God's long awaited definitive act of salvation. His God-experience allowed Jesus to address God as "abba" (loving parent), a name which is an invocation, not a description (as all divine names must be), and which tells us more about our own alienated situation and the way to redeem it than it tells us about the absolute mystery about God. "Abba" is the normal invocation Jesus henceforth used to address God, and to speak about God (Luke 10:21; Mark 14:36; John 11:41). In a religious tradition which stressed the transcendence of God to such an extent that his name was never spoken, this usage of Jesus was absolutely unique. God is never addressed as "Parent" in the Hebrew Bible. He/She is addressed as "Father" with a qualification ("Our father in the heavens" or "Our Father our King") in rabbinic texts of the time of Jesus. But nowhere in Jewish tradition is God ever addressed simply as "Father," much less by the far more informal and intimate locution "Abba." The language of Jesus is unique and points to a unique experience of God.

Like every great religious teacher, Jesus shares this experience with his not always receptive followers. "No one knows the parent but the child," he says, and those whom the child has chosen to reveal the parent" (Matt. 11:25). Jesus claims to "know" the Parent. In biblical language to "know" means to "experience," "to enter into an intimate relationship with," a relationship as intimate as that between man and woman in the closeness of the act of love (Gen. 4:1). Jesus therefore experiences God as a loving parent; and he gifts this experience to those who follow him.

Indeed to be a follower of Jesus means precisely to share in this God-experience of his. What makes a person a Christian is not professing certain beliefs, nor practicing particular rituals, nor undergoing an initiation rite, nor belonging to a recognizable social group, nor even confessing the name of Jesus, though all these are inevitable stages in the evolution of a religious tradition. To be a disciple of Jesus means *to experience God the way that Jesus experienced God*. That is why one can say "Lord, Lord" and prophesy in the name of Jesus, or cast out demons in his name or do many mighty works in his name, and still not be acknowledged by him as his follower (Matt. 7:21-24); and one may not have known Jesus at all and yet be recognized as one of his own, because one has fed the hungry, given shelter to the homeless, clothed the naked, cared for the sick and visited those in prison (Matt. 25:31-46). The routinization of charism, inevitable in the development of any movement, has transformed the community of disciples which Jesus gathered around him into a proliferating mass of competing (often squabbling) churches, defining themselves in terms of points of doctrine (*homoousios* or *homoiousios*), practices of ritual (communion under one species or under two), or issues of organization (monarchical papacy, collegial episcopacy or 'democratic' presbyterate). In the process we have perhaps forgotten that the one thing necessary for Christian self-definition is the experience of God's love which impels us to love in return and to reach out in effective compassion to those in need. But Jesus has not forgotten this. His fellowship is not limited to the churches which carry (and too often profane) his name. It reaches out to the many who will "come from east and west, and from north and south and sit at table in the kingdom of God" (Luke 13:29).

The Freedom of Jesus

The God-experience of Jesus frees him. For love experienced always leads to a freedom from inner conditioning, that is, from the compulsions and fears that hold us in bondage. For are not such bondages the result of an absence of love? Are not the concupiscence of the eyes (our consumerism) and the concupiscence of the flesh (our eroticism) ultimately compensation mechanisms through which we strive to make up for the emptiness caused by the absence of love in our lives; and is not the pride of life (our macho assertiveness and craving for power) ultimately a defense mechanism through which we try to cover up the absence of self worth we experience because we lack love? Is not the poverty of our people the result of such greed and the structures of exploitation it engenders? Is not their social rejection on grounds of race, caste or gender, and the profound psychic scars this leaves a result of "patriarchy," the urge to dominate, and of the vast structures of domestic and societal oppression it creates? Does not our unfreedom make others unfree? Does not Mammon (personal bondage) generate (and is it not generated by) Satan (structured evil)? Love leads to freedom (to personal freedom and ultimately to structural freedom) because it frees us from the constraints and fears, the doubts and compulsions that paralyze us.

Jesus, who has experienced God as love, was supremely free. We marvel at his freedom. He was driven by no demons of greed or ambition. "The Son of Man has nowhere to lay his head," he said (Luke 9:58), describing the state of religious indigence that he had freely chosen. "The Son of Man has come not to be served but to serve and to lay down his life as a ransom for many," he announced (Mark 10:45), offering a neat and pointed summary of his life and mission. In a society that was politically colonized, socially patriarchal, and religiously conservative, he moved around with absolute freedom and authority. His freedom is all the more remarkable because he lacked position or power. Jesus had no religious prestige: he was not a priest born into a priestly family. He enjoyed no intellectual status: he was not a recognized theologian who had been trained in a scribal school (John 7:15). He commanded no political power. He did not enjoy the privileges of wealth. Yet he taught with authority in word and deed. "The crowds were astonished at his teaching," we are told on the occasion of the first miracle he performed, (so Mark 1:2); and of the first "sermon" he delivered (Matt. 7:28), "because he taught as one having authority and not as the scribes." The scribes of course had great authority, because of their patiently acquired knowledge of the Torah and of the oral traditions which had grown up around it. But the authority of Jesus was not like theirs. It was not "legal" authority based on learning and institutional sanction. It was charismatic and prophetic authority derived from his experience of God. The authority of Jesus (as he will explicitly affirm when challenged by the priests to justify his cleansing of the temple) is associated with his baptism by John, that is, it derives from his foundational experience of God (Mark 11:27-33).

This authority of Jesus (a significant christological element) enables him to confront the religious, social and political establishment of his people with sovereign freedom. He reinterprets the Law with an authority which seems to parallel the authority of God. "It was said to them of old" (that is, "God said to our ancestors"), he announces, quoting not just rabbinic interpretations of the law but the written law itself (Matt. 5:21, 27, 31, 33, 38), and then goes on to correct this with his "but I say to you" (Matt. 5:21-48). No prophet has ever spoken like this. The prophets spoke in God's name, with God's authority, communicating God's message. "Thus says the Lord" was the prophet's way of speaking; but Jesus says: "I say unto you." Even if these antitheses of Matthew's Sermon on the Mount may be editorial compositions formulated at a time when Jesus was already interpreted as the founder of the new Israel standing over and against the formative Judaism of Yahweh representing the old, they carry the memory of the remarkable authority that Jesus must have shown in his interpretation of the Law.

Such authority is very evident in the Sabbath controversies which were a conspicuous feature of Jesus' ministry, attested to in all the gospel traditions (Mark 2:23-28; 3:1-6; Luke 13:10-17; John 5:1-18; 9:1-34). Jesus breaks the Sabbath whenever human need demands it, justifying his infringement of the sacred law of Sabbath rest with the radical principle that "the Sabbath is made for the human person not the human person for the Sabbath" (Mark 2:27). Every human institution or law (no matter how sacred) is thus subordinated to human need.

The pervasive law of purities which so restricted every aspect of Jewish life is abrogated by Jesus in the single striking observation that "nothing which enters anyone from the outside can make the person unclean: it is what comes out of the person that makes him or her unclean" (Mark 7:15). All purity lines are thus abolished in a stroke. Cleanness or uncleanness is not a matter of ritual purity, but of the disposition of the heart. "Nothing in itself is unclean," as Paul rightly understands Jesus to have said (Rom. 14:14). No *places* are of themselves holy, for God is to be worshiped not in Jerusalem or in Gerizim, but in spirit and in truth (John 4:21-23), wherever, that is, a community assembles in sincerity and love. No *person* is more sacred than another, for there is only one Parent God, and all humankind are brothers and sisters (Matt. 23:8-10). There is here a radical desacralization of the cosmos, a radical dehierarchization of society (that is, a radical affirmation of the equality of humankind) and a radical shift from an ethics of observance (ritual and legal) to an ethics of love ("the heart").

In a patriarchal society where *women* were numbered with children and slaves as "minors" with diminished responsibility and a restricted role in worship and in public life, Jesus admits them into his movement as helpers and disciples. Not only do women follow him to take care of his needs (Luke 8:2), but Mary who sits at his feet listening to what he teaches (and so assuming the role of a disciple) is commended for having chosen the "better part" (Luke 10:38-42). Even in a tradition which has suffered heavy editing, colored by patriarchal biases, the role of women in the gospels is striking. Three conspicuous incidents in the ministry of Jesus, each heavy with theological significance, feature women (John 4:4-42; 7:36-50; Mark 3:11). In all these the women are not only occasions of significant teaching, but emerge favorably in comparison with their male counterparts. The spontaneous testimony of the Samaritan woman, who after conversing with Jesus proclaims him as the Christ to her people (John 4:28-30) contrasts with the embarrassed silence of the disciples who do not care to question Jesus (John 4:27); the moving love shown to Jesus by the woman who "had lived a sinful life" but shows by her loving actions that she is a forgiven sinner who has experienced God's forgiving love, is contrasted by Jesus with the indifference of Simon the Pharisee, whose unloving behavior shows him to be the real unforgiven "sinner," one who cannot love because he has not experienced forgiveness. The sensitive loyalty as shown to Jesus on the eve of his passion by the woman in Bethany contrasts sharply with the ideological fixation of the disciples and the disloyalty of Judas. This contrast is carried a great step further in the stories of the passion and resurrection, where the women disciples of Jesus are found at the cross and his tomb when the male disciples have all abandoned him and fled (Mark 15:4-41, 47; 16:1-8).

Where the Pharisees (the Jews of strict observance) and the Essenes of Qumran sought to renew their society through a rigorism that sought to enforce the observance of the Law as strictly as possible, Jesus opted for a *radicalism* which sought to realize as perfectly as possible the spirit of the Law, which he saw embodied in love (*agape*), that is in inter-human concern.

The Love (Agape) of Jesus

That is why Jesus can sum up his ethic in his love commandment (Matt. 22:34-40) which he formulates by joining the great text of Judaism in Deuteronomy 6:4-5 ("The Lord your God is one God and you shall love the Lord your God with all your heart, with all your soul and with all your mind") to a little known text from the Holiness Code of Leviticus, Lev. 19:18 ("You shall love your neighbor as yourself"). As understood by Jesus this commandment does not ask us to love God and neighbor as if there were to be two different objects to our love. Rather Leviticus 19:18 is meant to be an interpretation of Deut. 6:4-5. The content of Deuteronomy ("You shall Love the Lord your God with all your heart") is spelled out by Leviticus ("You shall love your neighbor as yourself"). The love command of Jesus therefore reads: "You shall love the Lord your God with all your heart, with all your soul, and with all your mind, this means, you shall love your neighbor as yourself." To love God means, concretely, to love neighbor. The one commandment that Jesus gives us as the "great commandment," the one that founds and includes all the others is, then, that we *love God by loving neighbor.*

"Who, then, is my neighbor?" Is not this for Jesus a question as significant as that other christological question he will ask "Who do you say I am?" In defining "neighbor" Jesus allows no distinctions of caste, race, gender or class (Luke 10:30-37). For the love with which we love neighbor is not a human disposition (determined by human prejudices or preference) but it is the reflex of the experience of God's love for us. To the extent we experience God's love, we love neighbor the way that God loves us. But God loves us unconditionally. His love is not a response to our goodness. "God does not love us because we are good," as Augustine has somewhere said, "we are good because God loves us." God loves because God is love. God's love is not a reaction but an action. God loves the way the sun shines because it must. That is why our love for neighbor, which issues from (1 John 4:4) and images (Matt. 5:43-48) God's love for us, can make no conditions and put no limits. It reaches out to the unrewarding, undeserving, even those hostile to us (Luke 6:32-36).

But by "love" Jesus does not understand friendship or fellowship or erotic passion, all the other human affects which (more or less correctly) are understood as "love" today. The *agape* which the New Testament uses as its own very special term stands rather for an active, effective concern. It is best understood perhaps as the attitude of those who, because they have experienced God as Parent, experience (and not merely talk about) their fellow human beings as brothers and sisters and spontaneously respond to their needs. Like the Buddhist attitude of "mindfulness" the Christian attitude of "agape" is thus an existential attitude deriving from a change in one's being. The change is not (normally) a sudden one and for all transformation (as a "conversion" is usually understood to be), but a life-time's process of growth. Christian life is a life-long lesson in love.

Agape then is effective love. The New Testament defines it as "doing good to" (Luke 6:35; 1 Thess. 5:15) and understands this (as the parable of the Good Samaritan shows) as responding effectively to the real needs of the people we encounter. Love embraces the effective response to the whole spectrum of needs that we observe around us. Because it is increasingly evident that the effective response to many of our most urgent needs is necessarily a structural one, justice understood as a change of structures is an inescapable dimension of *agape*.

Jesus and Justice

Jesus may not have been as aware as we are aware today of the structural origins of the evils of the society in which he lived. But he was committed to justice and to structural change because his proclamation of the Kingdom implied the vision of a new society. The Kingdom that he announced was the realization of the "alternative community" previsioned in biblical history at the Exodus, where the Israelite was liberated from bondage in Egypt that it might become God's people (Exodus 6:2-7); and frequently invoked by the prophets who appear precisely when the monarchy has reversed the thrust of the Exodus (1 Sam 8:6-18; 1 Kings 5:13) to protest against the perversion of the community that Israel was meant to be (Isa. 3:13-15; Amos 2:6-8; Micah 2:1-1). The proclamation of the Kingdom by Jesus is both a promise and summons, looking towards the ultimate realization of this alternative community, depicted in the core metaphor of "the family of God," which is implicit in all the teaching of Jesus.

As part of the realization of this vision, Jesus (who shares the apocalyptic world-view of the time) sees the coming of the Kingdom of God as the end of Satan's rule. Satan is the "prince of the world" (John 12:31), ruling the world through demons and demonic people. Satan stands for structured evil, organized might (the "legion" of Mark 5:1-20). It is this satanic power-structure that Jesus combats through his controversies and his healings and exorcisms. The miracles of Jesus are therefore not to be taken as isolated actions of compassion (relief work). As such, the thirty or so healings and exorcisms that Jesus performed would not have amounted to very much. Rather they are an indication that God's rule has dawned and that Satan's rule has ended. "The strong man has been bound and his goods taken away" (Mark 3:27). The satanic power structure has been destroyed. The miracles of Jesus are thus the subversion of a power structure and so manifestations of a structural change.

Love as exercised by Jesus inevitably leads to conflict. This is because love, though it is universal in its object, is differentiated in its action. The *agape* of Jesus reaches out indeed to all. But it affects people in different ways. The same love which prompts Jesus to say "Blessed are the poor" leads him to announce "Woe to you rich" (Luke 6:20-27). The concern he shows when he identifies his mission as the proclamation of the good news to the poor (Luke 4:16; Matt. 11:5) is paralleled by the concern implied in his warning that "it is easier for a camel to pass through the eye of a needle than for the rich to enter the kingdom of God" (Mark 19:26). In an unequal world where class, caste, and race and gender conflicts exist, love must take sides. For nothing is more unjust (or more unloving), it has been said, than to divide equally among unequals, or treat oppressor and oppressed alike. The love of Jesus leads him to make (as the God of Bible makes) an unambiguous option for the poor and the outcast, because they are as the Bible sees them, always victims of oppression.

Because of this self-defining option, the life of Jesus is lived out in the twin dimensions of *solidarity and conflict*. These are the complementary expressions of his God-experience. The gospels show Jesus living a life of progressive identification with the poor and of growing conflict with those who oppress them.

Solidarity with the Poor: Incarnation

Born into what we would call a *petit bourgeois* family (the class of artisans, who own the tools of their trade), Jesus de-classes himself by becoming an itinerant religious beggar with nowhere to lay his head (Luke 9:58). He breaks with his family to join the family of God, made up of all those who do the will of God, which is to love (Mark 3:31-35). He abandons himself wholly to God's provident care (Matt. 6:28-34); depending for his livelihood on the casual help provided by sympathizing friends (Luke 38:1-2). A would-be religious teacher, he associates with outcasts, becoming an untouchable with the untouchables. He touches a leper (incurring ritual uncleanness) to welcome him back to human fellowship (Mark 1:40-42). He dines with the ritually unclean and socially ostracized tax-collectors and sinners, incurring the hostility of the religious elite: "this man receives sinners," they say, "and eats with them" (Luke 15:2; Mark 2:16).

The solidarity of Jesus with the poor and the outcasts finds its christological symbol in the *incarnation*. This particular "mystery" of the confessional history of Jesus has been best expressed in the marvelous Johannine *sutra*: "The word was made flesh *(sarx)*, and dwelt *(eskenosen)* among us. The Word (whose identity is never disclosed except in Jesus) does not become a male *(aner)*; nor even a human person *(anthropos)*. The Word becomes flesh *(sarx)*. Flesh stands for humankind, indeed for all life, in its transience and fragility. "All flesh is as grass," says the prophet, "and its beauty is like the flower of the field; the grass withers, the flower fades, but the word of our God endures forever" (Isa. 40:3). The word of God's creation, challenge, and love, which endures forever, becomes fleeting flesh.

But flesh also stands for *solidarity and relatedness*. Man and wife become one flesh (Gen. 2:24); members of a family are of the same "flesh and blood" (Gen. 37:27); the poor and needy of our people are our own flesh (Isa. 58:7). Flesh stands for the solidarity of humankind, for the fact that humankind is not a collection of isolated individuals, but an organic whole in which what happens to one happens to all. If the Word became flesh, it has graced, as Athanasius remarked, the whole human race. Humankind has now become the proper locus of our encounter with God. We meet God in neighbor; we love God by loving neighbor.

The individualism of Hellenistic philosophy, reinforced by the selfish individualism of bourgeois society, and legitimized by a psychology of personal fulfillment, which insists on the distinction between the "I" and the "you" ("I am I and you are you"), but forgets the oneness of the "we" ("you and I are we"), has made us forget this. We think of the incarnation, only in its implication for Jesus as an isolated individual. Jesus is then made the God-Man (or even God appearing as a human being), who becomes the God of the Christians, much in the way that, say, Krishna is a god of the Hindus. The challenge of his human life is lost. He becomes the object of our devotion but no longer a paradigm for action so that Christian life comes to mean worshiping Jesus, not following him. But the incarnation (whatever its mechanism) must be seen primarily as a call to follow Jesus in his solidarity with humankind, expressed concretely through a consistent and progressive identification with the outcasts and the poor.

Conflict with the Powerful: The Cross

The solidarity of Jesus with these victims of economic, social and political oppression is not merely a passive solidarity which assumes and endures their lot. It leads to a confrontation with the religious and political establishment which oppresses them, and to a struggle with Satan (structured evil) and Mammon (the mental causes of capitalism) which in his world view are the ultimate sources of oppression. Jesus confronts the *theological establishment* (the scribes) to free people from a burdensome interpretation of the ritual and moral law (Mark 2:1-3:6); the *religious establishment* (the chief priests) and their misuse of the temple, to protest against the exploitation of the people in the name of religion (Mark 11:15-19); and the *political establishment* (Herod) whose threat to kill him (a clear sign of the political impact of his ministry) he dismisses with contempt (Luke 13:31-33). The life of Jesus is thus riddled with conflict. Indeed conflict spills over even into the gospel narrative of his infancy, (Matt. 2:1-23; Luke 1:27-32), and finds its resolution only with the death of Jesus on the cross.

The *cross* is no arbitrary intrusion into the life of Jesus. It is the natural outcome of a life of solidarity with the poor and the outcasts and of confrontation with the powerful who oppress them. Conflict with the rich and the powerful leads inevitably to the fatal confrontation which could only end with a foreseen and freely accepted death. And this death becomes the appropriate fulfillment of a life lived out with and for the poor and the outcasts. For on the cross Jesus is wholly poor and totally outcast. Identification and confrontation have here reached their furthest possible limits. Jesus is one with all the marginalized and all the martyred victims of the earth. The journey from the center to the periphery which, as Kosuke Koyama reminds us, was the basic movement of his life, now reaches its goal. A life of freedom and love expressing itself in a radical identification with the poor and the outcasts and a resolute confrontation with all the oppressive powers of the world arrives at its paradoxical outcome baffling all human calculation, where "[God's] power is made perfect in weakness" (2 Cor. 12:9); and where "the foolishness of God is [shown to be] wiser than the human wisdom and the weakness of God stronger than human strength" (1 Cor. 1:25). For the cross shows forth not just the death of Jesus but announces his resurrection as well.

The Goal of Life: The Resurrection

The resurrection, of course, escapes the net of history. Unless it is conceived as the resuscitation of a corpse it is not an observable, locatable event which can be grasped by the historian's empirically oriented tools. It is, however, accessible through the two past historical traces it has left (the empty tomb and the appearances of Jesus to his first disciples), both of which can be reached (though not easily) through the confused, sometimes contradictory and not easily decipherable stories about them in the gospels. But above all, the resurrection is accessible to us in our present experience of the living Jesus, which assures us that *Jesus is alive.* "The resurrection is not a doctrine that we try to prove or a problem that we argue about," Thomas Merton has said. "It is the life of Christ himself in us by the Spirit."

Rooted in the past event of Jesus, made actual in the present experience of his living presence among us, the resurrection grounds our hope for the future, turning, as Leonardo Boff would say, all our *utopias* ("nowheres") into *topias* ("somewheres"). But this faith experience which grounds our hope is only available to us in a life of love. Because it anticipates the end of history, the resurrection, God's final and overwhelming answer to our cry for life, "can be understood only through a praxis that seeks to trans-form the world" (Sobrino).

Indeed the mystery of Jesus can be grasped only through praxis, because Jesus is essentially the way. It is not in constructing theoretical models about his being that we "understand" Jesus (indeed these alienate us from him) but in following him in the life of solidarity and conflict that is his way to life. All true christology is ultimately grounded on christo-praxis. It is in communities walking this way that we shall discover (as Aloysius Pieris has already told us) the "names" that we are to give Jesus in the Third World today.

Because our understanding of Jesus emerges in the dialectic of the Jesus of faith and the cry for life, it is unlikely that in Asia and possibly Africa this understanding of Jesus will be an exclusive one. Jesus is a saving name for the Absolute Mystery as it is experienced by us. But the inexhaustible Absolute Mystery has, as Hinduism teaches, a thousand saving names. Is not the radical Freedom (the total silencing of all desire), which the Buddha realized through strenuous mindfulness, as much a name of God as the unconditional Love which was the name revealed to us in Jesus? For six hundred million people it is. Or the ongoing current of pulsing Life received with awe and cherished with joy by the great indigenous religions of Africa, is not that too a name for God? Or again, the total harmony of the cosmos that the Chinese sages Confucius, or Lao-Tzu, or Mencius envisaged, does not that too name Absolute Mystery? All these names speak to us of the incredible richness of the religious experience of humankind, which throws up forms of religiosity as abundantly as the flowers in a forest. To fight about the superiority of one or the other of these would seem neither practical nor wise. Indeed the problem of the uniqueness of Christ as discussed in theology today seems to me an academic problem with little significance (for no one doubts that salvation exists outside the Christian community, and whether or not it is through "Christ" operating in some mysterious way, or does not really seem to matter), and of much presump-tion (for it presumes to know the mind of God). In Asia at least, it's God (not Christ) who will always remain at the center. That is why perhaps Asians have produced no notable christologies but many "theologies." The true "uniqueness" of Christ is the uniqueness of the way of solidarity and struggle (a way that is neither male nor female), that Jesus showed as the way to life. That uniqueness cannot be argued about but must be lived. We "follow" Jesus along this way because we have experienced the Absolute Mystery in him and have realized that his way is indeed the way of life. We invite others to walk along with us and share the experience we have had without affirming this is the only way or the best one. "The whole world is pervaded by the glory of the Lord," says the Isavasya Upanishad. It is when we forget this and reduce the Absolute Mystery to the dimensions of our own understanding that the saving name becomes a slogan, and christology instead of being a way to life becomes an ideology of death. *"Fullness there; fullness here; fullness from fullness comes. Take fullness from fullness, fullness still remains" (Isavasya Upanishad).*

Notes

1. For a useful survey of contemporary approaches to christology see J.A. Fitzmyer, *Scripture and Christology: A Statement of the Biblical Commission with a Commentary* (NY: Paulist, 1986), pp. 54-96.

2. Although occurring for the first time in John in this clear and explicit form the mystery of the incarnation is foreshadowed in Matthew's theme of Jesus as Emmanuel (1:23; 18:12; 28:20); in Paul's affirmation that "God was in Christ reconciling the world to himself" (2 Cor 15:15); and in Mark's eschatological *jus talionis* (sentence of holy law) which declares that a stance taken vis-à-vis Jesus will be sanctioned by corresponding eschatological consequence (Mark 8:38). A basic feature of the Jesus experience communicated in the New Testament is thus the conviction (expressed most clearly in the extreme and paradoxical form of the Johannine sutra) that in Jesus we encounter God comes into our world.

3. W.H.C. Frend, *The Early Church* (Philadelphia: Fortress, 1982), p. 233.

4. M. Wiles, *Working Papers in Doctrine* (London: SCM Press, 1976), pp. 39-40.

5. For a history of the christological controversies, see A. Grillmeier, *The Christian Tradition. Volume One. From the Apostolic Age to Chalcedon,* (Atlanta: John Knox, 1975) pp. 153-554; J. Pelikan, *The Christian Tradition, 1. The Emergence of the Catholic Tradition [100-600]* (Chicago: University Press, 1971), pp. 226-277; H. Lietzmann, *From Constantine to Julian [A History of the Early Church. Volume III]* (London: Lutterworth, 1950), pp. 94-136.

6. Grillmeier (no. 5 above), p. 251: "A historico-political theology emerges: the appearance of the Messiah and imperial peace, Christianity and the empire are bound together in an indissoluble unity by the idea of providence. We already saw hints of this in Melito and Origen. Eusebius provides the theory."

7. Nicea was attended by about 220 bishops from the East but only 5 from the West (Lietzmann, no. 5 above, pp. 116-17); Chalcedon in 451 by 520 bishops, of whom only the four papal legates were from the West (Frend, no. 3 above, p. 230). The first ecumenical councils had almost no Western bishops; those of the second millennium hardly any from the East.

8. The extent of Constantine's influence on conclusions of the council is disputed, but in spite of Grillmeier's elaborate apologia of the council's independence (no. 5 above, pp. 250-264) it was certainly considerable. Even the crucial expression *homoousios* (one in substance) with the father, which has become the basic expression of christological belief in the Christian tradition and a source of trouble in subsequent generations, appears to have been inserted into the council decrees at his behest, Pelikan (no. 5 above), pp. 201-202; Lietzmann (no. 5 above), pp. 118-119; Frend (no. 3 above), pp. 140-141.

9. Frend (no. 3 above), pp. 212-13. The different christologies were based (as always) on different soteriologies which Frend has neatly described as follows: "In the last resort the Antiochene Christ redeemed through his baptism and self-sacrifice on the Cross, 'drawing all men unto him,' the Alexandrian through the death-destroying power of the divine elements in the Eucharist"; p. 213).

10. Grillmeier (no. 5 above), p. 544.

11. Pelikan (no. 5 above), p. 263.

12. Ibid, p. 266.

13. Walter Bauer, *Orthodoxy and Heresy in Earliest Christianity* (London: SCM, 1972) offers a now classic description of the origins of "orthodoxy" as representing the form of Christianity supported and actively propagated by the church of Rome, but never accepted elsewhere.

14. Pelikan (no. 5 above), p. 266.

15. R. Panikkar, *Salvation in Christ: Concreteness and University, the Supername* (Santa Barbara: 1972), p. 3.

16. K. Rahner, "Basic Theological Interpretation of the Second Vatican Council," in his *Theological Investigations* XX (N.Y.: Crossroad, 1981), pp. 77-79 [-83].

17. K. Rahner, *Inspiration in the Bible* (N.Y.: Herder, 1961), pp. 47-50. As Rahner points out it is precisely this fact that they are the self expression of the faith of the apostolic church which makes the scriptures inspired; inspiration is thus rightly seen as the quality of a text, not as some mysterious influence on an elusive 'author.'

18. Works on New Testament christology are too numerous to be listed here. There is a useful discussion on recent New Testament christology in *Semeia* 30 (1985), an issue on "Christology and Exegesis: New Approaches" and in Heinz Kremers, "Der Beitrag des Neuen Testaments zu eine nichtantijudischen Christologie" in E.L. Ehrlich, B. Klappert and U. Ast (eds.), "Wie gut sind deine Zelt Jaakow" [Festschrift Rheinhold Meyer] (Gerlingen: Bleicher, 1986), pp. 196-207.

19. Raymond Brown, *The Birth of the Messiah* (N.Y.: Doubleday Image, 1979), pp. 29-32.

20. On Jewish messianic beliefs in New Testament times, see Jacob Neusner, William Scott Green and Ernest Frerichs (eds.), *Judaism and the Messiahs at the Turn of the Christian Era* (Cambridge University Press, 1987).

21. For the future christology of Q see Edward Schillebeeckx, *Jesus—An Experiment in Christology* (London: Collins, 1979), pp. 406-407.

22. J.D.G. Dunn, *Christology in the Making: An Enquiry into the Origins of the Doctrine of the Incarnation* (London: SCM, 1980), p. 258: "only with the Fourth Gospel can we speak of a full blown conception of Christ's personal pre-existence and a clear doctrine of incarnation" (p. 258). This is the basic thesis of Dunn's book. For a critical discussion on it see *Semeia* 30 (1985), pp. 65-121, with contributions by Carl Holladay, Alan Segal, Reginald Fuller and Donald Juel.

23. Dunn (no. 22 above), p. 196.

24. M. Casey, *From Jewish Prophet to Gentile God: The Origins and Development of New Testament Christology* (London: James Clarke, 1991).

25. Panikkar (no. 16 above), p. 24.

26. Edward Schillebeeckx, *Interim Report on the Books Jesus and Christ* (London: SCM, 1980), pp. 14-15.

27. See J. Sobrino, *Christology at the Crossroads* (New York: Orbis Books, 1978), pp. 1-16, for an excellent discussion on the starting point of christology.

28. The old quest for the historical Jesus, which read the gospels as biographies of Jesus colored by myth, and sought to reconstruct a life of Jesus by removing mythical elements from the harmonized gospel narratives, was brought to an end by Albert Schweitzer's, *Quest of the Historical Jesus* (1906), which brilliantly demonstrated how the "historical Jesus" in every case turned out to be the historian's Jesus. The new quest initiated by Ernst Käsemann in 1954 after a period of Bultmannian

skepticism when any quest for the Jesus of history was given up as impossible and illegitimate, gave up attempting to reconstruct a life of Jesus but was content to show some continuity between the "Jesus of history" and the "Christ of faith." It has died a quiet and unadvertised death. Though Jesus books continue to appear, no consensus has emerged about the "intention" of Jesus. The new "Jesus research" pretends to hold greater promise because it uses new evidence (from Nag-Hammadi and Qumran) and new sociological methods for investigating the social setting of Jesus. But it has so far (in my opinion) been no more successful in disclosing the Jesus of history than in previous attempts, cf. R. S. Sugirtharajah, "'What Do Men Say Remains of Me?' Current Jesus Research and Third World Christologies," *Asia Journal of Theology* Vol. 5 (1991), pp. 331-37.

29. I have taken the distinction between "confessional" and "critical" history from G. von Rad, *Old Testament Theology, Volume I-II* (Edinburgh: Oliver & Boyd, 1965), pp. 1,107.

30. See G. Soares Prabhu, "The Historical Critical Method. Reflections on Its Relevance for the Study of the Gospels in India Today," in M. Amaldoss, T.K. John and G. Gispert-Sauch (ed.), *Theologizing in India* (Bangalore: TPI, 1981), pp. 314-67 (sp. pp. 340-41).

31. Panikkar (no. 15 above), p. 33.

32. Mahatma Gandhi, in *Modern Review* (October 1964) p. 67, referred to in Panikkar (no. 15 above), p. 46, no. 1.

33. See specially M.K. Gandhi, *Christian Missions: Their Place in India*, edited by B. Kumarappa (Ahmedabad: Navjivan, 1957); and his *In Search of the Supreme, Volume III*, compiled by B.G. Kher (Ahmedabad: Navjivan, 1962), pp. 313-42.

34. H. Staffner, *Baba Amte's Vision of a New India* (Sangamnar: Nitre Prakash, 1990).

35. Bhagwan Shree Rajneesh, *The Mustard Seed*, Vols. I-II (Pune: Rajneesh Foundation, 1975); *Come Follow Me, Vols. I-IV* (1976-77); *I Say Unto You, Vols. I-II* (1977-78). All three works contain the Bhagwan's discourses on the sayings of Jesus. The first on sayings taken from the Gospel of Thomas; the other two on sayings from the canonical gospels.

36. Reflections about Jesus tend to be, to use a convenient distinction proposed by E. Schillebeeckx, either "theologies of Jesus" or "christologies" proper. A theology of Jesus locates the saving event in the ministry of Jesus. It focuses on the human Jesus of Nazareth "experienced as a saving reality and interpreted as orientation and inspiration for Christian living." It finds in him "an inspiration and an orientation for working, not uncritically but committedly, to achieve a better world here on earth, without expressly introducing any vista of a life eternal or an eschatological encounter with Christ, sometimes even expressly denying it." A christology on the other hand locates salvation primarily (if not exclusively) in the death and resurrection of Jesus and so "celebrates and thematizes the Christ who is present in the ritual worship of the Church." It places, therefore, "a total emphasis on the God 'Jesus Christ,' the Lord exalted to the Father's side, who is active and alive among us even now, is celebrated in the liturgy and sheds upon us the spirit as pledge of an eternal life to come which is perpendicular, more or less, to our historical existence in this world, whereof the form passes away." See Schillebeeckx (no. 21 above), pp. 29-30.

37. W. Balddensperger commenting on John 1:9-10, quoted in E. Käsemann, "The Prologue to John's Gospel," in his *New Testament Questions of Today* (London: SCM, 1969), pp. 138-167.

Response from Latin America

JOSÉ MÍGUEZ BONINO

The excellent and fruitful paper and presentation deserve a much more detailed and reflected-upon response than these comments in ten quick minutes. I shall confine myself to, first, an affirmation of his methodological approach (the first section of the paper), and second, a suggestion of what it could mean to ask the question of "the experience of Jesus in Latin America."

I

I fully agree with Fr. Soares's methodological decision to approach the subject as that of "the Christian experience of Jesus." The use of this methodology does not imply a denial of the Christ event as "the mystery of Christ's divinity," nor a reduction of the historical nature of this event, the concrete historicity of the incarnation, to a subjective experience. The mystery is apprehended in faith and this apprehension is always mediated in an experience. The historical witness of the Gospels is enough to assess the basic facts and character of Jesus but it is, as all critical scholarship would today accept, mediated in an apostolic witness which unavoidably interprets that historical reality and which, in turn, we always interpret in the conditions of our own context.

While I fully concur with Fr. Soares's approach, I would suggest the need to pursue more thoroughly two points:

First, is the either/or "metaphoric" vs. "conceptual" language about Jesus such a basic issue as the paper at some points suggests? Are we not in both cases dealing with two ways of trying to give expression to a mystery which can never be fully apprehended intellectually or expressed in language? Cannot we admit, therefore, that different conceptual "instruments" and types of language can be legitimate as long as we recognize their insufficiency and ambiguity? Is not this problem of rigidity which the paper rightly denounces due not so much to the "conceptual" approach as to the use by the churches of the christological formulations as a "law" to judge the authenticity of the faith of people, with the consequence that this implies in a church, or churches, wielding political power?

Second, the paper speaks on the one hand of "a christological development" in the New Testament (in which different christologies unavoidably
appear as "stages"), and on the other hand of a variety, a plurality of New
Testament christologies which are born from the experience and witness of
different Christian communities. It seems to me that this second interpretation is more adequate both to the present state of historical research and
to the nature of New Testament variety. The truthfulness and the power of
the New Testament witness does not issue from the unanimity of its
formulations or the "development" of *one* progressively more perfected
christology, but precisely from the "freedom" of this multiplicity with its
differences and even its contradictions, but its unanimous affirmation of
Jesus as God's saving and liberating presence and its invitation to enter *now*,
in our own contexts, into Jesus' liberating work in our world.

II

An attempt to account for "the experience of Jesus" in Latin American
popular Christianity should take into account not only the *explicit* christological references in Catholic or Protestant popular piety but also the
implicit christological dimensions or possibilities of the total experiences of
such pieties. In this sense I would suggest some possible "tracks" for
exploration.

First, in Catholic popular piety, as expressed, for instance, in early Latin
American iconography it has been noted that there are two dominant
images of Christ: the "heavenly king," an image of the Spanish king with
all the attributes of power, in fact, the image and the legitimation of the
conqueror, and "the crucified Christ," tortured, wounded, bleeding, with
the face of the Indian, the powerless victim (see, for instance, G. Caralis in
Faces of Jesus, Orbis Books).

But if these are the explicit christologies, I would suggest at least three
other "images" where an *implicit* christology is found:

1) the devotion of the Virgin in her multiple manifestations, the "material" accessible image of God; the God that befriends the outcast and "the
little ones"; the Jesus of the poor, always ready to listen, always at hand;

2) the devotion of the many saints, sometimes images of the old Indian
pantheon, who can miraculously come to the rescue in the needs of life—the
face of the God who accompanies us in the questions of everyday life:
sickness, need of bread, of love, of fertility, of work. The saints are the
"mediators" of the Jesus "who went about doing good and healing the
sick";

3) the popular human figures which people perceived as "on their side:
the side of the poor and oppressed, redressing conditions of injustice and
fighting for liberation, sometimes an "outlaw" or "bandit," sometimes a
charismatic political leader, sometimes a messianic figure (like in two
"black" messianic movements in Brazil and the Caribbean): human figures

on which the people invested a religious dimension and explicit christological attributes.

In Protestant popular piety there is a christological concentration usually around two axes:

1) Christ the Savior who rescues the poor from the evil world (the sea, sinking sands, the storm) which destroys and leads to death, and opens a new world in the community of joy, power, solidarity and participation, which is the anticipation of the perfect new world of heaven or "the Second Advent."

2) Jesus, the friend who is always near, ready to help in comfort, healing, who speaks personally in revelations, dreams or through a prophet. The more we move in Protestantism to the pentecostal or charismatic movements, the movement thus becomes a christology of the Spirit rather than a christology of the Word.

In both cases, but particularly in the former, I find that the growing "popular reading of the Bible" is creating the "integration" of these diverse images into one—the Jesus of the Gospels. Thus a certain "christological hermeneutics" seems to emerge in which the christological expectation of the poor reflected in these figures is a framework of references to read "the story of Jesus" in the Bible; at the same time, the biblical texts give a name as well as correct, deepen, purify and add newer meaning to the people's christological expectations. This seems to me one of the most promising aspects of what is happening in significant groups, although by no means imaginatory of popular Catholic and Protestant spirituality. It is in the growth and deepening of this "hermeneutics" where I think theology may render a significant service.

Response from the United States

JACQUELYN GRANT

In this paper, George Soares Prabhu has presented some interesting ideas that can aid us in broadening our understanding and conceptions of christology. He has given us some tools to develop innovative theological ideas and to free ourselves from traditional narrow views.

His first point is that New Testament christology is pluralistic. For this reason, it is possible to talk about christologies rather than christology. This pluralism has not been manifested in the history of the Christian tradition, and we have, therefore, been oppressed by a static, normative christology. Consequently, classical christology is not functional in a positive way for all people today. Its formula is composed essentially of abstractions of the experiential dimensions of the Jesus Christ figure. All in all, theological formulations have not been entirely helpful for the liberation struggles of oppressed peoples as most traditional christological formulations have provided static and absolute answers. But our christological task today is not to develop or to create mechanisms for christological answers, but to do christological reflections exploring the mysticism of Jesus Christ.

The task of Third World theologians is to develop their own christologies in a way that moves us beyond the abstractness of traditional theologians. Thus, Soares proposes to focus upon the Jesus of faith, who lies somewhere between the Jesus of history and the Christ of faith. The author's discussion of the "meaning of Jesus of faith" yields some interesting theological insights. This Jesus of faith is the Jesus as encountered, experienced, and lived in the community. This is important because the community's faith is often what tells the story, for what the people believe is often of more significance than what can be proven. It is the community whose faith gives life to its object/subject of worship and adoration. Either one without the other is inadequate. The community without faith is directionless, and faith without community is meaningless. This notion relocates the focus from the technical requirements of traditional discussions about both the Jesus of history and the Christ of faith.

By accenting the Jesus as experienced in the lives of oppressed people, Soares is able to move beyond the facts to embrace also what people have come to believe. "Every community evolves its own understanding of Jesus, responding to its own cry for life." Consequently, the Jesus of faith is where the consciousness of history and the abstractness of Christ converge. This convergence brings concreteness and thus meaning to traditional christological formulations.

Soares provides fresh insights into christological discussions that are worthy of further exploration. His introduction of the abbreviated formula of "Jesus of faith" challenges us to discard the "staticness" of merely duplicating the efforts of mechanisms and to liberate ourselves to the possibilities of communal explorations of mysteries. Again, it is the community that gives meaning to faith and that enables the dynamic quality of faith to emerge.

Soares states that "because life changes christology changes too." Our challenge is "to discover our own particular christology, that is, the specific significance of Jesus for our situation in the Third World today." This is a mandate for both the Third World and the First World. The former must be empowered and the latter must be disempowered. The Third World must be empowered in the sense that its people must be able to take seriously their own context. The First World must be disempowered in order to realize that its social context is not normative for all people everywhere. Furthermore, First World people must be re-empowered to put into perspective their own experiences alongside others. Only then can we become true neighbors.

I find it intriguing that the christological question is broadened by Soares to embrace another dimension reflected in the question "Who is thy neighbor?" There is a sense in which the question "Who do you say that I am?" is intricately related to the question regarding one's neighbor. An explication of Christ cannot remain solely focused on the "I am" or the individualism implied in the question. Rather, to talk about who Jesus Christ is forces us into a relational stance—"we-ness" must be addressed.

The christological symbol in the incarnation is used to demonstrate the solidarity of Jesus with the poor and outcast. Using John's gospel and focusing on the Word becoming flesh, the author suggests an egalitarianism that we all have beneath the skin, perhaps in our souls. The above-mentioned process of empowerment, disempowerment, and re-empowerment makes a way for this to happen and to be understood. Accepting the Jesus of faith provides the basis for this process.

Reflection upon Soares's Reflections

The freedom suggested by George Soares challenges us to move beyond the mere recognition of issues to their appropriation. His challenge to move beyond mechanisms is quite appropriate. My concern, however, is with the consistency with which this principle is applied. For example, in my initial reading of the paper, I wondered why, if God is mysterious, why is God's gender locked in at the point of mechanism? As I read further, the author soon acknowledged that God is beyond gender: "For God is not a 'he' or a 'she' or an 'it' but an I." That is, God is not object, but subject. However, even as this exciting notion is acknowledged, the author continues to name God in the masculine gender. In this regard, God is still held captive by the imitations of mechanisms. God, the mystery, is in fact circumvented.

Yes, everyone of us may in fact be the "thou art" uttered by the "I am." However, in reality, we are not all treated as "thous." There is a hierarchy of "thous" that in fact still renders some as "its." The "its" status of women is reflected in the fact that women are not seen as being in the image of God, and this is represented by their exclusion, even in the way we speak about and image God.

However, in spite of this, a demasculinization of the divine can perhaps be seen in the choice of love to describe Jesus' God-experiences, which free Jesus from inner conditioning. It is love that frees Jesus to relate to "others" (outcasts) differently. Further, focus upon relationship rather than gender is reflected in the author's explications of Jesus' use of "Abba" in reference to God.

In doing theology and christology, the author, while arguing for a dialectical relationship, seems to lean toward the functional over the onto-logical, the confessional over the critical, or the concrete over the abstract. Perhaps this is necessary if the emphasis on the Jesus of faith is to make sense. Yet, after affirmation of the experiential model, the discussion of the God-reality slips remarkably back into abstract language; thus, for exam-ple, the reliance on such phrases as "God as the ground of being."

The affirmation of God as subject is perhaps an attempt to give concrete content to the vastness of a concept as "the ground of being." God is the big "I," the "I am." Yet how do we speak of this "subject"? The author says that "any statement about God is always a statement about the world." If this is true (and I believe it to be so), then any statement about the subject is in fact a statement about the object, which (or who, in this case) in reality is the subject, who in fact is the object.

Are we not merely opting for intellectual theological double-talk in the place of a non-intellectual/academic (sometimes) fundamentalistic theo-logical double-talk? The question remains: how or in what ways does the community experience and speak about God? The fact of the matter is that we are more than just flesh. Acknowledging ourselves by our least common denominator does not in actuality indicate the physical, social, psychologi-cal, political, or economic realities that define who we are in the world. We are flesh impacted by all of these realities, which accents differences.

Indeed, some have been empowered to assume the privileges of "I" and "thou," while others forever remain "its"—objects. In other words, the use of incarnational theology is helpful for our understanding of the relation-ship of Jesus Christ to us; however, this does not resolve our human relationship dilemma. For as long as the mystery of the divinity is violated and mechanisms in any form are allowed to prevail, relationships (personal, professional and political) are problematic.

Interestingly, at one level the author appears to do what in his paper he critiques quite well. There is no focus on the abstract notion of the two natures of Christ; there is no attempt to explicate the meaning and nature of the Godhead. Rather, there is the interesting discussion of the God experience of Jesus. In fact, the bulk of the reflection is centered upon scriptural evidence that Jesus' God experience leads to the freedom of Jesus. Yet, is not the central thesis of the work (or at least the presupposition) the idea that Jesus must be experienced in the context where we are? Is this not yet another explication of how ancient sources are made normative over contextual experiences? Why isn't our central question that of how Jesus is experienced in the Third World, or at least how that God experience of Jesus is manifested in the Third world?

Sister Bernard Ncube of South Africa raised a question abut the validity of normatizing an ancient culture to the point of negating our own stories. Sister Teresa Okure of Nigeria pointed out the descriptive nature of the text, noting that we so often insist upon making it prescriptive. Indeed, while the paper presents some interesting and refreshing ideas, it still seems to be locked into traditional theological language and sources, which, in fact, normatize ancient cultures and employ prescriptive rather than descriptive methodologies.

Perhaps one way of getting out of this theological maze is to go back to the language of the people and begin there—with their stories, myths, folklore, sermons, and tales. Sister Bernard might begin, "There still lives a people in the beautiful Black country of South Africa." My story would begin, "There still lives a people in the context of North America who have survived against all odds. They've been dehumanized, disenfranchised, discriminated against; they've been lied to, cheated, stolen from, and they were themselves stolen. Yet in the womb of their community they nurtured a spirituality that not only contained their cries for life, but which produced their struggle for survival and liberation."

Out of that womb came a spirituality that emerged partially by their understanding that Jesus Christ inspired and guided their advocacy quest for human dignity. Out of the context of this spirituality comes the possibility for the development of a christology within the context of Black theology and womanist thought. Unlike most perspectives in liberation theology, womanist theology understands the interconnected nature of oppression. Thus, it seeks to develop a wholistic analysis that addresses various components of human existence. It represents a spirituality that brought forth individuals and communities who have struggled to restore the humanity of African-American peoples in general and African-American women in particular. It made them sing "Steal away to Jesus" and "Sweet Little Jesus Boy." It made them claim Jesus as friend; it caused them to proclaim Jesus as liberator; it led them to claim that Jesus means freedom, as they put their lives on the line for justice, freedom, and liberation. This is the meaning of the Jesus of faith; it is faith in this historical figure that empowers the oppressed to rise up against oppression in whatever form, directing them toward liberation.

13

Spirituality of the Third World: Conversion and Commitment

FRANK CHIKANE

This Third Assembly of the Ecumenical Association of Third World Theologians (EATWOT) is meeting at a critical time in the history of our struggles in different parts of the world.

We meet at a time of momentous events of cosmic proportions. Since our last Assembly in 1986, we have witnessed negotiations between Moscow and Washington which resulted in the closing of the era of the Cold War, which caused enormous pain and suffering to many people, particularly those in the Third World. We have witnessed the beginning of the resolution of regional conflicts and wars which were mainly inspired by the Cold War between the West and East, as they used to be known. We have witnessed the collapse of the Berlin Wall between East and West Germany. We have seen the excitement of the people of the so-called Eastern Bloc as they took to the streets to secure and also celebrate their freedoms.

As we witnessed these events our hopes for a new world order where there will be justice and lasting world peace were raised. We had hoped that the Third World would no longer be used as a battleground for the wars of the First and Second Worlds. We hoped and believed that with the ending of the Cold War we would be given the opportunity to develop our own just socio-political and economic models without being beaten into submission by the superpowers and forced to use their old models which have produced misery for many people around the world.

But our hopes and expectations were dashed before long. The talks between Moscow and Washington have led to the collapse of the Soviet Union, as it was known, leaving us with one superpower. The Gulf War brought the message home that we were now totally at the mercy of that power. The celebrated freedoms of the peoples of the former Eastern Bloc countries have ended in frustrations and disappointments. The expectation of better life by opening themselves to capitalist systems were not fulfilled. Some are beginning to see that capitalism is not necessarily the answer to their problems. That which was hoped for could not therefore be realized. In some instances their excitement was turned into civil wars devastating their countries, causing thousands of deaths.

At home in South Africa we have gone through a similar experience. We started with the unbanning of people's liberation movements, the release of the people's leaders, particularly Nelson Mandela. I am sure most of you watched ecstatic masses of our people who celebrated the release of Mr. Mandela. But this excitement and expectation for the birth of a new South Africa were violently ended by the outbreak of the type of violence we had never experienced before.

Although all efforts were made to salvage this situation resulting in the Convention for a Democratic South Africa (CODESA), held at the end of 1991, and although this raised new hopes for the demise of apartheid, as the negotiation process gained more momentum we began to worry about the risks now inherent in this process which might result in the abandonment of the noble ideals people struggled and died for. As the struggle moves from the terrain of liberation to the terrain of political power dynamics, we fear that the struggle for power might be waged at the expense of the course of justice.

All these events, coupled with the reality and negative impact of the unjust international economic order, have brought home the fact that although the Reign of God is already present, with us in our struggles for liberation it has not yet reached its complete fulfillment. Liberation is a precondition for the new society, but this is not all it is. While liberation is implemented in liberating historical events, it also denounces their limitations and ambiguities, proclaims their fulfillment, and compels them effectively towards total communion.[1]

We are reminded that God's mission (*missio Dei*) is not yet completed. The cry of our people can still be heard, the cry for justice, the cry for life. It has thus become clear to many of us that the struggle has not come to an end as a result of the "toenadering" of Moscow and Washington or a settlement of some regional conflict elsewhere in the world. This struggle will continue until the "new thing" is born in the world.

Some, even among us, were beginning to doubt whether or not there was still room for a theology of liberation in the light of the conclusion of liberation struggles in various parts of the Third World. But this cannot be. Simon Maimela's argument in defense of Black theology in a future South Africa is helpful. He says that "because of sin and human limitations and propensity towards evil, making it unlikely that human beings can ever hope to create a perfect state of justice in such a way that we can claim that any future transformed society will be totally free from violating the dignity and personal freedom of all its members, it seems obvious that Black theology of liberation must have a role to play in any future South African society."[2]

I want to submit that our goal and vision of the reign of God goes beyond these settlements and resolutions of regional and national conflicts. Our vision is for a new society, a new world, where there shall be justice for all.

This new world order and reality requires us, and EATWOT in particular, to critically reflect on it with the hope of discovering where and how God is at work and how God is continuing ceaselessly to transform it to come close to the ideal of the reign of God. Nothing short of this ideal is satisfactory. God is at work and our task is simply to be "converted" and be realigned with God's mission for the world. We need simply to participate in the ongoing liberating work of God in this historical process of the salvation of the world.

But for us to be part of this liberating act of God we need to be committed to God, and to this project of liberation. This commitment, I submit, must be a result of conversion to the God of liberation if it has to be a commitment to liberation rather than oppression. This brings me to the sub-theme I have been asked to speak on at this Assembly, namely "Christian Commitment (Conversion)."

The formulation of this sub-theme suggests to me that there is either a tension between "commitment" and "conversion," an attempt to express both at the same time, or that the two are simply collapsed into one. Whatever the position, I wish to submit that conversion is the foundation of authentic Christian life, and that it is out of this conversion experience that commitment issues.

For this reason I have taken the liberty to rephrase my theme to "The Spirituality of the Third World: Conversion and Commitment." I will thus critically reevaluate the concept of conversion and then redefine Christian commitment on the basis of this understanding of conversion. My thesis is that limiting or reducing the meaning of conversion and its socio-political and economic implications to that of commitment robs the liberation motive of the revolutionary dimension of the meaning of conversion.

In an attempt to establish this thesis I will briefly look at the perspectives of the biblical roots of the dogma of conversion followed by contemporary perspectives on conversion, and then link this up with the concept of commitment to the struggle. I will then conclude by showing how these perspectives of conversion and commitment were developed and illuminated in practice, through our struggle for liberation in South Africa.

Perspectives from the Biblical Roots of the Dogma of Conversion

Biblical sources show that the nexus of being a Christian is located at the point of conversion, a radical turning point and redirection of one's life.

Conversion is turning away from sin and turning towards God. Being a Christian here means being a new creature (2 Cor. 5:17), a new life (Rom. 6:4); being born again (John 3:3). In emphasizing the radical nature of this change, Albert Nolan argues that the Gospel is not a call "to renewal but to new life," "to transcend the past, to make a fresh start, to be born again."[3] Both Johannine and Pauline theology go beyond a demand for one to be converted to imbuing a Christian (one converted) with a "converting mission" and consciousness (Weltanschaaung).

The first Christian community to whom this message was preached was an economically poor, socio-religiously marginalized, and politically persecuted community. But it was a converted community. An act of conversion delimited it from the rest of society. This the Bible puts out clearly. What is not put out clearly is whether this conversion was expressing itself in a passionate "converting vision" of their reality in its totality, which includes their unenviable econo-political position.

Different explanations have been given in this regard, and I do not intend discussing them in this paper. What is clear though is that the early Christians never lived in absolute acquiescence to the powers that be; and this, we argue, is borne out by their understanding of conversion as an imperative of Christian discipleship to view all reality as crying out for improvement and transformation. Even in the period of decadence which came following the reign of Constantine as a Christian emperor, monastic orders emerged as critical witnesses to the appropriate Christian attitude towards the world.

Contemporary Perspective on Conversion

Since the first interpretation of the biblical sources we have on conversion, particularly beginning with the debates between Augustine of Hippo and Pelagius during the fourth century, the Christian conception of conversion has developed within the vicissitudes of two conflicting understandings.

The first is the traditional understanding, which refuses to relate to socio-historical reality and which in our contemporary world is represented by the so-called fundamentalist evangelical and Pentecostal church groups. This position has been subsequently critiqued in various publications of EATWOT and its members and thus I do not intend elaborating on it. The second understanding is a corrective of the first, what I see as the real meaning of conversion. This understanding of conversion as a wider process which has to realize itself as transformation of all reality is one common theme of the theology of liberation.

What we need to engage in at this stage of development of our joint reflection process as people from the oppressed communities of this world is a critical evaluation of some of the aspects of this understanding, or perhaps the highlighting of a number of aspects of this interpretation for strategic emphasis to strengthen our concept of commitment to God's project of liberation.

Conversion and Traditional Theology of Liberation

The maturing in Christian consciousness of the idea of the universality of salvation, and the question of the possibility of being saved while outside the visible frontiers of the church, resulted in the whole problem of salvation making "a quantitative leap," as Gustavo Gutiérrez puts it. From this perspective one can no longer talk about profane and sacred histories but one history of salvation. Thus, salvation here is not "something other-worldly, in regard to which the present life is merely a test," but salvation is "something which embraces all human reality, transforms it, and leads it to its fullness in Christ." Gutiérrez continues to say that "this fulfillment embraces every aspect of humanity: body and spirit, individual and society, person and cosmos, time and eternity."[4]

But it is precisely this "leap" which, I believe, has resulted in a de-emphasis of the concept of conversion. With universal salvation, conversion as part of the process of the salvific act of God seemed to be irrelevant. Liberation theologies have in a sense leaped from the concept of universal salvation to the concept of commitment to the liberation struggle. The concept of conversion here is somehow collapsed or equated to that of commitment. Conversion is thus reduced to commitment to the process of the liberation of the poor and oppressed. Personal salvation is found in an act of commitment to the struggle of the poor and oppressed.

I would like to submit that conversion is more than commitment. To be a Christian is not just to be committed, as a first act to the historical struggles. But to be a Christian is to be converted, to change perspectives, out of which issues not only commitment but a *constraint* to work for the conversion (change) of the entire world (cosmos). Once converted, one has no choice but to be committed. Turning to God requires total commitment to God's mission in the world.

The concept of commitment assumes that conversion has already taken place. The risk here is that conversion is then taken for granted. What remains is simply for one to be committed. For me conversion is what makes commitment meaningful because it becomes commitment to radically change the world.

A failure to delineate and to be specific about conversion as a radical experience of change rubs on the next stage where this conversion has to be applied as a model for social revolution. The de-emphasis, though, is understood if one considers the way in which evangelical-pentecostal groups have restricted this concept to an individualistic interpretation. I believe that the concept of conversion must be reappropriated in the same way as Maimela did with that of "atonement."[5]

The Case of South Africa

The oppressed Christian communities of South Africa have always seen and understood their mission as that of turning South Africa from the criminal and sinful system of apartheid to a just non-racial and democratic country. Apartheid or racism was seen as the total embodiment of all evil which distorted human reality and deformed God's creation. As if this was not enough, the Dutch Reformed Church (DRC) developed a heretical theological justification for this evil. Desmond Tutu takes this heretic justification of apartheid even further. He says that the heretic aspect of apartheid is not just the pain and suffering that it causes but the fact that it made the people of God doubt that they were made in the image of God.[6]

It is this evil nature of apartheid which made the converting mission and vision a priority. In South Africa to be born Black was to be doomed to a second-class citizenship. When you were Black you were classified as a "non-white," which meant that you were a "non-person." What is worse, Black people began to believe this, subjecting themselves to mental and psychological bondage. It is for this reason that Black Christian communities saw as the first priority the liberation of the minds of Black people. Early Black consciousness called this process "psychological liberation." Through Black consciousness Black people had to reassess their humanity and destiny. In a world which negated the humanity of Black people, our people had to reject all negative descriptions accorded to them and reassert that "Black is beautiful," and call on Black people to be "on their own" by rejecting white paternalism and liberation. Black theology took this struggle further by asserting that Blacks were made in the image of God and that the oppression of Blacks was in fact an attack on God. This affirmation of "blackness" in the face of all that negated it amounted to a "total conversion and experience of rebirth on the part of Black people."[7]

This view, of course, could be rejected outright by my evangelical-pentecostal family. But in South Africa it soon became clear that even conversion in the classical limited sense of individualistic form could not be fully realized as the very converted, or "born agains" as they would say, remained mentally and physically prisoners of the dehumanizing societal system. Total freedom (physically and mentally) was not realized. The oppressed remained subjects of racist oppressors. Thus even evangelical and pentecostal groups began to challenge the apartheid system as satanic and evil, although these were prophetic groups on the periphery of the mainline evangelicalism and pentecostalism. The document titled "Evangelical Witness in South Africa," produced and published by a group called "Concerned Evangelicals," expresses the mood and understanding of these emerging groups. An elaboration of the pentecostal dimension of this movement was articulated in another later document titled "Towards a Relevant Pentecostal Witness."

Changing (converting) a subjugated people who had been so psychologically deformed that they themselves doubted their own humanity became an absolutely necessary stage to be able to challenge the whole system of apartheid. Black people had to be converted themselves to develop a new consciousness which made it imperative to eliminate the system of apartheid. This conversion event happened in the course of a struggle to resist apartheid. It is this new consciousness which became the basis for the new vision, the vision of eradicating the system of apartheid to replace it with a just, non-radical democratic South Africa where Blacks and Whites would live together as human beings.

The concept of conversion was also inspired by the seriousness of the situation in South Africa. This reality ruled out any doubt as to the need for a metanoia of the reality in which Black people lived. Instead of rejecting the dogma of conversion, this was taken as an inspiration that the God whom we worship is a God who is for change. This view produced a crop of church activists who were captured by this realization and led into actual struggle against the apartheid regime at great personal costs.

This is where commitment became manifest: people of God facing guns and being prepared to die for a cause rather than surrender to the power of evil. We shall come to this matter later.

An attempt was also made to call on Whites to repent and turn from the god of oppression, the idol of death, to the God of life, the God of liberation. In the early seventies so-called white community programs were initiated to try and change the attitudes of Whites, with the hope of getting them committed to the elimination of apartheid. But these programs collapsed within the decade of the seventies because not many Whites were prepared to sacrifice their privileges by responding to the message of salvation. The closing report of one of these programs admitted that there was no necessary "yeast" among Whites to make this change possible.

From this experience it became clear that the only way to change Whites in the country was to mobilize Blacks to resist the apartheid system, to create a crisis to an extent that the regime would be forced to abandon the system. To do this we needed total commitment from the converted to lay their lives down for the liberation of all, both Whites and Blacks.

Following the collapse of these programs, "converted" White Christians could only be involved in the project of liberation by committing themselves to support and act in solidarity with the Black masses on their struggle for liberation. These Whites, like Beyers, Horst Kleinschmitt and others, were radicalized by the frustration trying to change Whites. Most of them were later banned and some went into exile.

Christian Commitment

The concept of conversion, as outlined above, became the basis and motivation for a total commitment to the liberation struggle in South Africa. It moved oppressed Christian communities from a liberal, reformist approach of ending apartheid to demands for a radical change of the system. And as we have said earlier, conversion did not only lead to commitment to this struggle, but it made Christians feel constrained to work for the conversion or change of the entire system.

In the last twenty years or so, various Christian groups and organizations were formed to undertake this mission with a religious zeal. For them, God required that they do so. Many were detained and tortured, some imprisoned. Many were attacked in various ways and others were killed. In the midst of this persecution, more and more Christians saw their actions as that of witnessing to the vision of the Reign of God. They witnessed to the God who was concerned about the victims of oppression and exploitation, a God who takes sides with the oppressed, a "fighting God," as Biko described this God.

At the height of the worst repression during the latter part of the eighties, church leaders were compelled as well to take to the streets in defiance of the regime. They understood this act of defiance as an act of obedience to God. As the regime demanded total allegiance, church leaders asked who they should obey: "God or human beings." And in a decisive choice they said, "We shall obey God rather than human beings." This was a demonstration of total commitment to God. Christians engaged in the struggle took seriously the fact that love for the neighbor required one to lay down one's life for one's brothers and sisters. This was the cost of discipleship.

The Spirituality of Struggle

This commitment to the struggle for liberation occasioned the development of a spirituality of struggle. According to the *Kairos Document*, church activities had to be transformed to be "fully consistent with a prophetic faith which is related to the Kairos."[8] This amounted to a call for the revision and writing of liturgy and church structures so as to convert them into instruments for the total conversion of the Christian church and the society at large.

It was clear to everyone that once the regime was declared illegitimate one could not pray for "our President," but had to pray for the "downfall of the government." One could not experience God as the God of liberation and then worship God as the "almighty dictator." The traditional acts of worship were appropriated to serve the liberation struggle. In fact there is no spirituality on this view of the church which is outside the acts of struggle for liberation. The acts of worship simply become acts of celebration, meditation and reflection on these struggles.

The new publication titled *We Shall Overcome: Spirituality of Liberation*[9] on South Africa is an attempt to articulate this process of interpreting the spirituality of South African Christians and to relocate it within the terrain of the people's struggles.

References

1. Gutiérrez, G., *A Theology of Liberation* (Maryknoll, N.Y.: Orbis Books, 1988), Revised Edition, pp. 103-105.

2. Maimela, S., *Proclaim Freedom to My People* (Johannesburg: Skotaville, 1987), p. 72.

3. Nolan, A., *God in South Africa: The Challenge of the Gospel*, (Cape Town: David Philip, 1988), p. 200.

4. Gutiérrez, G., p. 85.

5. Maimela, S., pp. 87 ff.

6. Serfontein, H., *Apartheid Is a Heresy*.

7. Maimela, J., p. 65, referring to Allan Boesak.

8. *The Kairos Document* (Johannesburg: Kairos Theologians, 1985), p. 23.

9. Worsnip, M. and Van der Water, D. (eds.), *We Shall Overcome: Spirituality for Liberation* (Pietermarizburg: Cluster Publication, 1991).

Response from the Philippines: Commitment

MARY JOHN MANANZAN

In 1987, Dean Alejandro, a very promising young man and secretary general of the biggest network of cause-oriented organizations in the Philippines (BAYAN), was brutally murdered in front of his office in Manila. At almost the same time, in Leyte, a woman, Cecilia Udtujan, a pregnant organizer for AMIHAN, a peasant women's organization, was slit open and her unborn child carved out of her. Last November (1991) a young priest, Neri Sator, who was known for his struggle against illegal logging, was gunned down while on his motorcycle on his way to say mass. One thing is common to these brave people: They had all been warned that if they continued their activities, they would be killed. Yet they continued. Why? One word comes to mind, commitment: commitment to justice.

Wellsprings of Commitment

Actually, one does not need theology to be committed to justice. One does not even have to believe in God. Any decent human being could decide in the midst of oppression and exploitation to work for justice for the sake of oppressed and exploited people. However, those who have a Christian tradition and faith do find an inspiration to do the same thing from their religious conviction. The church people mentioned in the previous paragraph belong to those who have found a new meaning to their faith. They have come to the conviction that to preach the good news of salvation means to work for justice and transformation of the world. They have understood that salvation is an integral salvation that is to be accomplished within the church's declared preferential option for the poor and the oppressed and in solidarity with the struggling and suffering people of God. The people I have referred to above have begun to understand the social dimension of their faith. They have realized that salvation is not the "salvation of the soul from sin, hell and death, in order to go to heaven" but rather the total and concrete salvation of the human person, body and soul, not only individually but in the context of a social milieu. This holistic understanding of salvation has urged them to struggle against the obstacles to an integral human liberation that they have discovered imbedded in economic, political, and social structures. This has led them to make a consequent option for the oppressed, which, of course, has had political consequences and has drawn the ire of the rich and powerful who benefit from the oppressive systems that continue to exploit and oppress the great majority of the people. To the extent that they pose a threat to the powers that be, church people have become targets of retaliation or elimination by those whose interests are threatened by their commitment.

The Stages of Commitment

Experience as a Starting Point of Commitment

How did these people begin to come down from the realms of theory to actual involvement? Many can formulate beautiful theological treatises on justice without actually having their hands dirtied, so to speak. I think the crucial thing is experience—the actual experience of oppression, exploitation, injustice. Unless one gets a skin-to-skin contact with these realities, there is no sense of urgency to involve oneself. Allow me to share my own experience, since it is the only one I know. I call it my baptism of fire.

I had just come from a six-year study leave in Germany and Rome, and I was teaching contemporary philosophy in a Jesuit university. I joined a group called "Interfaith Theological Circle," which aimed at evolving a "Filipino theology" in the air-conditioned library of the university. Needless to say, we came under critique for undertaking "intellectual gymnastics," in spite of producing what appeared to us as extremely erudite papers on the subject. After a period of defensiveness, we realized that it was indeed futile to evolve such a theology without getting involved in the struggle of the people. That was what made me respond to the invitation of the workers of a wine factory "La Tondeña" to accompany them when the military threatened to arrest them. This was at a time of martial law when strikes were illegal. During this first encounter with military brutality, I felt helpless when the military came, beat the workers, and herded the bloody mass of humanity like animals into waiting military buses. That was my starting point. Other people have other starting points—perhaps more dramatic ones, such as a friend of mine who happened to be working with a German pastor who was under surveillance. She was implicated in his arrest and gang-raped by the military. That started her involvement. Whatever its form, experience is the starting point.

It is amazing how commitment can grow like a weed into a plant, a fruit-bearing tree. And with it, of course, come growing pains. The La Tondeña strike inspired a hundred more strikes in a period of three months as we went from one factory to the other, gaining valuable learning experiences from persons, getting an insight into the root causes of their problems. Helping workers immersed us in the problems of slum dwellers, for this is where the workers live. We joined human barricades to stop demo-litions. We formed composite groups that spearheaded rallies and marches. We were recruited into negotiating teams to face the military in mass actions. And, inevitably, we got involved in the fate of political detainees who were arrested in marches and rallies and who were snatched from their houses during midnight raids.

Much later we realized that our whole effort for a total human liberation could not be total if we did not pay attention to the gender issue. If women, who form at least half of society, remain oppressed and exploited, then half of society remains unliberated despite any economic and political libera-tion. So we began organizing and educating women and launching cam-paigns against violence toward women and the trafficking of women. We encountered initial difficulties because even so-called progressive men who were our companions in the struggle for justice were so gender blind that they felt our efforts to be "watering down the main contradiction" or dissipating energies. It took time before we could make them see that the emancipation of women was a constitutive dimension of social transforma-tion.

The Anguish of Awareness

Initiation into the struggles of people can shake the framework of one's religious existence. In an article describing my first experience of involve-ment, I wrote:

> Social awareness can mean real anguish. Exposures even on a minor scale to the miseries of people and a serious reflection on this misery can confront us with facts that question our former values. And yet it takes time to adopt and synthesize a new set of values one is just beginning to perceive. One is back to zero during this period. One is barren. One stops giving talks or writing articles, because one feels empty, one needs to be reeducated. This awareness gives one a sense of urgency that may seem fanatic to those who either do not see or who do not have the same sense of urgency. Here is where one can make a mistake in strategy, become over-zealous, or turn off people. But there is, indeed, a constriction of the heart that one feels when one talks with persons who see no further than the four protective walls of their houses or convents. Here is where awareness can cause real loneliness. All of a sudden one is on a different plane when talking with one's own family, one's closest friends and colleagues. Not to be able to share values can be painful and the slow, painstak-ing trial-and-error attempts to share these new values and new imperatives—without turning people off—can bring one to a point of helplessness and frustration further aggravated by one's clearer and closer perception of the magnitude of the problem and the uncertainty, risks, and corresponding magnitude of the proposed

solutions. To confront time and time again one's own prejudices, one's own blind spots, one's own doubts, is to relive time and time again one's own metanoia without a sense of relief at the thought that the decision and choice lie within one's power. But perhaps the greatest anguish is the yawning gap between one's insight and one's generosity. Insight brings with it imperatives to action that may mean crucial decisions; to perceive and yet not to have the courage or moral energy to act is a real agony. To conscientize is truly a serious business, because the price of awareness is anguish. (Quoted in Mananzan, "Redefining Religion Commitment Today," *Women Religious Now*, Manila, 1993.)

The Cost of Commitment

In the end, those who totally involve themselves in the struggle for justice and the complete transformation of society begin to feel the consequences of their commitment. On the occasion of the killing of Father Dionisio Malalay and Rufino Rivera on April 2, 1989, the bishop, clergy and people of the diocese of Pagadian in the Philippines wrote the following statement of protest:

> Since 1987 we have grieved at the loss of nine Church leaders from the diocese who have been killed by government forces (four others had already been killed during the Marcos regime). Combine this high rate of killing of Church personnel with the constant harassment of Church people through blatant attempts of intimidation by propaganda, lies and threats to their very lives, it becomes relatively clear why we consider ourselves to be living in a period of Church persecution in the Philippines. It is not an exaggeration to say that practically all efforts of Church people to promote life, even such attempts as organizing the people for health, farming for reforestation, for liturgical celebration and Bible sharing, for protection and promotion of Tribal communities, are labelled as communist activities. To the outsider this may seem a harmless enough accusation, but to the people accused, it is a life and death issue, because anyone who is associated with such activities is considered by the military to be communist and therefore can be summarily executed by military force. ("Statement of Protest," Pagadian, 1989.)

What is sad is that except for a few incidents such as this that evoked the support of the bishop, other cases of persecution of church people have not elicited active protests of the hierarchy. Many bishops, easily taken in by the "Red scare," readily acquiesce in the accusations of civil authorities and the tactics of the military who conveniently provide them with "evidences" of the "moral lapses" of the accused, especially if they are priests or religious. These people are even marginalized in the church because their ideas and activities disturb and their questioning threatens the more traditional elements, which are, of course, the majority.

Test of Commitment

Aside from the persecution of inimical forces, commitment can be put to the test by other factors. In the recent global happenings—the failure of the so-called socialist bloc, the return of reactionary forces and values in struggles that have achieved victory, and so forth—have caused committed people all over the world to rethink their own struggles.

In addition, internal problems within liberation movements have also given rise to so-called "burned-out" activists. Some have given up and have decided to focus on their careers. Others have become directionless, indifferent. Some have even joined those they used to denounce. In the women's movement in the developed countries, young women are taking for granted the rights and opportunities that are now theirs because of the struggle waged by their mothers and grandmothers in the 1960s.

The question is: Has anything really and fundamentally changed? Have the goals for a better society become irrelevant? Has there been an end to exploitation and oppression?

Challenge to EATWOT Members

I think the world needs our commitment more than ever. The oppressed people all over the world have not given up their struggles. Some persons who are steadfast in their commitment have listened to our words and taken them seriously, so seriously that they have given their lives as a witness to their convictions. Surely, this gives us grave reason to reflect on our responsibility. They force us to examine our own commitment, the integrality of our own spirituality. We sometimes think that our theologizing is our contribution to our people's struggle. It sometimes gives us an excuse not to actually be in the fray. But have we the right to reflect theologically on vicarious experience? Do we have the right to be spectators? Can we consider our verbalization of "looking on"—even though we are not really in their midst—as genuinely liberating theology? How faithful have we been to the provision that commitment to transforming action is a criterion for EATWOT membership?

The fact that so many have suffered the consequences of their commitment should sober us; it should, however, likewise inspire us to continue drawing out the liberating factors in our otherwise truly oppressive religion. And even if we suffer in our own churches suspicion, marginalization, or outright persecution, we know that our vision is to see to it that the truest, the noblest, and the most authentic part of the church and Christianity will continue forward. And it is actually the "loyalists" in the church who in their intransigent clinging to the past are, in fact, digging the grave for an obsolete church.

It is relatively easy to wax eloquent about prophetic spirituality. But it is when we are called to share the fate of the prophets of history that our words assume a consequent reality. The effectiveness and the achievement of EATWOT does not lie in how many continental and intercontinental conferences we have launched or in how many books we have published. The significance of EATWOT is in the commitment of its members to live day by day the consequences of their theological insights.

14

The Statement of the Assembly:
A Cry for Life

Cry, Cry, Cry for Life

Cry, cry, cry for life
For the living, for the dead
For the desert, for the sea
Poisoned fish, birds with broken wings
Poets with no words
Singers without a song.

Cry, cry, cry for life
For the little children, fighting in the streets
Playing with toys, guns and grenades
For Afro-Amerindian mothers, weeping out of sorrow
Wondering about their children's fate.

Cry, cry, cry for life
For South Africans, robbed of motherland
Fighting apartheid, denied of liberty
For Korean people, ridden with han
Yearning to be united, for half a century.

Cry, cry, cry for life
For natives in the Americas, guardians of wisdom
Staring at the sun, not allowed to dance
For Jamaican youths, captives in Babylon
Wanting to return, but no promised land.

Cry, cry, cry for life
For the Indian Dalits, outcasts in their own land
From day to day, burying hundreds who die
For the refugees, exiled in diaspora
On the willow tree, hanging their harps and sigh.

Cry, cry, cry for life
For the peasants who produce our food
But go to bed with empty stomachs
For workers who keep the wheel turning
But carry heavy burdens on their backs.

Cry, cry, cry for life
For the courage, for the hope
For the forest, for the stream
Bodies may die, spirit never dies
In our struggle, we burst in songs
As a new day dawns, we will shout in joy.

Introduction

The Third Assembly of the Ecumenical Association of Third World Theologians (EATWOT) met at the Methodist Conference Center in Nairobi, Kenya, from 6 to 13 January 1992.

For EATWOT members, friends, and observers, it was a historic occasion. EATWOT was conceived here in Nairobi in 1975, and inaugurated at the University of Dar-es-Salaam a year later. It is gratifying that after fifteen years of steady growth in membership and programs EATWOT has again come to Africa.

The Assembly meets at a time when the Third World in general and Africa in particular are going through unprecedented changes. The poor and the marginalized groups have discovered their collective power, and the impact of their corporate cry for life is opening up avenues for their participation in decision-making processes. Signs of hope are clearly discernible all over the African continent from Cape to Cairo; encouraging changes have taken place and continue to take place in South Africa, Zimbabwe, Angola and Kenya.

These signs of hope, however, are countered by new problems and the frustrations they give rise to: ethnic conflicts in South Africa, Somalia, and the Sudan and Liberia, and the continuing civil war in Mozambique and the consequent exodus of refugees and displaced people, foreign interference in local affairs, deteriorating economic situation, population explosion, the growing incidence of AIDS, deforestation, the growing gap between the rich North and the poor South and among the Third World politicians who siphon off national resources into foreign banks and cling to power, and the worsening poverty of the people.

While African theologians have been reflecting on these problems, the gathering on the African continent of EATWOT members from Asia, Latin America, the Caribbean, and Native American and minority people in the USA, together with EATWOT's long-time friends and observers from other countries has been a source of great encouragement. This has given African theologians on the continent strength to be more determined and to cry much louder a cry for life, in all its fullness.

The cry of the Third World is not a passive cry of resignation to the realities of death. It is a strident witness to the persistence of life. The cry for life is not a cry of despair, sorrow, hopelessness or grief. It is a cry that denies victory to torture, detainment, starvation and military might. It is a cry for bread, rice, water, land, housing, jobs, health care.

The cry of the Third World is indeed raised from the midst of misery and from within situations in which the forces of death are rampant; in which children die by the thousands from diseases related to malnutrition while elsewhere food is wasted, milk and grain are destroyed, and resources are hijacked from life's need to a life of luxury and to the production of weapons of annihilation.

The cry of the Third World is from the midst of the politics of the powerful who rule by torture, assassination and the contriving of the disappearance of women and men, and who commit aggression through proxy wars. The cry rises from the midst of structures designed for our subjugation, marginalization and extinction, through distorted priorities, skewed agricultural policies, unjust trade arrangements and inhuman economic manipulations and pressure tactics, all practiced and imposed in brutal and subtle ways by neo-colonialism and the international imperialism of money built up through atrocities, cruelties and robberies during the era of military colonialism. The cry is from places where people are killed every day for maintaining that the poor have a right to live and for believing that children must be given food, and justice must be practiced. The cry comes from within situations in which domination is transnational, and it counts on allies in our own midst.

The Third World cry for life is *one multi-tonal* cry. It reflects the various ways oppression assaults Third World life. It carries the cries of countries protesting economic indenture to IMF and the World Bank. It contains the cries of nature against technological devastation. It contains the cries of religious cultures oppressed by the dominant ones. It carries the cries of the innocent massacred by the bombs of the sophisticated technology of war. It carries the cries of indigenous, tribal and aboriginal peoples for land, civil rights, autonomy and cultural respect. It carries the cries of refugees, children, displaced people and those afflicted with AIDS, the cries against the discrimination of homosexuals, of those who suffer from economic oppression, women forced into prostitution, victims of drug abuse and the unjust politics of health care. It carries the cries of Blacks against apartheid.

It carries the cries of the Dalits against the apartheid of caste oppression. It carries the cries of women against patriarchal dominance and sexual violence.

The urgency of the Third World cry for life drew EATWOT to Nairobi. We gathered to listen to the challenges posed by that cry. What does the cry mean for our spirituality? What does the cry say about Jesus? What does the cry do to our commitment? EATWOT assembled in Nairobi to boldly proclaim that even in the midst of the "new world order" of racism, sexism and capitalism, God has not disappeared. God has not failed the Third World people. God IS PRESENT in the Third World cry for life.

Structures of Oppression

Structures of oppression are global and local, external and internal. We are faced with a new global coalition that controls world economy, world politics, and world information and communication systems. These involve an international security system into which the internal security of every Third World country is annexed. We are under the grip of a market economy that is being directly controlled by the financial institutions of the powerful countries. It is a foregone conclusion that under that kind of economic arrangement the condition of the poor and socially disabled will not become better. While increasing globalization of market economy would seem inevitable, what safeguards can prevent its catastrophic effects on the poor and the marginalized?

Developments in the last few years make us wonder whether such safeguards are possible at all. Global institutions are intimately connected with the political process. The disappearance of the Cold War and the break up of the socialist system in Europe have left us in a situation where world politics tends to be under the increasing control of a single power maintained by aggressive militarism targeted primarily at the Third World. In the new military and political configurations the poor in the Third World are expendable. It is this reality that compels us to believe that the emerging new world order is anti-people and anti-life. Meeting in 1992, the year that marks the five hundredth anniversary of the colonial conquest, we are painfully aware that the tentacles of power are still colonial in one form or another.

The collapse of the historical expressions of socialism in Eastern Europe and the Soviet Union raises with urgency questions about alternative ways for Third World development. It is now clear that the major causes for the failure of historical socialism are non-democratic forms of government, imposition of a centralized economy, denial of people's participation and their ethnic and cultural identity and of freedom for the spiritual development of the people. The present crisis was brought about by people asserting and fighting for their rights and freedom in a context where imperialist frameworks persisted.

The collapse of this historical model of socialism does not mean the demise of the values, goals and utopias of socialism. However ambiguous historical socialism might have been, some of its achievements cannot be ignored, as, for example, advances in economic democracy and towards the elimination of absolute poverty, and towards education and health for all, full employment and the development of sciences and sports. One would hope these gains will be preserved in the changing circumstances.

Our analysis of the global context is incomplete if we do not address ourselves to the growing divisions among our own people in the Third World and the violence committed on one another. To a large extent they are the result of a process of internalizing the aggressive values of dominant societies. Our elites perpetuate their dominance over the majority, increasing the misery of the poor. Among our religious institutions there are churches in most places which tend to be elitist, racist and sexist. By and large these churches have lost the moral credibility to respond to the cry of the world for life.

Emerging Currents

Yet our situation is not completely dismal and hopeless. We hear the stirrings of people, we see their resistance to oppression. There are movements which assert their hope and life. They provide inspiration and vision for a new way of living.

The Irruption of Women: A Cry for Life

For many decades, women of the Third World have been active participants in struggles for justice, for human rights, for economic and political freedom and in movements for the integrity of creation. Around the '70s there was a fresh wave of activism when women of Asia, Africa and Latin America and US minorities started identifying themselves as women and naming the specific forms of violence and marginalization they experience, while continuing their active solidarity within and critical support for the struggles of other oppressed groups in their societies. The need for some measure of autonomous existence and an agenda of action focussing on women arose out of their disillusionment with political processes and movements that did not recognize the gender-specific forms of oppression women experience.

Out of such experiences, women have articulated new paradigms of political and social analysis as they discovered that traditional ways of understanding society were far from adequate. They have also provided a strong critique of the Euro-centered development paradigm, and the untold levels of suffering it causes, particularly to women and children. They search for a new anthropology—a new way of understanding what it means to be human. Patriarchy, as a system of graded subjugation, has been identified, and its pernicious roots that weave into other structures of oppression have been exposed and targeted for concerted action. Patriarchal structures have legitimized scandalous forms of dehumanization of women and men, and have violated women's rights to self-identity and dignity.

The violence that women experience can be overt and even brutal—rape, incest, battery in the domestic sphere, prostitution, especially related to tourism and the rest and recreation industry for defense personnel, and violence related to certain religious and cultural practices. This overt form of violence against women can be extended to the abuse of women's bodies by medical technologies, particularly reproductive technologies, and the rampant use made of Third World women for testing new pharmaceutical formulations. There have been forced and sometimes surreptitious and massive sterilization of Third World women.

The subtle forms of violence women experience cannot be so easily articulated but have for centuries been eating into the psyche of women, eroding their self-esteem. This takes various forms—denying to women their right to self-expression out of their own wisdom, which expresses a perspective different from the dominant mode, or rendering women invisible. The oppression of women by patriarchal religion, including Christianity, and the androcentric language and interpretation of Scriptures are other expressions of this. The marginalization women experience in the church is indeed another form of violence against them.

But hope lies in the fact that women affirm that they will not be silenced as they reclaim their own history and heritage and celebrate their own religious and spiritual resources. Hope lies in their affirmation that holistic and creation-centered theological feminist and womanist paradigms are important for the empowering of the communities in which they live and for the healing of the broken relationship between humanity and creation. Hope lies in the solidarity of women around the world in opposition to any structure or system that threatens their rights.

Movements of Black Peoples

The civil rights and Black power movements of the 1960s were the resistance movements against white racism in the United States of America. The Black poor came out to assert their dignity and to fight for freedom. The source of their resistance is their spirituality and their hope is found in the power to say "no" to death and "yes" to life.

In South Africa the anti-apartheid struggle gave birth to the Black consciousness movement. Blacks in South Africa have set foot on the path to being autonomous subjects of their history. The current movement of liberal democracy in Africa is not seen as life-saving. The poor will be even more powerless. They will be alienated from their land and get deeper and deeper into the culture of violence. In this situation we witness young people's anger and resistance against marginalization.

Black women have begun to articulate the multi-dimensional nature of black oppression. For them it is not just an issue of race, or class, but also an issue of gender. Black women are saying "no" to racist, classist, patriarchal oppression and "yes" to freedom for all Black people. Black women and men throughout the diaspora are saying "yes" to the richness of Black cultural heritage.

Out of the development of Black consciousness throughout the diaspora emerged Black theologies, particularly in the US and South Africa. Black liberation theology (US) today is continuing to articulate the empowering message of the Gospel of Jesus in the struggles of Black and other oppressed peoples throughout the Third World. The Black poor believe in the God of life who affirms their dignity and empowers them to fight against the forces of death.

In South Africa, in the first ten years during which Black theology concentrated on enabling Black people to rediscover their God-given humanity which was denied by White people, White Christians and White theologians, they faced an uphill task. The Black theology (S. Africa) has been challenged to respond to other concerns and issues as well. They have come up with radical perspectives on christology and ecclesiology, while anti-apartheid and anti-racism commitments remain the context of their theology.

Recognizing the invisibility of their experience within the Black theology movement, Black women are developing their own distinctive theologies. They are attempting to articulate the meaning of God, Christ, the church and culture from their own perspectives. The womanist theology (US) and women in theology in Africa are significant manifestations of this movement.

Indigenous Movements and Religions

Those who have been the most oppressed and dispossessed for the last five hundred years are today emerging as a great source of new life and energy. The autochthonous peoples of our Third World, called Indios or Indigenous in the American continents, are coming forth with new proposals for life which radically question our modern societies, churches and theologies. Even though these peoples have been consistently exploited, and excluded from the economic structures of society, they possess a life-giving force which is unlimited. Their demands for their traditional rights to the land and for their religious- cultural identities constitute a great reserve of life and offer new hope for all the peoples of the world, especially for the poor.

In the face of the social models imposed by the First World on the peoples of the periphery, the indigenous people cry out to be seen and recognized not through the images of western mirrors, but through their own proper mirrors so that others might see them as they really are and want to be.

The indigenous peoples have always been deeply spiritual and live in communion with God. As their old cultures relook at Christianity through their own traditions and struggles for life and survival, they can provide the churches and their theologies with possibilities of great enrichment and profound renewal. This offers opportunities of discovering and manifesting other faces of God that throughout the ages have been known by the native peoples, but not known or appreciated by the western churches. These insights will greatly enrich other religious traditions of the world. As western civilization continues to self-destruct through avarice, moral depravity, individualism and the overall ethic of death, indigenous peoples can offer new hope for life for these dying peoples. The ancestral rites, traditions, myths and utopias of the indigenous people constitute an important source of spiritual energy. This energy has kept the indigenous peoples alive, and sustained them with hope amidst the most adverse circumstances of their long and painful historical journey throughout many generations. In today's very fragile new world order, which is desperately looking for alternatives for survival, especially the survival of the poor and starving peoples of the world, the ways of life and beliefs of the indigenous peoples offer an important humanizing force and thus an important saving force for the very survival of our common humanity.

Twice Conquered, Twice Colonized, Twice Oppressed: The Hispanic Struggle in the United States

In spite of being considered for many years as pilgrims, migrants, strangers, foreigners, temporary and transitional communities, today the Hispanic/Latino people in the United States feel moved to personal and collective recuperation that includes both their spiritual strength and their transforming energies with the end of affirming a new identity based on the full recognition of their alterities. This new identity is expressed by the growing self-awareness of being a people with its own characteristics, its own ways of reading, communicating, celebrating and sharing life. So far, despite numbering around twenty million in the United States, the dominant structures have designated the "minority" category to address this people, thus affecting not only its self-understanding as a people but its experience of God as well. Therefore, in addition to suffering the consequence of the unjust present order, this people has been forced to develop an inferiority complex that leads to the personal and collective perpetuation of an attitude of servility to benefit the dominant minority.

For Hispanic/Latino people, however, hope has not vanished. Even though the traditional religious vision has alienated this people from its responsibility towards its own reality and destiny, the experience of faith has also been, and continues to be, a source that allows it to recognize its own values and resist the current aggressiveness caused by religious, spiritual and cultural colonization. In this respect, the theological task is to strengthen its transforming potential as well as its solidarity in linkage with other peoples and the capacity to struggle and resist the forces of death.

We celebrate with joy those indicators that already reveal signs of the emergence of the Hispanic/Latino people as a cry for, but also a smile towards, life. Among these are the refusal to disappear within the Anglo-Saxon "melting pot" at the cost of losing its identity, the refusal to continue as strangers and foreigners in their own land or to be second-class citizens, and the reaffirmation that in Spanish or "tex-mex," or "Spanglish," or "poncho," it is possible to be a vital part of a people with their own identity. Among them are also the affirmation of women, not only as agents of their own destiny, but also as a changing force with their own initiative and their own unique ways of verbalizing the experience of faith, the discovery that true identity consists in preserving intrinsic human dignity and the responsibility we have assumed in supporting our families left behind in our respective countries, including a serious commitment to improve their real condition of life and affirming that there is no salvation if it is not collective and communitarian. We rejoice in the increasingly committed faith of those whose God is not the one in whom, according to its currency, America trusts.

Ecological Movement

The interconnectedness between commitment to the renewal of society and the renewal of the earth is clearly seen in the struggle of many marginalized groups all over the world. Indigenous people everywhere and many groups who have been traditionally dependent upon land and sea—farmers, fisherfolk, agricultural laborers—have kept these two dimensions together in their movements for liberation. The stubborn resistance of the poor tribal women in the now famous Chipko movement in India against the government's decision to turn their habitat into a mining area, and the cry of the poor in many other countries whose habitats are threatened by the demands of modernization have brought home to us the inseparable link between the struggle of the poor and ecological issues. Integral to the struggle for justice and liberation is the struggle for preserving the integrity of creation.

Such movements remind us that the ecological crisis is created by modern industrial and technological growth and modern lifestyle. The western industrial growth model is uncritically and universally accepted as a paradigm of development. Ruthless exploitation of nature and fellow human beings is the necessary consequence of this development. Decisions about the kind of goods to be produced and the type of technology to be used are influenced by the demands of a consumerist economy where the controlling logic of growth is greed and not need. This creates imbalances between different sectors and allows the massive exploitation of the rural and natural environment for the benefit of dominant classes. Much of the profit-oriented growth which destroys the ecobalance is engineered and controlled by multinationals based in the US, Europe, Japan and a few other countries. They often use the Third World as a market for powerful pesticides and drugs which are banned in their own countries.

The ecological movements are demanding an alternative form of development which calls for a halt to the violence committed on nature and human beings and the unlimited demand for nonrenewable resources. These movements are bringing to our awareness how some countries are forced to trade their forests and national resources for debt relief and to become dumping places for nuclear and chemical wastes from rich nations, causing massive ecological destruction. They have brought a new awareness about our dependence on the earth. We belong to the earth. We share a common destiny with the earth. This has sharply challenged the modern view of reality and demands a revaluation of currently held values and perhaps a recovery of old values. The issue is about all of humanity living in right relations with nature. The impact of this perception on our vision for an alternate society is critical for our theologizing. In this regard our own spirituality can be informed by the spirituality of the indigenous people whose fundamental principle is harmony with the universe.

Our theology should be, and largely is, shaped by these emerging currents in the movements of our people. We learn from their experience of struggle and their resistance to the situations of oppression. We drink from their wells (Gustavo Gutiérrez) the spiritual resources that sustain them. We have been insisting that our "method is our spirituality." It is therefore appropriate that the spirituality of the Third World became the focal point of our theological reflection at this conference.

Theological Reflections

Spirituality of Life

The very word "spirit" is an acknowledgement that human life is propelled by a principle beyond human power and knowledge. Unable to define this sense of being touched by the beyond, the word spirituality has come to our aid as a convenient term to articulate the sense of our being moved by a spiritual energy to hold on to life and to live it to the fullest. Spirituality spells our connectedness to God, to our human roots, to the rest of nature, to one another and to ourselves. Our spirituality is our experience of the Holy Spirit moving us and our communities to be life-giving and life-affirming. The Spirit itself makes intercession for us with groaning which cannot be uttered (Rom. 8:26).

We live our spirituality in creative response to the cry for life, the cry for God. We celebrate our spirituality in songs, rituals and symbols which show the energizing Spirit animating the community to move together in response to God. All existence is spiritual, our way of life as Third World peoples is spiritual. The spiritual traditions of indigenous peoples—Native Americans, Aborigines, Maoris, Dalits, Tribal peoples of India and Black Africans in Africa—are a powerful reminder of this fact. The spirituality of these people recognizes the "personhood" of all things in creation and leads therefore to a deep respect for nature. They are rooted in nature and therefore live a life of reciprocal dependence with the rest of creation. There is a life force that urges them to seek the glory of God and of creation by seeking the glory of the whole of humanity, for to do so is to seek a humanity fully alive. Spirituality is described as that which fuels theological reflection to generate a more immediate and attainable vision of a just and peaceful world.

There is no room for romanticizing spirituality. It is a cry for life, a power to resist death and the agents of death. Spirituality is the name we give to that which provides us with the strength to go on, for it is the assurance that God is in the struggle. Spirituality involves people's resistance to dehumanization and fulfills the quest for self-discovery, self-affirmation and self-inclusion, for in each of us in the whole human community is the urge to live and to live fully as human beings. It is the strength of the call to life that leads to various life-giving rituals of Native Americans and other indigenous peoples.

This quest for life is one that seeks to be attained in an environment that is imbued with and reflects the justice and glory of God. Our language about spirituality uses expressions such as "spirituality for liberation, spirituality for struggle, spirituality of involvement, spirituality of combat." The current use of spirituality is not one that directs us to the next world but to justice here and now. Spirituality is not a call away from life but the life force that urges us on to do justice and to resist evil. We are dealing here with Jesus' spirituality, one that is the source of justice and righteousness.

What are the springs of this spirituality among indigenous peoples? One encounters spiritual experiences and praxis that reveal God in creation. Their spiritualities are deeply rooted in land. The alienation of such peoples from their lands is a cause of spiritual and often even physical death. The violation of their space and place becomes the violation of the very spiritual values that hold the people together. In Black Africa the cosmic religions that undergird the cultures of peoples have provided their spirituality and have continued to do so in the Afro-Caribbean cults. African peoples call us to a life-force that is earthed and efficacious. Life now is celebrated by and through myths and symbols. This enables the construction in this world of a world beyond oppression, a celebration of hope. It is a spirituality that creates and sustains community. Recognizing this demands that we share spiritualities across religions whenever fullness of life and justice are sought. Women relate positively to this spirituality. Women's cry for life, women's sharing and caring, is a way of resisting death and struggling for life for the whole of humanity, men, women and children, and for all creation. The cry for balance, harmony, mutuality and reciprocity comes from the womb of life; it is the spirit groaning to give birth to a new humanity and community. In all communities of women and men reaching out to life and resisting death, prayer becomes a threat to those who violate life.

The authenticity of one's spirituality is demonstrated by one's involvement in the struggle and the theology that results from it. That is why the context of our lives influences both our spirituality and our theology. Consumerism and pollution have us in their bondage. We constantly face the clash of conflicting ideas. In the context of the gathering threat to health and life itself, we can have recourse only to the deep spiritual resources that are available to us, God's children. These forces of fragmentation threaten to create in us a life-denying passivity. This we resist, for spirituality is expressed in activities that defeat death. Spirituality is linked with commitment to life.

The Jesus of Faith

As Christians our spirituality is rooted in the Jesus spirituality, even as our struggles for liberation are rooted in our experience of Jesus, which awakens us to the need for struggle and empowers us to sustain the struggle. This empowering experience of Jesus is not that of the Christ of the christological dogmas, who has little relevance to life, but that of the Jesus we meet in the Gospels. This Jesus is the Jesus who experiences the conflicts we face, undergoes sufferings as we do, shares in our joys and sorrows, and remains faithful to his mission even when it brings him to death on the cross.

The many faces of Jesus that are encountered in the experiences of our people need to be identified. They provide a genuine guide for interpreting the mystery of the Jesus reality. They help us avoid the pitfall of intellectual abstraction and root ourselves in the reality of people.

To follow the Jesus of faith, first, is to follow one who is unrelentingly critical of the power relations in the structures of society that engender injustice and oppression. Second, it is to follow someone who believes that it is necessary to embody in community our vision of the new, more just society, as well as the discipline to work to realize our vision in this world. Third, following the Jesus of faith means following one who was dedicated to feeding the hungry, clothing the naked and fighting for the liberation of oppressed people.

But if the Jesus we encounter in the Gospels as our inspiration and empowerment is seen as merely the human Jesus, it may be asked why we should follow him instead of some other spiritual leader like Mahatma Gandhi or Martin Luther King. In the ultimate analysis there is no answer to this outside our faith.

For us Jesus is the Lord, and fully Lord, but this does not mean that we need to impose him on everyone else. For though Jesus, we believe, truly puts us in touch with God so that God is present to us in him, the absolute mystery of Godhead cannot be wholly comprehended in Jesus. For God is beyond all name and form, and the many insights we have into God cannot singly or collectively exhaust the mystery of God's being.

Our christology, then, must not be an imperial christology, such as developed in the post-Constantine era or such as was brought to us by a colonial Christianity which denied other religions (and other cultures) the right to exist, and claimed a monopoly for salvation. Jesus' own words are not the triumphalistic words of the imperialist Christ of the colonial Christianity, but words of love and service. He comes so that we may have life and have it in abundance; he comes that we may be one; he comes not to be served but to serve and to lay down his life as a ransom for many (John 1:10; Mark 10:45).

It is his followers who give him religious titles and make him into a militant conquering Christ. Such an understanding of Jesus does not cohere either with our experience of struggles nor with our Third World spirituality. In our struggles for liberation we have discovered a common commitment in people belonging to quite different faiths; and our religious life as Third World Christians is, in fact, lived out of two great traditions—both the Christian tradition and the traditions of our indigenous religions.

The Bible and People's Life and Traditions

Similarly, the reading and interpretations of the Bible too must obtain within a context of life. The poor read the Bible in the context of their struggles, their cultures as women, Third World Christians and indigenous peoples. They do it in their communities, animated by their spirituality. In the past we have read the Bible to the people. Now the people read it for themselves. The Bible begins to live in the lives of the people and the lives of the people bring the Bible to life.

For many centuries the Bible has been interpreted from the point of view of a western patriarchal and dominant culture. The Bible was used as an instrument for the spiritual conquest of America, Africa and Asia. It continues to be a tool of class, race and gender oppression of the large majorities of Third World peoples.

The people are now freeing the Bible from these wrong interpretations and recovering its text, its history and its inspiration on the basis of their own tradition of revelation and salvation.

God has revealed God's nature and being from the beginning of creation, and God continues to be revealed in nature, peoples' cultures and religious traditions. Revelation has always been alive and effective in the lives and religions and cultures of indigenous peoples, in the liberation movements and in the day-to-day struggles of the downtrodden. This kind of revelation is the first book of God. God gave the Bible to us as a second book to reveal the fullness of God's word and to transform the cosmos and the lives of our people in a big epiphany of God's presence. The Holy Spirit itself guides us in the discovery of God's revelation in our personal existence and in our community.

The Bible constitutes a historical memory and consciousness of the people. The people maintain their tradition and re-read it continuously to discover God in the changing situations. In the Bible itself one can see the struggle of people against the manipulation of scribes and the teachers of the law. The Bible teaches us to get over those texts which are oppressive in the new context. The Bible is self-critical and has the capacity to expose the oppressive elements in the lives, traditions and cultures of our people.

The Bible is read and interpreted in the Third World in a communitarian way. The community appropriates the Bible in a spirit of prayer, faith and celebration. This enables the people to make critical discernment in the society and in the church. We are encouraged by witnessing the contribution to this significant movement by women who are re-reading the Bible.

Commitment

As our method is incarnate in our theology, so our spirituality is enfleshed in our commitment to and work for the liberation of the oppressed.

Samuel Rayan

A crisis of commitment is a reality for the people of the Third World. As new governments come to power with promises of a better life, our people's movements are muted. As political leaders compromise away justice, our people are left in a quandary. What are the people of the Philippines and South Korea to do now that they have toppled one oppressive regime and another regime comes to power which falls far short of their vision for life? What are the student resisters of South Africa to do as "high level" talks proceed for a more "democratic" South Africa? What are the people of Nicaragua and Haiti to do as they face countless obstacles in hoping and struggling for liberation? What does it mean to be committed when governments talk endlessly of freedom, justice, and democracy, but grant it to only a few?

The rapidly changing world situation forces us to examine the nature of commitment. Commitment means a radical conversion to the God of liberation and life. Conversion is becoming aligned with God's mission for the world. Sometimes this conversion forces persons into struggle. For others conversion emerges out of the struggle, and for yet others it is an ongoing experience. What is important is that conversion takes place. Conversion is not merely to an institutional church, a particular religion, or even to a social system. Conversion is to the God of justice, peace and life. It is the radical experience of conversion that helps maintain one's commitment to the Reign of God. Conversion makes commitment meaningful because it becomes a commitment to radically change the world.

To be committed to the people's struggle for life is to be committed to a world where there shall be justice, freedom and new respect for all of creation. To be committed means not just settling for resolutions of regional and national conflicts. To be committed means not selling out the vision for personal gain. To be committed means standing fast until anything which threatens the full humanity of any person is destroyed.

Commitment varies with the particular context of struggle. To a Ghanaian it might mean speaking for the rights of women in church and society. For a Mexican-American it might mean leading a group of poor men and women to stymie the daily function of a local bank. For a Filipino it might mean mobilizing to oust the U.S. military bases from its shores. To a South Korean it might mean working towards the reunification of the Korean people and for peace.

There is a price to commitment. Commitment might lead to harassment, marginalization, ecclesiastical sanctions, arrest, torture or even death. To be committed means there is no cost too great when one joins God's mission to make the world a place where life is valued for all of God's creation.

Within the lines of commitment to justice, there may be legitimate differences in the strategies and priorities for reaching our goal. Our task is not to judge the justice commitments of others. The cry for life challenges us to continually affirm our commitments to transform all reality so that all life can thrive.

A Specific Challenge

1492: The Beginning of Today's New World Order

In the last two decades of the fifteenth century "a new world order" was born: the Portuguese went around the Cape of Good Hope into the Indian Ocean (1485); Columbus, in search of a passage to the "Indies," arrived in the Caribbean Islands (1492); and Vasco da Gama touched Mombasa in Kenya on his journey to Calicut in India (1498). Soon after, France, England, Holland and the other countries of Europe began competing in their efforts to conquer, colonize, missionize and exploit all the other continents and their peoples.

Africa, the Americas and Asia were now destined to become absorbed into this new European world order! Europe's growing and expanding trade, strengthened by its military, political and economic power, imposed its culture and religious traditions all over the other peoples of the world.

When the ruling elites of Spain, England and other European countries are celebrating 1992, the "Discovery of America" and "The Encounter between Two Worlds," the native peoples of the Americas are launching another campaign, "500 Years of Indian, Black and Popular Resistance." This "encounter of two worlds" was experienced by the indigenous peoples of the Americas not as encounter but as a tragic genocide. A Maya-Quiche poet described the arrival of the Spaniards in Guatemala in 1528 as follows:

> They taught us fear.
> They came just to wither the flowers

So that their flower may blossom
They damaged and swallowed our flower.

In Africa, the Europeans provoked the birth of modern slavery with a tremendous upsurge of the traditional Islamic slave trade by the opening of the "middle passage," the Atlantic slave trade. According to Lerone Bennett, Jr., an African-American historian, in his classic book *Before the Mayflower*, in the period between 1444 and 1850 Africans lost an estimated forty million people, many of whom died in Africa during and after their capture or on the ships in the middle passage. South Africa was colonized; the land was forcefully taken from the Africans by White settlers. The abominable system of apartheid was created. It was also during this time that Asians from today's Philippines were carried as slaves to Mexico.

Henceforth humanity was divided into two: White Christian Europe versus all others; western civilization and culture versus all others; the western academic tradition versus all others; the capitalist system versus all others; the White peoples versus all others. Through a coming together of various forces, European White men would henceforth see themselves and their way of life as normative for all the other peoples of the world and themselves as the natural masters of the rest who by "God's eternal will" were born inferior and hence had developed inferior ways of life based on false religions.

Through the process of modernization, Europe and later North America were so convinced of their own superiority that they would develop historical, philosophical and theological teachings about the fundamental inequality of the races. This would further the moral legitimation to colonialism with all its mechanisms of exploitation of the colonies and their peoples.

In terms of the expansion of the Christian faith, the sword and the cross came together. So evangelization came to Africa, America and Asia supported and enforced militarily and politically. Thus colonialism was, generally speaking, justified religiously. Many of the first missioners were opposed to the violence of the enslavement and exploitation of the indigenous populations in America, but the Christian religion was an essential part of the colonial order. Hence even the best of the missioners were, in effect, agents of the ultimate violence: the destruction of the religious systems which were the inner roots of the life of the people.

When the missioners opposed the colonizers, they were persecuted and expelled and their missions, for example, Jesuit Guarani projects in Paraguay, were simply destroyed. This collusion between western Christianity, Catholic or Reformed, and the colonial powers carried with it the religious legitimization of the Black enslavement and produced a theology of enslavement instead of offering the gospel of liberation.

So evangelization as spiritual conquest, especially after the military conquests, distorted the gospel and profoundly hurt the Indian spiritual life. The Aztec theologians replied to the Franciscan missionaries in Mexico:

> Let us die
> Let us Perish
> Because our Gods are dead.

Search for Alternatives

Beyond Capitalism and Socialism

The historical expressions of socialism have failed in Eastern Europe and the former Soviet Union. But we do not accept international capitalism, dominated by the TNCs and the main capitalist countries, as an acceptable social order for the future. Unbridled capitalism, with its emphasis on technology and productivity, offers no acceptable future for the masses of the poor and for nature, and it provides an atmosphere for the growth of insidious racism.

We commit ourselves to a more community-responsible form of social organization that ensures life for all and uses the resources of nature caringly.

In our search for new alternatives we reaffirm certain fundamental values, which can help evaluate and correct deficiencies in each historical experience.

Every society should endeavor to ensure sustainable economic growth to meet human needs without exploitation of persons and nature; a just distribution of income and wealth without overly curbing the need of initiative and due reward for work; fair trade with and among nations, without permitting a few oligopolies to control and manipulate the markets for resources and products; the civil and political as well as economic, social, cultural and religious rights of all, especially the poor and the marginalized; and international social justice based on relationships of solidarity and mutuality.

These require an ongoing effort to meet the basic needs of all: food, work, land, shelter, health, education and leisure. The fullest democratic participation of all persons at all levels is a means of treating all persons and groups with dignity, of providing space for ethnic and cultural identity and spiritual development, of promoting relationships of mutuality irrespective of gender and sexual orientation, as well as of (at least) reducing exploitation, competition and waste.

It is not within our competence to provide one blueprint for the structures of future development everywhere. We are, however, more than ever convinced that the power and strength for our future should emerge from the accumulated experience for survival and resistance of oppressed and poor people, and also subjugated or marginalized cultures.

Along with the peoples' movements emerging throughout the world, we can endeavor to influence different social systems and areas of social life in the direction of practically realizing the values we hold and correcting unwholesome trends. We urge a new style of politics and a paradigm of relationship in which people can be truly fulfilled and not exploited and dehumanized. Both private and public enterprise should be made efficient, meaningful in productivity and socially responsible. Individuals, companies, elites and all power holders are subject to the higher demands of the right to life of each and all persons, and the common good of humanity. We should resist the efforts at "privatization" merely because of capitalistic pressure. The public sector often needs to be safeguarded to serve the people.

We should work to bring about effective checks on the accumulation of private profit by companies, and of power by rulers. This is a most difficult and challenging task in the present world situation, and more so with the capitalistic so-called "new world order."

The TNCs must be brought under effective forms of public control at national and international levels by people's pressure. Public enterprises, especially in poor countries, and the international agencies such as UNCTAD and GATT can be valuable agents in developing countervailing power vis-à-vis the TNCs and the world political powers that exploit and dominate the poor. The Non-Aligned Movement needs to be strengthened.

Within nations the rulers and elites must be obliged to serve the people and not misuse power, generally in collusion with the TNCs and foreign powers that often come as donors of aid.

People Power

In the present national and global situations, it is the enlightened and sustained commitment of alliances of peoples' movements that can bring about practical action towards reaching such desirable goals. The very magnitude of the crisis and its global nature can motivate such movements in all countries to try to work together to save humankind from this present misery.

As an organization of theologians we can contribute by participating in the peoples' efforts, learning from them and supporting them by our faith, analysis and commitment.

We need to work everywhere to share in existing movements, and help to form, strengthen and correlate peoples' groups and movements around their felt needs. Such basic Christian and basic human groups can be the primary bases for national and global peoples' movements.

For this we need to develop our methodologies of analysis of situations at all levels to see the deeper causes of our problems and ways of promoting practical commitment, undeterred by opposition and the difficulties of the tasks.

The core inspiration of our faith and of the other faiths and persuasions of the peoples can be a powerful motivation for such commitment. We can develop inter-faith relations while mutually correcting non-liberative trends in each of them.

In the face of the enormous power of the forces of exploitation and the destructiveness of war and violence, we need to develop effective means of resistance. Ultimately our hope lies in creating a non-violent society. Recent experience has shown how governments and even superpowers can be impacted by the organized non-violent movements of people power.

We can participate in the emerging movements of people power, working for justice in the relationships of gender, racial, ethnic and social groups, among cultures and religions and with nature. The hope for the future lies in the convergence of such efforts towards desirable goals as against the combined exploitation by economic, political, military and cultural superpowers. Our hope is especially in the new movements such as those of women, indigenous peoples, Blacks, the urban poor, farmers, Dalits and others. Environmental movements have sometimes prevented companies and governments from doing damage to nature. Women's movements have contributed immensely to safeguard human rights against sexual abuse, and worked for peace within and among nations.

While working at local and national levels we can help generate peoples' movements for the reform of the United Nations and its agencies such as the Security Council and the UNCTAD. It is imperative that the IMF and the World Bank be made responsible, at least, to the governments of all the nations, and not be dominated as at present by the rich countries to the utter detriment of the poor almost everywhere.

15

Taking the Poor Seriously:
An Interpretative Report

K. C. ABRAHAM

The Ecumenical Association of Third Word Theologians (EATWOT) was founded to foster the growth of theologies relevant to the lives, religions and cultures of Third World people, theologies able to sustain them in their struggles for full humanity.

The initiative for EATWOT's first meeting in Dar-es-Salaam, Tanzania, in August 1976 came from several Asian, African and Latin American theologians present at the World Council of Churches' Nairobi Assembly (1975). The twenty-one theologians who came to that first meeting adopted the Dar-es-Salaam Declaration, which has become EATWOT's charter of identity, the point of reference for all subsequent assemblies and conferences. The declaration is forthright about the organization's stance: "We reject as irrelevant an academic type of theology that is divorced from action. We are prepared for a radical break in epistemology which makes commitment the first act of theology and engages in critical reflection on the praxis of the reality of the Third World."

Evolving Insights

Every five years EATWOT has met in assembly to assess its work and set future directions. Reflections at the First Assembly (Delhi, India, 1981) centered on the "Irruption of the Third World: Challenge to Theology." While identifying poverty and oppression as the overriding reality in the Third World, the conference took note of the irruption of the exploited classes, marginalized cultures and humiliated races, "expressed in revolutionary struggles, political uprisings, and liberation movements." A striking feature of this new uprising was that it was of "a world that is not

Christian, bursting into history with a voice of its own, demanding justice and equality, reaffirming its age-old religions and cultures and challenging the West-oriented and narrowly Christian understanding of the world and history."

Five years later, in Oaxtepec, Mexico, participants examined "common and diverse aspects in the theologies developing in Asia, Africa and Latin America in terms of theological issues, orientation and methodology, as well as the possibilities and need of mutual enrichment and cross fertilization." As EATWOT continued to reflect on the situation of deprivation in the Third World, it was also led to deal with problems of oppression specific to each of the three continents and to minorities in the United States. Among those that received special attention were cultural and religious oppression, racism and male domination. Encounter with such immediate forms of oppression within the global system of injustice posed a new challenge to EATWOT.

Could there be a more adequate framework of analysis that would link these specific forms of oppression? How could we initiate a dialogue among the liberation theologies evolving in different cultural situations? Regrettably, such a dialogue did not begin in Oaxtepec. But it did become clear that "Third World theology" is not a monolithic system of thought. Divergences were acknowledged, and the internal dialogue among partners was accepted as an important function of the association.

A New Situation

When EATWOT returned to Africa for its Third Assembly in Nairobi in January 1992 there was an overriding feeling that the condition of the poor in the Third World has deteriorated since Dar-es-Salaam. As the Third World poor face a "new world order," projected by the powerful nations, they do not see that it holds much hope for them. Often in EATWOT meetings we used to speak of the power of the poor. Today, what is threatened in many countries is their very survival.

- Racism is rampant everywhere. Different manifestations of it, subtle or blatant, vitiate our relationships and continue to keep large sections of society in bondage.

- Violence committed on women is increasing.

- Unjust trade arrangements and inhuman economic manipulations have increased the debt burden of Third World countries.

- We are in the grip of a market economy directly controlled by the financial institutions of a few developed countries.

- A revolution is taking place in the area of communication, and information technology is opening up new possibilities. But the power-brokers have already captured these technologies in order to make even more complete their control.

It was against this background of the grim realities of our day and of the shattered dreams of socialist experiments that the Nairobi meeting began to reflect on possible Third World responses in theology and praxis. One could say that "theology after the socialist crisis" was the paramount concern of the Nairobi conference. The choice of the theme "A Cry for Life: The Spirituality of the Third World" and the reflections on it marked a new style of thinking and approach to Third World realities and to doing theology within that context.

Moving away from a rigidly ideological approach to analysis, often influenced by Marxian thinking, the participants were groping for a more holistic approach and life-centered symbols and paradigms to articulate their experiences of suffering and oppression. In that context, the word "cry" captured the mood of the situation. The cry of the Third World today is a cry for life. It is a cry for the freedom and dignity without which life is less than human. It is a cry for rice and bread, eaten in company, a cry for community and belonging. It is a cry of protest as well as a cry of hope. In the worship services and the recurring review of daily reflections, several symbols were used to communicate powerfully the experience of both suffering and longing.

Ideologies, particularly of the Marxian variety, are useful only up to a point. In fact, the conference was clearly ideological when it categorically rejected thoroughgoing capitalism as inhuman and evil. Ideology has an important negative function insofar as it provides clarity about what one rejects. Ideology helps one to see the logic of power in the established system.

Latin American delegates reminded us of the historical significance of 1992, the year that marks the five-hundredth anniversary of the European "discovery" of a continent where civilization flourished long before Europe had any, and the beginning of the colonial era, which in turn led to the buying and selling of people and the institutionalization of racism. In our analysis we once again dwelt at length on the colonial collusion of conversion and exploitation, which continues even today.

If "cry" points to the present realities, "life" provides the vision of the new. That vision too, should break out of its ideological captivities.

The relation between theology and ideology, whether articulated or assumed, continued to influence much of our reflection. But there was greater stress on moving away from traditional formulas and an increasing realization that the vision for the future and the resources for theologizing should emerge out of the collective experience of the resistance of the poor in the last five hundred years. We need to be more sensitive to the logic of the faith of the poor and the power of their cry.

God is involved in the cry for life. That conviction is the source of Third World spirituality. And that should determine the forms it takes. The active participation of indigenous groups from the US and Latin America was a powerful reminder of this new dimension of the spiritual. We are challenged by their age-old experience of resistance against the forces of death, whether these come in the guise of development or modernization. Their celebration of life and hope has its source in their belonging to the earth and to one another.

Nairobi will be remembered for initiating a new style of theologizing. It was evident in the worship services and celebrative events. We heard it articulated in the stories of resistance told by black women and native Americans, in the songs of suffering and hope by black Americans, in the Filipino testimonies of struggle and the minjung dance from Korea. Thus EATWOT will continue to provide a critique of the dominant theologies in Third World churches. More significantly, in that process it compels the churches to take seriously the ecclesial reality of the poor and the deprived in their theology and mission.

Contributors

K. C. Abraham is president of EATWOT and professor of theology and ethics at the United Theological College in Bangalore. He is the editor of *Third World Theologies: Commonalities and Divergences*.

Elizabeth Amoah is a Methodist lecturer in the Department for the Study of Religion, University of Ghana and teacher of Phenomenology of Religion and African religions.

Frank Chikane is General Secretary of the South African Council of Churches and the author of *No Life of My Own*.

Virgil Elizondo is director of the Mexican-American Cultural Center in San Antonio and the author of several books, including *Way of the Cross: The Passion of Christ in the Americas*.

Ivone Gebara, a Roman Catholic Sister from Brazil, is co-author of *Mary: Mother of God, Mother of the Poor* and of several books in Portuguese.

Jacquelyn Grant is an associate professor of systematic theology at the Interdenominational Theological Center, Atlanta, Georgia.

Franz J. Hinkelammert is presently a staff member of the Departmento Ecuménico de Investigaciónes in San José, Costa Rica, and director of the postgraduate program in economics at the National University of Honduras.

Dwight N. Hopkins teaches theology at Santa Clara University, Santa Clara, California. His most recent book is *Shoes That Fit Our Feet: Sources for a Constructive Black Theology*.

José Míguez Bonino is a Methodist theologian from Argentina who has been active in the ecumenical movement, serving on the Faith and Order Commission of the World Council of Churches. His books include *Doing Theology in a Revolutionary Situation* and (as editor) *Jesus in Latin America*.

Mary John Mananzan, a Missionary Benedictine Sister from the Philippines, is dean of St. Scholastica's College in Manila and the founder of GABRIELLA, a women's movement in the Philippines.

Bernadette Mbuy-Beya, an Ursuline Sister from Zaire, is Mother Superior of the Ursuline Sisters and Director of the Institut Supérieur des Sciences Réligieuses in Lubumbashi, Zaire. She is the vice-president of EATWOT.

Takatso Mofokeng is a professor of theology at the University of South Africa, Pretoria.

Pablo Richard is a Chilean theologian who serves on the team of the Departamento

Ecuménico de Investigaciónes (DEI) in Costa Rica. He is the author of *Death of Christendoms, Birth of the Church.*

Rosa Adela O. Sierra, a Brazilian Franciscan Missionary of Notre Dame, lives in a slum with poor women. She is a founder of KUNAITE, a group working to articulate theological reflection and pastoral practice.

George Soares Prabhu, an Indian Jesuit, is professor of Scripture at Pontifical Seminary, Pune, India.

Lawrence Surendra, former co-ordinator of the Asia Regional Exchange for New Alternatives (ARENA), Hong Kong, is a social activist and freelance writer from Madras, India.

Ana María Tepedino, a Roman Catholic laywoman, teaches theology at the Catholic University and at St. Ursula's University, both located in Rio de Janeiro, Brazil.

George E. Tinker, a Native American, is professor of theology at the Iliff School of Theology in Denver, Colorado, and author of *Missionary Conquest: The Gospel and Native American Cultural Genocide.*

Sergio Torres is a Chilean priest who teaches systematic theology at the Alfonsin Institute of Pastoral Theology in Santiago, Chile. He is the editor of four previous EATWOT books, including *The Challenge of Basic Christian Communities* and *Doing Theology in a Divided World.*

Maria Vidale, a Catholic sister, is a professor of missiology at the Faculty of Theology (FAI) in Sao Paulo, Brazil.

Publications of EATWOT

The Ecumenical Association of Third World Theologians

(All published by Orbis Books, Maryknoll, New York)

1976   *Theology in the Americas*, edited by Sergio Torres and John Eagleson (the Detroit Conference of Theologians from the Americas held in Michigan in 1975).

1979   *The Emergent Gospel: Theology from the Underside of History*, edited by Sergio Torres and Virginia Fabella (EATWOT Dialogue held in Dar-es-Salaam, Tanzania in 1976; official founding of EATWOT).

1979   *African Theology En Route*, edited by Sergio Torres and Kofi Appiah-Kubi (Pan-African Conference of Third World Theologians held in Accra, Ghana in 1976).

1980   *Asia's Struggle for Full Humanity: Towards a Relevant Theology*, edited by Virginia Fabella (Asian Theological Conference of EATWOT held in Sri Lanka in 1979).

1981   *The Challenge of Basic Christian Communities*, edited by Sergio Torres and John Eagleson (International Ecumenical Congress of Theology held in São Paulo, Brazil in 1980).

1983   *Irruption of the Third World: Challenge to Theology*, edited by Virginia Fabella and Sergio Torres (Fifth International Congress of EATWOT held in New Delhi, India in 1981; the first general assembly).

1985   *Doing Theology in a Divided World*, edited by Virginia Fabella and Sergio Torres (Sixth International Conference of EATWOT, known as the Dialogue between First and Third World Theologians, held in Geneva, Switzerland in 1983).

1988   *With Passion and Compassion: Third World Women Doing Theology*, edited by Virginia Fabella and Mercy Oduyoye (Women's Conference of EATWOT meeting at EATWOT's First Assembly in New Delhi, India in 1981).

1990   *We Dare To Dream: Doing Theology as Asian Women*, edited by Virginia Fabella and Sun Ai Lee Park (EATWOT's Women's Commission and the Asian Women's Resource Centre in Hong Kong).

1992   *Asian Christian Spirituality: Reclaiming Traditions*, edited by Virginia Fabella,

Peter Lee, David Suh (Asian Theological Conference of EATWOT III held in Korea in 1989).

1993   *Third World Theologies: Commonalities & Divergences*, edited by K. C. Abraham (Second General Assembly of EATWOT held in Oaxtepec, Mexico in 1986).

1994   *Spirituality of the Third World: A Cry for Life*, edited by K. C. Abraham and Bernadette Mbuy-Beya (Third General Assembly of EATWOT held in Nairobi, Kenya in 1992).